D1069150

Equity
derivatives

Founded in 1807, John Wiley & Sons is the oldest independent publishing company in the United States. With offices in North America, Europe, Australia, and Asia, Wiley is globally committed to developing and marketing print and electronic products and services for our customers' professional and personal knowledge and understanding.

The Wiley Finance series contains books written specifically for finance and investment professionals as well as sophisticated individual investors and their financial advisors. Book topics range from portfolio management to e-commerce, risk management, financial engineering, valuation, and financial instrument analysis, as well as much more. For a list of available titles, please visit our web site at www.WileyFinance.com.

Equity
derivatives

Theory and Applications

Marcus Overhaus
Andrew Ferraris
Thomas Knudsen
Ross Milward
Laurent Nguyen-Ngoc
Gero Schindlmayr

John Wiley & Sons, Inc.

This book is printed on acid-free paper. ∞
Copyright © 2002 by Marcus Overhaus. All rights reserved.

Published by John Wiley & Sons, Inc., New York.
Published simultaneously in Canada.

No part of this publication may be reproduced, stored in a retrieval system
or transmitted in any form or by any means, electronic, mechanical,
photocopying, recording, scanning, or otherwise, except as permitted
under Section 107 or 108 of the 1976 United States Copyright Act,
without either the prior written permission of the Publisher, or authorization
through payment of the appropriate per-copy fee to the Copyright Clearance
Center, 222 Rosewood Drive, Danvers, MA 01923, (978) 750-8400, fax
(978) 750-4744. Requests to the Publisher for permission should
be addressed to the Permissions Department, John Wiley & Sons, Inc.,
605 Third Avenue, New York, NY 10158-0012, (212) 850-6011,
fax (212) 850-6008, E-Mail: PERMREQ@WILEY.COM.

This publication is designed to provide accurate and authoritative information
in regard to the subject matter covered. It is sold with the understanding
that the publisher is not engaged in rendering professional services. If
professional advice or other expert assistance is required, the services of a
competent professional person should be sought.

Library of Congress Cataloging-in-Publication Data:

Overhaus, Marcus.
    Equity derivatives: theory and applications / Marcus Overhaus.
      p. cm.
    Includes index.
    ISBN 0-471-43646-1 (cloth : alk. paper)
      1. Derivative securities. I. Title.
    HG6024.A3 O94 2001
    332.63'2–dc21   2001026547

Printed in the United States of America.

10 9 8 7 6 5 4 3 2 1

Marcus Overhaus is Managing Director and Global Head of Quantitative Research at Deutsche Bank AG. He holds a Ph.D. in pure mathematics.

Andrew Ferraris is a Director in Global Quantitative Research at Deutsche Bank AG. His work focuses on the software design of the model library and its integration into client applications. He holds a D.Phil. in experimental particle physics.

Thomas Knudsen is a Vice President in Global Quantitative Research at Deutsche Bank AG. His work focuses on modeling volatility. He holds a Ph.D. in pure mathematics.

Ross Milward is a Vice President in Global Quantitative Research at Deutsche Bank AG. His work focuses on the architecture of analytics services and web technologies. He holds a B.Sc. (Hons.) in computer science.

Laurent Nguyen-Ngoc works in Global Quantitative Research at Deutsche Bank AG. His work focuses on Lévy processes applied to volatility modeling. He is completing a Ph.D. in probability theory.

Gero Schindlmayr is an Associate in Global Quantitative Research at Deutsche Bank AG. His work focuses on finite difference techniques. He holds a Ph.D. in pure mathematics.

preface

Equity derivatives and equity-linked structures—a story of success that still continues. That is why, after publishing two books already, we decided to publish a third book on this topic. We hope that the reader of this book will participate and enjoy this very dynamic and profitable business and its associated complexity as much as we have done, still do, and will continue to do.

Our approach is, as in our first two books, to provide the reader with a self-contained unit. Chapter 1 starts with a mathematical foundation for all the remaining chapters. Chapter 2 is dedicated to pricing and hedging in incomplete markets. In Chapter 3 we give a thorough introduction to Lévy processes and their application to finance, and we show how to push the Heston stochastic volatility model toward a much more general framework: the Heston Jump Diffusion model.

How to set up a general multifactor finite difference framework to incorporate, for example, stochastic volatility, is presented in Chapter 4. Chapter 5 gives a detailed review of current convertible bond models, and expounds a detailed discussion of convertible bond asset swaps (CBAS) and their advantages compared to convertible bonds.

Chapters 6, 7, and 8 deal with recent developments and new technologies in the delivery of pricing and hedging analytics over the Internet and intranet. Beginning by outlining XML, the emerging standard for representing and transmitting data of all kinds, we then consider the technologies available for distributed computing, focusing on SOAP and web services. Finally, we illustrate the application of these technologies and of scripting technologies to providing analytics to client applications, including web browsers.

Chapter 9 describes a portfolio and hedging simulation engine and its application to discrete hedging, to hedging in the Heston model, and to CPPIs. We have tried to be as extensive as we could regarding the list of references: Our only regret is that we are unlikely to have caught everything that might have been useful to our readers.

We would like to offer our special thanks to Marc Yor for careful reading of the manuscript and valuable comments.

The Authors
London, November 2001

contents

CHAPTER 1
Mathematical Introduction   1

1.1   Probability Basis   1
1.2   Processes   2
      Where in Time?   3
      Martingales and Semimartingales   4
      Markov Processes   7
1.3   Stochastic Calculus   8
      Itō's Formula   9
      Girsanov's Theorem   10
1.4   Financial Interpretations   11
1.5   Two Canonical Examples   11

CHAPTER 2
Incomplete Markets   15

2.1   Martingale Measures   15
2.2   Self-Financing Strategies, Completeness, and
      No Arbitrage   17
2.3   Examples   21
2.4   Martingale Measures, Completeness, and
      No Arbitrage   28
2.5   Completing the Market   30
2.6   Pricing in Incomplete Markets   37
2.7   Variance-Optimal Pricing and Hedging   43
2.8   Super Hedging and Quantile Hedging   46

CHAPTER 3
Financial Modeling with Lévy Processes   51

3.1   A Primer on Lévy Processes   52
      First Properties   52
      Measure Changes   58
      Subordination   61
      Lévy Processes with No Positive Jumps   66

3.2   Modeling with Lévy Processes   68
        Model Framework   69
        The Choice of a Pricing Measure   69
        European Options Pricing   70
3.3   Products and Models   72
        Exotic Products   72
        Some Particular Models   77
3.4   Model Calibration and Smile Replication   88
3.5   Numerical Methods for Lévy Processes   95
        Fast Fourier Transform   95
        Monte Carlo Simulation   95
        Finite-Difference Methods   97
3.6   A Model Involving Lévy Processes   98

CHAPTER 4
Finite-Difference Methods for Multifactor Models   **103**

4.1   Pricing Models and PDEs   103
        Multiasset Model   104
        Stock-Spread Model   105
        The Vasicek Model   106
        The Heston Model   106
4.2   The Pricing PDE and Its Discretization   106
4.3   Explicit and Implicit Schemes   109
4.4   The ADI Scheme   110
4.5   Convergence and Performance   113
4.6   Dividend Treatment in Stochastic Volatility Models   116
        Modeling Dividends   117
        Stock Process with Dividends   117
        Local Volatility Model with Dividends   122
        Heston Model with Dividends   123

CHAPTER 5
Convertible Bonds and Asset Swaps   **125**

5.1   Convertible Bonds   125
        Introduction   125
        Deterministic Risk Premium in Convertible Bonds   127
        Non–Black-Scholes Models for Convertible Bonds   132
5.2   Convertible Bond Asset Swaps   137
        Introduction   137
        Pricing and Analysis   140

CHAPTER 6
Data Representation   **147**

6.1 XML   149
     Tags and Elements   150
     Attributes   151
     Namespaces   151
     Processing Instructions   152
     Comments   152
     Nesting   152
     Parsing XML   153
     Multiple Representation   154
6.2 XML Schema   154
6.3 XML Transformation   157
     XML Document Transformation   158
     Transformation into HTML   160
6.4 Representing Equity Derivative Market Data   162

CHAPTER 7
Application Connectivity   **165**

7.1 Components   166
7.2 Distributed Components   167
     DCOM and CORBA   168
7.3 SOAP   168
     SOAP Structure   171
     SOAP Security   173
     State and Scalability   175
7.4 Web Services   177
     WSDL   177
     UDDI   179

CHAPTER 8
Web-Based Quantitative Services   **181**

8.1 Web Pricing Servers   183
     Thread Safety Issues in Web Servers   186
8.2 Model Integration into Risk Management and
     Booking Systems   187
     A Position Server   190
8.3 Web Applications and Dynamic Web Pages   191
     Option Calculator Pages   193
     Providing Pricing Applications to Clients   195

CHAPTER 9
Portfolio and Hedging Simulation   **199**

9.1   Introduction   199
9.2   Algorithm and Software Design   199
9.3   Example: Discrete Hedging and Volatility
      Misspecification   201
9.4   Example: Hedging a Heston Market   205
9.5   Example: Constant Proportion Portfolio Insurance   206
9.6   Server Integration   209

REFERENCES   **211**

INDEX   **219**

Equity
derivatives

CHAPTER 1

Mathematical Introduction

T he use of probability theory and stochastic calculus is now an established standard in the field of financial derivatives. During the last 30 years, a large amount of material has been published, in the form of books or papers, on both the theory of stochastic processes and their applications to finance problems. The goal of this chapter is to introduce notions on probability theory and stochastic calculus that are used in the applications presented afterwards. The notations used here will remain identical throughout the book.

We hope that the reader who is not familiar with the theory of stochastic processes will find here an intuitive presentation, although rigorous enough for our purposes, and a set of useful references about the underlying mathematical theory. The reader acquainted with stochastic calculus will find here an introduction of objects and notations that are used constantly, although maybe not very explicitly.

This chapter does not aim at giving a thorough treatment of the theory of stochastic processes, nor does it give a detailed view of mathematical finance theory in general. It recalls, rather, the main general facts that will be used in the examples developed in the next chapters.

1.1 PROBABILITY BASIS

Financial models used for the evaluation of derivatives are mainly concerned with the uncertainty of the future evolution of the stock prices. The theory of probability and stochastic processes provides a framework with a form of uncertainty, called *randomness*. A *probability space* Ω is assumed to be given once and for all, interpreted as consisting of all the possible paths of the prices of securities we are interested in. We will suppose that this probability space is rich enough to carry all the random objects we wish to construct and use. This assumption is not restrictive for our purposes, because we could always enlarge the space Ω, for example, by considering a product space. Note that Ω can be chosen to be a "canonical space," such as the space of continuous functions, or the space of *cadlag* (French acronym for "continuous from the right, with left limits") functions.

We endow the set Ω with a σ-field $\mathcal{F}$ which is also assumed to be fixed throughout this book, unless otherwise specified. $\mathcal{F}$ represents all the events that are or will eventually be observable.

Let $\mathbb{P}$ be a probability measure on the measurable space $(\Omega, \mathcal{F})$. The *(Lebesgue) integral* with respect to $\mathbb{P}$ of a random variable X (that is, a measurable function from $(\Omega, \mathcal{F})$ to $(\mathbb{R}^N, \mathcal{B}^N)$, where $\mathcal{B}^N$ is the Borel σ-field on $\mathbb{R}^N$) is denoted by $\mathbb{E}[X]$ instead of $\int_\Omega X\, d\mathbb{P}$ and is called the *expectation* of X. If we need to emphasize that the expectation operator $\mathbb{E}$ is relative to $\mathbb{P}$, we denote it by $\mathbb{E}_\mathbb{P}$. We assume that the reader is familiar with general notions of probability theory such as independence, correlation, conditional expectation, and so forth. For more details and references, we refer to [9], [45], or [49].

The probability space $(\Omega, \mathcal{F}, \mathbb{P})$ is endowed with a *filtration* $(\mathcal{F}_t, t \geq 0)$, that is, a family of sub-σ-fields of $\mathcal{F}$ such that $\mathcal{F}_s \subset \mathcal{F}_t$ for all $0 \leq s \leq t$. The filtration is said to be $\mathbb{P}$-complete if for all t, all $\mathbb{P}$-null sets belong to every $\mathcal{F}_t$; it is said to be right-continuous if for all $t > 0$,

$$\mathcal{F}_t = \bigcap_{\epsilon > 0} \mathcal{F}_{t+\epsilon}$$

It will be implicit in the sequel that all the filtrations we use have been previously completed and made right-continuous (this is always possible).

The filtration $\mathcal{F}_t$ represents the "flow of information" available; we will often deal with the filtration generated by some process (e.g., stock price process), in which case $\mathcal{F}_t$ represents past observations up to time t. For detailed studies on filtrations the reader can consult any book concerned with stochastic calculus, such as [44], [63], and [103].

1.2   PROCESSES

We will be concerned with random quantities whose values depend on time. Denote by $\mathcal{T}$ a subset of $\mathbb{R}_+$; $\mathcal{T}$ can be $\mathbb{R}_+$ itself, a bounded interval $[0, T]$, or a discrete set $\mathcal{T} = \{0, 1, \ldots\}$. In general, given a measurable space $(E, \mathcal{E})$, a *process* with values in E is an application $X : \Omega \times \mathcal{T} \to E$ that is measurable with respect to the σ-fields $\mathcal{E}$ and $\mathcal{F} \otimes \mathcal{B}_\mathcal{T}$, where $\mathcal{B}_\mathcal{T}$ denotes the Borel σ-field on $\mathcal{T}$.

In our applications we will need to consider only the case in which $E = \mathbb{R}^N$ and $\mathcal{E}$ is the Borel σ-field $\mathcal{B}^N$. From now on, we make these assumptions. A process will be denoted by X or $(X_t, t \in \mathcal{T})$; the (random) value of the process at time $t \in \mathcal{T}$ will be denoted by X_t or $X(t)$; we may sometimes wish to emphasize the dependence on ω, in which case we will use the notation $X_t(\omega)$ or $X(t, \omega)$. The jump at time t of a process X, is denoted by ΔX_t and defined by $\Delta X_t = X_t - X_{t-}$, where $X_{t-} = \lim_{\epsilon \downarrow 0} X_{t-\epsilon}$.

Where in Time?

Before we take on the study of processes themselves, we define a class of random times that form a cornerstone in the theory of stochastic processes. These are the times that are "suited" to the filtration $\mathscr{F}_t$.

DEFINITION 1.1

A random time T, that is a random variable with values in $\mathbb{R}_+ \cup \{\infty\}$, is called an $\mathscr{F}_t$-*stopping time* if for all $t \in \mathscr{T}$

$$\{T \leq t\} \in \mathscr{F}_t$$

This definition means that at each time t, based on the available information $\mathscr{F}_t$, one is able to determine whether T is in the past or in the future. Stopping times include constant times, as well as hitting times (i.e., random times τ of the form $\tau = \inf\{t \in \mathscr{T} : X_t \in B\}$, where B is a Borel set), among others.

From a financial point of view, the different quantities encountered are constrained to depend only on the available information at the time they are given a value. In mathematical words, we state the following:

DEFINITION 1.2

A process X is said to be *adapted* to the filtration $\mathscr{F}_t$ (or $\mathscr{F}_t$-adapted) if, for all $t \in \mathscr{T}$, X_t is $\mathscr{F}_t$-measurable.

A process used to model the price of an asset must be adapted to the flow of information available in the market. On the other hand, this information consists mainly in the prices of different assets. Given a process X, we can define a filtration $(\mathscr{F}_t^X)$, where $\mathscr{F}_t^X$ is the smallest sub-σ-field of $\mathscr{F}$ that makes the variables $(X_u, u \leq t)$ simultaneously measurable. The filtration $\mathscr{F}_t^X$ is said to be generated by X, and X is clearly adapted to it. One also speaks of X "in its own filtration."

Because we do not make the assumption that the processes we consider have continuous paths, we need to introduce a fine view of the "past." Continuous processes play a special role in this setting.

DEFINITION 1.3

1. The *predictable σ-field* $\mathscr{P}$ is the σ-field on $\Omega \times \mathscr{T}$ generated by $\mathscr{F}_t$-adapted processes whose paths are continuous.

2. A process X is said to be *predictable* if it is measurable with respect to $\mathscr{P}$.

That is, $\mathscr{P}$ is the smallest σ-field on $\Omega \times \mathscr{T}$ such that every process X, viewed as a function of (ω, t), for which $t \mapsto X(t)$ is continuous, is $\mathscr{P}$-measurable. It can be shown that $\mathscr{P}$ is also generated by random intervals $(S, T]$ where $S < T$ are stopping times.

A process that describes the number of shares in a trading strategy must be predictable, because the investment decision is taken before the price has a possible instantaneous shock.

In discrete time, the definition of a predictable process is much simpler, since then a process $(X_i, i \in \mathbb{N})$ is predictable if for each n, X_n is $\mathscr{F}_{n-1}$-measurable. However, we have the satisfactory property that if X is an $\mathscr{F}_t$-adapted process, then the process of left limits $(X_{t-}, t \geq 0)$ is predictable. For more details about predictable processes, see [27] or [63].

Let us also mention the optional σ-field: It is the σ-field $\mathcal{O}$ on $\Omega \times \mathscr{T}$ generated by $\mathscr{F}_t$-adapted processes with right-continuous paths. It will not be, for our purposes, as crucial as the predictable σ-field; see, however, Chapter 2 for a situation where this is needed.

We end this discussion by introducing the notion of localization, which is the key to establishing certain results in a general case.

DEFINITION 1.4

A *localizing sequence* (T_n) is an increasing sequence of stopping times such that $T_n \to \infty$ as $n \to \infty$.

In this chapter, a property is said to hold *locally* if there exists a localizing sequence such that the property holds on every interval $[0, T_n]$. This notion is important, because there are many interesting cases in which important properties hold only locally (and not on a fixed interval, $[0, \infty)$, for example).

Martingales and Semimartingales

Among the adapted processes defined in the foregoing section, not all are suitable for financial modelling. The work of Harrison and Pliska [60] shows that only a certain class of processes, called *semimartingales* are good candidates. Indeed, the reader familiar with the theory of arbitrage knows that the stock price process must be a local martingale under an appropriate probability measure; Girsanov's theorem then implies that it must be a semimartingale under any (locally) equivalent probability measure.

DEFINITION 1.5

A process X is called an $\mathcal{F}_t$-*martingale* if it is integrable (i.e., $\mathbb{E}[|X_t|] < \infty$ for all t), $\mathcal{F}_t$-adapted, and if it satisfies, for all $0 \leq s \leq t$

$$\mathbb{E}[X_t|\mathcal{F}_s] = X_s \qquad (1.1)$$

X is called a *local martingale* if there is a localizing sequence (T_n) such that for all n, $(X_{t \wedge T_n}, t \geq 0)$ is a martingale. X is called a *semimartingale* if it is $\mathcal{F}_t$-adapted and can be written

$$X_t = X_0 + M_t + V_t \qquad (1.2)$$

where M is a local martingale, V has a.s. (almost surely) finite variation, and M and V are null at time $t = 0$. If V can be chosen to be predictable, X is called a *special semimartingale* and the decomposition with such V is called the *canonical decomposition*.

If we need to emphasize the underlying probability measure $\mathbb{P}$, we will say that X is a $\mathbb{P}$-(semi)martingale.

With a semimartingale X are associated two increasing processes, called the quadratic variation and the conditional quadratic variation. These processes are interesting because they allow us to compute the decomposition of a semimartingale under a change of probability measure: This is the famous Girsanov theorem (see Section 1.3). We give a brief introduction to these processes here; for more details, see for example [27], [44], [63], [100], [103], [104], [105].

We first turn to the quadratic variation of semimartingale.

DEFINITION 1.6

Let X be a semimartingale such that $\mathbb{E}[X_t^2] < \infty$ for all t. There exists an increasing process, denoted by $[X, X]$, and called the *quadratic variation* of X, such that

$$[X, X]_t = \plim_{n \uparrow \infty} \sum_{t_i \in \tau^{(n)}} (X_{t_i} - X_{t_{i-1}})^2 \qquad (1.3)$$

where for each n, $\tau^{(n)} = (0 = t_0 < t_1 < \cdots < t_{p_n} = t)$ is a subdivision of $[0, t]$ whose mesh $\sup_{1 \le i \le p_n}(t_i - t_{i-1})$ tends to 0 as n tends to ∞.

The abbreviation "plim" stands for "limit in probability." It can be shown that the above definition is actually meaningful: The limit does not depend on a particular sequence of subdivisions. Moreover, if X is a martingale, the quadratic variation is a compensator of X^2; that is, $X^2 - [X, X]$ is again a martingale. More generally, given a process X, another process Y will be called a *compensator* for X if $X - Y$ is a local martingale. Because of the properties of martingales, compensation is the key to many properties when paths are not supposed to be continuous.

Given two semimartingales X and Y, we define the quadratic covariation of X and Y by a polarization identity:

$$[X, Y] = \frac{1}{2}([X + Y, X + Y] - [X, X] - [Y, Y])$$

Let M be a martingale. It can be shown that there exist two uniquely determined martingales M^c and M^d such that: $M = M^c + M^d$, M^c has continuous paths and M^d is orthogonal to any continuous martingale; that is, $M^d N$ is a martingale for any continuous martingale N. M^c is called the *martingale continuous part* of M, while M^d is called the *purely discontinuous part*. If X is a special semimartingale, with canonical decomposition $X = M + V$, X^c denotes the martingale continuous part of M, that is $X^c \equiv M^c$.

Note that the jump at time t of the quadratic variation of a semimartingale X is simply given by $\Delta[X, X]_t = (\Delta X_t)^2$. We have the following important property:

$$[X^c, X^c]_t = [X, X]_t^c = [X, X]_t - \sum_{s \le t} \Delta[X, X]_s \qquad (1.4)$$

where the last sum is actually meaningful (see [100]).

We now turn to the conditional quadratic variation.

DEFINITION 1.7

Let X be a semimartingale such that $\mathbb{E}[X_t^2] < \infty$ for all t. If

$$\operatorname*{plim}_{n \uparrow \infty} \sum_{t_i \in \tau^{(n)}} \mathbb{E}\left[(X_{t_i} - X_{t_{i-1}})^2 | \mathscr{F}_{t_{i-1}}\right] \qquad (1.5)$$

exists, where for each n, $\tau^{(n)} = (0 = t_0 < t_1 < \cdots < t_{p_n} = t)$ is a subdivision of $[0, t]$ whose mesh $\sup_{1 \le i \le p_n} t_i - t_{i-1}$ tends to 0 as n tends to ∞, and the limit does not depend on a particular subdivision, this limit is called the *conditional quadratic variation* of X and is denoted by $\langle X, X \rangle_t$. In that case, $\langle X, X \rangle_t$ is an increasing process.

In contrast to the quadratic variation, the limit in (1.5) may fail to exist for some semimartingales X. However, it can be shown that the limit exists, and that the process $\langle X, X \rangle$ is well-defined, if X is a special semimartingale, in particular for a Lévy process or a continuous semimartingale, for example.

Similar to the case of quadratic variation, the conditional quadratic covariation is defined as

$$\langle X, Y \rangle = \frac{1}{2} \left(\langle X + Y, X + Y \rangle - \langle X, X \rangle - \langle Y, Y \rangle \right)$$

as soon as this expression makes sense.

It can also be proven that when it exists, the conditional quadratic variation is the predictable compensator of the quadratic variation; that is, $\langle X, X \rangle$ is a predictable process and $[X, X] - \langle X, X \rangle$ is a martingale. It follows that if X is a martingale, $X^2 - \langle X, X \rangle$ is also a martingale, and the quadratic variation is the predictable compensator of X^2. The (conditional) quadratic variation has the following well-known properties, provided the quantities considered exist:

- The applications $(X, Y) \mapsto [X, Y]$ and $(X, Y) \mapsto \langle X, Y \rangle$ are linear in X and Y.
- If X has finite variation, $[X, Y] = \langle X, Y \rangle = 0$ for any semimartingale Y.

Moreover we have the following important identity (see [100]):

$$[X^c, X^c] = \langle X^c, X^c \rangle$$

so that if X has continuous paths, $\langle X, X \rangle$ is identical to $[X, X]$. The (conditional) quadratic variation will appear into the decomposition of $F(X)$ for suitable F, given by Itō's formula, which lies at the heart of stochastic calculus.

Markov Processes

We now introduce briefly another class of processes that are memoryless *at stopping times*.

DEFINITION 1.8

1. An $\mathcal{F}_t$-adapted process X is called a *Markov process* in the filtration $(\mathcal{F}_t)$ if for all $t \geq 0$, for every measurable and bounded functional F,

$$\mathbb{E}[F(X_{t+s}, s \geq 0)|\mathcal{F}_t] = \mathbb{E}[F(X_{t+s}, s \geq 0)|X_t] \qquad (1.6)$$

2. X is called a *strong Markov process* if (1.6) holds with t replaced by any finite stopping time T.

In other words, for a Markov process, at each time t, the whole past is summarized in the present value of the process X_t. For a strong Markov process, this is true with a stopping time. In financial words, an investment decision is often made on the basis of the present state of the market, that in some sense sums up its history.

A nice feature of Markov processes is the Feynman-Kac formula; this formula links Markov processes to (integro-)partial differential equations and makes available numerical techniques such as the finite difference method explained in Chapter 4. We do not go further into Markov processes and go on with stochastic calculus. Some relationships between Markov processes and semimartingales are discussed in [28].

1.3 STOCHASTIC CALCULUS

With the processes defined in the previous section (semimartingales), a theory of (stochastic) integral calculus can be built and used to model financial time series. Accordingly, this section contains the two results of probability theory that are most useful in finance: Itō's formula and the Girsanov theorem, both in a quite general form.

The construction and properties of the stochastic integral are well known, and the financial reader can think of most of them by taking the parallel of a portfolio strategy (see Section 1.4 and Chapter 2).

In general, the integral of a process H with respect to another one X is well-defined provided H is locally bounded and predictable and X is a semimartingale with $\mathbb{E}[X_t^2] < \infty$ for all t. The integral can then be thought of as the limit of elementary sums

$$\int_0^t H_s \, dX_s = \text{``} \lim_{n \uparrow \infty} \sum_{t_i \in \tau^{(n)}} H_{t_i}(X_{t_{i+1}} - X_{t_i}) \text{''}$$

where for each n, $\tau^{(n)} = (0 = t_0 < t_1 < \cdots < t_{p_n} = t)$ is a subdivision of $[0, t]$ whose mesh $\sup_{1 \leq i \leq p_n}(t_i - t_{i-1})$ tends to 0 as n tends to ∞. See [27], [100], [103], or [104] for a rigorous definition.

Note an important property of the stochastic integral. Let X, Y be semimartingales and H a predictable process such that $\int H_s dY_s$ is well-defined; the following formula holds:

$$\left[X, \int_0^{\cdot} H_s dY_s \right]_t = \int_0^t H_s d[X, Y]_s \tag{1.7}$$

where $\int_0^{\cdot} H_s dY_s$ denotes the process $(\int_0^t H_s dY_s, t \geq 0)$. The same formula holds with $[.,.]$ replaced with $\langle.,.\rangle$, provided the latter exists; this follows from the linearity of the quadratic variation and the stochastic integral.

Itō's Formula

We can now state the famous *Itō's formula*. More details can be found in the references mentioned previously. Let $X = (X^1, \ldots, X^n)$ be a semimartingale with values in $\mathbb{R}^n$ and F be a function $\mathbb{R}^n \to \mathbb{R}^m$ of class C^2. Then $F(X)$ is a semimartingale, and

$$\begin{aligned} F(X_t) = F(X_0) &+ \sum_{i=1}^{n} \int_0^t \frac{\partial F}{\partial x^i}(X_{s-}) dX_s^i \\ &+ \frac{1}{2} \sum_{i=1}^{n} \sum_{j=1}^{n} \int_0^t \frac{\partial^2 F}{\partial x^i \partial x^j}(X_s) d[X^i, X^j]_s^c \\ &+ \sum_{s \leq t} \left\{ F(X_s) - F(X_{s-}) - \sum_{i=1}^{n} \frac{\partial F}{\partial x^i}(X_{s-}) \Delta X_s^i \right\} \end{aligned} \tag{1.8}$$

where ΔX is the jump process of X. Itō's formula is often written in the differential form

$$\begin{aligned} dF(X_t) = &\sum_{i=1}^{n} \frac{\partial F}{\partial x^i}(X_{t-}) dX_t^i \\ &+ \frac{1}{2} \sum_{i=1}^{n} \sum_{j=1}^{n} \frac{\partial^2 F}{\partial x^i \partial x^j}(X_t) d[X^i, X^j]_t^c \\ &+ dZ_t \end{aligned} \tag{1.9}$$

where

$$Z_t = \sum_{s \leq t} \left\{ F(X_s) - F(X_{s-}) - \sum_{i=1}^{n} \frac{\partial F}{\partial x^i}(X_{s-}) \Delta X_s^i \right\}$$

Itō's formula shows that the class of semimartingales is stable under the action of C^2 functions. In fact, it can be shown that the class of semimartingales is stable under the action of convex functions; this is the Itō-Meyer-Tanaka formula (see [100] or [103]). We will not need it in this book and we content ourselves with (1.8) and (1.9).

Girsanov's Theorem

Together with Itō's formula, Girsanov's theorem is probably the best-known theorem in the world of finance. It allows one to compute the decomposition of a semimartingale under a change of probability. Let us state the result:

Let $T > 0$ be fixed and Z be a strictly positive, uniformly integrable $\mathbb{P}$-martingale with $\mathbb{E}[Z_t] = 1$. We can then define a probability $\mathbb{Q}$ on $\mathscr{F}_T$ by the formula

$$\mathbb{Q}(A) = \mathbb{E}[1_A Z_T]$$

Let $X = M + V$ be a $\mathbb{P}$-semimartingale, where M is a $\mathbb{P}$-local martingale. Then

$$M'_t := M_t - \int_0^t \frac{1}{Z_s} d[M, Z]_s \tag{1.10}$$

is a $\mathbb{Q}$-local martingale. Note that the process $V'_t = V_t + \int_0^t \frac{1}{Z_s} d[M, Z]_s$ has finite variation, hence X is a $\mathbb{Q}$-semimartingale with decomposition $X = M' + V'$.

If the predictable covariation of M and Z exists, then

$$M''_t := M_t - \int_0^t \frac{1}{Z_{s-}} d\langle M, Z \rangle_s \tag{1.11}$$

is a $\mathbb{Q}$-local martingale. In particular if X is a special $\mathbb{P}$-semimartingale, with canonical decomposition $X = M + V$, then X is a special $\mathbb{Q}$-semimartingale, with canonical decomposition $M'' + V''$, where

$$V''_t = V_t + \int_0^t \frac{1}{Z_{s-}} d\langle M, Z \rangle_s$$

Girsanov's theorem states that the class of semimartingales is stable under a locally equivalent change of probability. The same result holds with weaker assumptions on the density process Z (see [100] or [103]). In this book we will always deal with processes such that Equation (1.11) is true, which is the most interesting case of Girsanov's theorem.

1.4   FINANCIAL INTERPRETATIONS

In this section, we hint at basic financial interpretations of the notions introduced earlier. The financial meaning should become clearer in further chapters as more practical examples are developed. The reader may also consult [69] or [89].

First of all, the use of stochastic processes in financial modeling refers to the uncertainty about the future evolution of stock prices. As already mentioned, the notion of a filtration $\mathscr{F}_t$ is used to represent the flow of information. Note that the use of a filtration assumes *no loss of information* as time goes on. This is somehow balanced by the use of Markov processes and the renewal property. Adaptedness of price processes means that the price of the assets is determined on the basis of the information available. Predictable processes will be used to represent portfolio strategies (the number of shares the investor chooses to hold); the decision has to be made before a jump happens—if any.

The stochastic integral expresses the result of a portfolio strategy; that is, the sum of the gains and losses experienced by the portfolio in elementary intervals of time. Here "elementary interval" means "infinitesimal interval" (or dt) in continuous time, or the smallest interval in a subdivision $(t_i - t_{i-1})$ in discrete time.

A martingale is a translation of the concept of a *fair game*, hence of no arbitrage (see next chapter for details). Semimartingales can be interpreted as martingales seen from another probability measure, such as asset prices seen not from the market point of view but from the personal point of view of an investor.

Girsanov's theorem allows us to transfer from the market point of view to a subjective point of view and vice versa; Itō's formula expresses that products based on primary assets have the same price structure and do not change the nature of the market. Moreover, these two results give us the decomposition of processes as semimartingales, which can be seen, loosely speaking, as a mean-variance decomposition in infinitesimal time.

The Markov property can be interpreted as a translation of the market efficiency hypothesis: At a given time, all the information is revealed by the present value of prices or state variables. The models we will present in subsequent chapters all use strong Markov processes; although the price process itself is not necessarily a Markov process, the (multidimensional) process that also incorporates state variables does possess the Markov property.

1.5   TWO CANONICAL EXAMPLES

To illustrate the theory described previously, we present its application to two very common processes that will be used extensively in the sequel:

Brownian motion and Poisson processes. Both these processes are Lévy processes, a class of processes that will be studied in detail in Chapter 3.

Let us first turn to Brownian motion. Most of the financial models in use today are based on Brownian motion and on derived processes such as diffusion processes. These processes are studied in great detail in [68] and [103]. Recall the basic setting: We have a probability space $(\Omega, \mathscr{F}, \mathbb{P})$ endowed with a filtration $\mathscr{F}_t$.

DEFINITION 1.9

A process $W : \Omega \times \mathbb{R}_+ \to \mathbb{R}$ is an *$\mathscr{F}_t$-Brownian motion* if

1. For all t, W_t is $\mathscr{F}_t$-measurable.
2. For some $\sigma > 0$, for all $0 \leq s \leq t$, the variable $W_t - W_s$ is independent of $\mathscr{F}_s$ and has a Gaussian distribution with mean 0 and variance $\sigma^2(t - s)$.
3. With probability 1, its paths $t \mapsto W_t$ are continuous.

For $\mu \in \mathbb{R}$ and $\sigma > 0$, the process $X_t := \mu t + \sigma W_t$ is called a Brownian motion with drift.

Because of condition 2 in Definition 1.9, we have for $s \leq t$:

$$\mathbb{E}[W_t|\mathscr{F}_s] = \mathbb{E}[W_t - W_s + W_s|\mathscr{F}_s]$$
$$= W_s$$

so W is a martingale (hence also a semimartingale). Moreover it is easy to see that $W_t^2 - t$ is also a martingale, so the quadratic variation of W is $[W, W]_t = t$ (and $\langle W, W \rangle_t = [W, W]_t$ because the paths are continuous). The important result that these two properties characterize an $\mathscr{F}_t$-Brownian motion was discovered by Paul Lévy (see [103]).

Consider the process $S_t = e^{\mu t + \sigma W_t}$ for $\mu \in \mathbb{R}$ and $\sigma > 0$. By Itō's formula, we have

$$S_t = S_0 + \int_0^t S_u \mu du + \int_0^t S_u \sigma dW_u + \frac{1}{2}\int_0^t S_u \sigma^2 d\langle W, W \rangle_u$$
$$= S_0 + \int_0^t S_u(\mu + \sigma^2/2)du + \int_0^t \sigma S_u dW_u$$

or in the differential form (1.9)

$$dS_t = S_t\left((\mu + \sigma^2/2)dt + \sigma dW_t\right)$$

Consider now the process $Z_t = e^{\theta W_t - \theta^2 t/2}$ ($\theta \in \mathbb{R}$): Z is a positive, uniformly integrable martingale with expectation 1. Define a probability measure by $\mathbb{Q}(A) = \mathbb{E}[Z_T 1_A]$ for $A \in \mathscr{F}_T$. By Girsanov's theorem,

$$W'_t = W_t - \int_0^t \frac{1}{Z_s} d\langle W, Z \rangle_s$$

is a $\mathbb{Q}$-martingale. Because $\langle W, Z \rangle_t = \int_0^t \theta Z_s ds$, we see that $W'_t = W_t - \theta t$; because $\langle W', W' \rangle_t = t$, we conclude, by Lévy's result, that W' is a Brownian motion under $\mathbb{Q}$.

Let us now turn to the Poisson process, and follow the same lines as we did for the Brownian motion. The underlying probability space and filtration remain.

DEFINITION 1.10

A process $N : \Omega \times \mathbb{R}_+ \to \mathbb{N}$ is an $\mathscr{F}_t$-*Poisson process* if

1. For all t, N_t is $\mathscr{F}_t$-measurable.
2. For some $\lambda > 0$, for all $0 \le s \le t$, $N_t - N_s$ is independent of $\mathscr{F}_s$, and has a Poisson distribution with parameter $\lambda(t - s)$; that is,

$$\mathbb{P}[N_t - N_s = k] = e^{-\lambda(t-s)} \frac{(\lambda(t - s))^k}{k!}$$

3. With probability 1, the paths of N are continuous from the right, and all the jumps have size 1.

λ is called the *intensity* of the process.

Note the similarity to the definition of the Brownian motion. N itself is not a martingale, but one can check that $\overline{N}_t = N_t - \lambda t$ is a martingale, called a *compensated Poisson process*. It is also easy to check that $[N, N] = [\overline{N}, \overline{N}]_t = N_t$ and that the conditional quadratic variation exists and is given by $\langle N, N \rangle = \langle \overline{N}, \overline{N} \rangle = \lambda t$. Similar to the result of Lévy for the Brownian motion, Watanabe showed that these properties characterize an $\mathscr{F}_t$-Poisson process (see [103]).

Consider the process $S_t = e^{\mu t + \sigma N_t}$. By Itō's formula, we have

$$S_t = S_0 + \int_0^t \mu S_u du + \int_0^t \sigma S_{u-} dN_u + \sum_{u \le t} (S_u - S_{u-} - \sigma S_{u-} \Delta N_u) 1_{\Delta N_u \ne 0}$$

$$= S_0 + \int_0^t \mu S_u du + \sum_{u \le t} S_{u-}(e^\sigma - 1) 1_{\Delta N_u \ne 0}$$

or, in the differential form (1.9)

$$dS_t = S_{t-}(\mu dt + (e^\sigma - 1)dN_t)$$

In particular, we see that S is a martingale if $\mu = -\lambda(e^\sigma - 1)$ (or, equivalently, $\sigma = \ln(1 - \mu/\lambda)$).

For $\zeta > -1$, consider the process $Z_t = e^{\ln(1+\zeta)N_t - \lambda\zeta t}$; according to the preceding remark, this is a positive martingale, with expectation 1. Define a probability $\mathbb{Q}$ by $\mathbb{Q}(A) = \mathbb{E}[1_A Z_T]$ for $A \in \mathscr{F}_T$. By Girsanov's theorem,

$$N'_t = \overline{N}_t - \int_0^t \frac{1}{Z_{s-}} d\langle \overline{N}, Z\rangle_s$$

is a $\mathbb{Q}$-martingale, where by (1.7)

$$\langle \overline{N}, Z\rangle_t = \left\langle \overline{N}, \int_0^{\cdot} \zeta Z_{s-} d\overline{N}_s \right\rangle = \int_0^t \zeta Z_{s-} d\langle \overline{N}, \overline{N}\rangle_s = \lambda\zeta \int_0^t Z_s ds$$

So we have $N'_t = \overline{N}_t - \lambda\zeta t = N_t - \lambda(1 + \zeta)t$. By the characterization result of Watanabe just mentioned, N is a Poisson process under $\mathbb{Q}$, with intensity $\lambda(1 + \zeta)$.

The two examples presented above highlight the use of Itō's formula and Girsanov's theorem in very simple cases. These can be considerably generalized: Brownian motion is the basis for the construction of a large class of processes with continuous paths, called diffusion processes, which have been extensively studied and are used in most financial models today. Poisson processes can be generalized in many ways. Their intensity λ can be taken as a function of time; as a function of an underlying stochastic process, leading to so-called Cox processes or marked point processes (see [18] or [35]); or even as a measure on a measurable space. The characterization result mentioned previously remains valid in most of these cases.

In this chapter we have tried to summarize very briefly the principal mathematical notions of the theory of stochastic processes and stochastic calculus, without restricting attention to the case of continuous paths, as is often the case in finance. By adopting an intuitive point of view, we hope to facilitate comprehension for the reader who is not necessarily familiar with this theory; we lose a little precision and generality from a theoretical point of view, but we try to maintain a certain level of rigor. The two examples we studied show typical uses of the tools of stochastic calculus in the context of financial applications.

In the following chapters we will not always explicitly refer to the concepts introduced here. However, they are the ground upon which the theory and applications developed in the following chapters rely.

CHAPTER 2

Incomplete Markets

A ssume we model the prices of a set of assets as a stochastic process on some probability space. It is then well known that there is a close connection between the no arbitrage of the market in this model and the existence of a measure under which the discounted prices are martingales (a martingale measure). Furthermore, there is a connection between completeness in the model and the uniqueness of a martingale measure. In this chapter, we illustrate why these connections are in some ways quite obvious (at least at an intuitive level) and we describe the exact relationships between martingale measures and completeness/no arbitrage. The rest of the chapter is devoted to incomplete markets and to how to make incomplete markets complete by adding more tradeable instruments. We explore the relationship between the "number of martingale measures" and the number of traded assets needed to make the market complete, and finally we discuss hedging and pricing in incomplete markets (as every real market is).

The aim of this and the following chapter is to explain quite technical concepts in a way that is of value both to an audience without a background in the general theory of stochastic calculus and to those with a solid knowledge of stochastic processes. In order to achieve this we will describe every concept in a fairly nonmathematical way before the mathematical definitions are given.

2.1 MARTINGALE MEASURES

The concept of equivalent martingale measures is a key point in the theory of derivatives pricing, because it turns out that completeness and the absence of arbitrage can be determined from the existence and uniqueness of equivalent martingale measures.

15

We are considering a market with a money market account

$$B(t) = \exp\left(\int_0^t r(s)ds\right)$$

where r is interpreted as the continuously compounded short rate. That is, $r(t)$ is the interest rate for the period t to $t + dt$. Furthermore, we assume there are N "risky" assets $S = (S_1, \ldots, S_N) = (S_1(t), \ldots, S_N(t))$. Even though the money market is called riskless, r can certainly be (and in general is) a stochastic process. However, B is less risky than S in the sense that the short-term return on B is known, whereas it is generally completely unknown for S.

Clearly, the fact that S and r are stochastic processes must reflect the fact that future values are unknown. However, at time t, we know $S_i(u)$ and $r(u)$ for all $u \leq t$. As described in Chapter 1, these properties are modeled by the increasing family of σ-algebras $\{\mathcal{F}_t, t \in [0, \infty)\}$. We require that r and S be *adapted* to $\{\mathcal{F}_t\}$. Loosely speaking, this means that events that can be described by the values of r and S up to time t are part of $\{\mathcal{F}_t\}$, the information available at time t. Events like $\{S_i(t) \in I\}$ and $\{\sup_{\{u \leq t\}} S_i(u) \in I\}$ (provided S is continuous from left or right), where I is some interval, are typical, but events like $\{\mathbb{E}[B(t)/B(T) \mid \mathcal{F}_t] \in I\}$ are also interesting. If $\mathbb{E}$ is expectation under a suitable measure, $\mathbb{E}[B(t)/B(T) \mid \mathcal{F}_t]$ is actually the price at time t of the zero-coupon bond maturing at T.

Since $\mathcal{F}_t$ is interpreted as the knowledge we have at time t, $\mathcal{F}_t$ should not contain too much information about what happens after time t. In fact, it would be natural to work exclusively with filtrations consisting of the minimal σ-algebras such that the traded assets are adapted. For technical reasons, this is not possible, but such filtrations describe the framework we are working in pretty well, and this should normally be the way one thinks about $\mathcal{F}_t$. Exceptions include models with an unobservable state variable, such as most stochastic volatility models, which we will describe in further detail later (see Example 2.4).

DEFINITION 2.1

The mathematical framework in which we are working consists of a probability space $(\Omega, \mathcal{F}, \mathbb{P})$ endowed with a filtration $\{\mathcal{F}_t, t \in [0, \infty)\}$ which is right-continuous and complete (it satisfies the "usual conditions"). The tradeable assets S and B as defined above are assumed to be progressively measurable with respect to $\{\mathcal{F}_t\}$.

REMARK

Progressive measurability of a process s means that for any $t > 0$, the map

$$(s, \omega) \in [0, t] \times \Omega \mapsto S(s, \omega)$$

is measurable with respect to $\mathscr{B}[0, t] \times \mathscr{F}_t$ where $\mathscr{B}[0, t]$ is the Borel σ-algebra on $[0, t]$.

In this general framework, an equivalent martingale measure $\hat{\mathbb{P}}$ is any probability measure that is equivalent to $\mathbb{P}$ (i.e., for any set $A \in \mathscr{F}$, $\hat{\mathbb{P}}(A) = 0$ if and only if $\mathbb{P}(A) = 0$) and such that the deflated asset prices

$$\tilde{S}_i(t) := \exp\left(-\int_0^t r(s)ds\right)S_i(t) = \frac{S_i(t)}{B(t)}$$

are martingales under $\hat{\mathbb{P}}$. We note that the deflated money market asset is trivially a martingale under all probability measures. In fact, it constantly equals 1, and *all* traded assets deflated are thus martingales under a martingale measure.

A $\hat{\mathbb{P}}$ martingale is a stochastic process X such that $\hat{\mathbb{E}}[|X(t)|] < \infty$ and $\hat{\mathbb{E}}[X(t) \mid \mathscr{F}_s] = X(s)$ for all $t \geq 0$ and all $0 \leq s \leq t$ (cf. (1.1)). So under a martingale measure the expected returns on all traded assets are the same even though they are not all equally volatile. For this reason, a martingale measure is also called a risk-neutral measure. Of course, the equivalence of measures is very important, and it is also imposes significant restrictions on the martingale measures we can consider. For instance, the Girsanov theorem implies that if we have a Brownian motion on a probability space, then under any equivalent measure, this process will be a Brownian motion with drift.

2.2 SELF-FINANCING STRATEGIES, COMPLETENESS, AND NO ARBITRAGE

Pricing of derivatives in complete markets with no arbitrage opportunities is simply a question of replicating the payout of the derivative by a self-financing trading strategy and then using the value of the replicating portfolio as the price of the derivative in question. A self-financing trading strategy is a way of trading the underlyings without adding or withdrawing money from the total portfolio. To illustrate these concepts, let us look at an almost trivial example that replicates a forward contract and therefore determines the price of the forward.

Assume asset number 1 does not pay dividends. Borrow $S_1(0)$ at time $t = 0$ and buy 1 unit of asset number 1. Then at time $T = 1$ year sell the stock for $S_1(T)$ and pay back the loan at $S_i(0)B(T)$. If interest rates are deterministic (or if it is possible to borrow money for 1 year at a fixed rate, which it normally is) the payment on the loan is known already at time 0, and this self-financing strategy replicates the payoff on a forward contract on asset 1. To continue this example, let us assume that interest rates are in fact deterministic and that party A would like to do a forward contract with party B to buy one stock of asset 1 for K at time $T = 1$ year in the future. Hence at time T, A receives $S_1(T) - K$. Now if party B receives $S_1(0) - K/B(T)$ at time 0 (remember that B is deterministic, so $B(T)$ is known at time 0), then by taking out a loan of $K/B(T)$, B can buy the stock. At time T, the stock is sold to the customer for the contract price of K, which will exactly pay back the loan. Hence B would be happy to sell the product for any price greater than or equal to $S_1(0) - K/B(T)$, and A should not buy the product for more than $S_1(0) - K/B(T)$. So clearly, the forward can be replicated, and in an arbitrage-free market the fair price would be $S_1(0) - K/B(T)$. Of course, in principle there could be another self-financing trading strategy that replicates the payoff and that requires a different initial endowment from $S_1(0) - K/B(T)$. This would be an example of arbitrage.

Loosely speaking, a given financial market is complete if every contingent claim (derivative) can be exactly replicated by trading the assets S and the money market account, and no arbitrage means that it is impossible to make a positive profit (over and above the money market return) with no risk of an actual loss. More precisely:

DEFINITION 2.2

A contingent claim that pays out at time T is a $\mathscr{F}_T$ measurable random variable.

A self-financing trading strategy is a triple (x, V, X), where $x \in \mathbb{R}$ and V and X are adapted processes such that

$$\int_0^t X(u) \cdot dS(u) \qquad \text{and} \qquad \int_0^t r(u)(V(u) - S(u) \cdot X(u))du \qquad (2.1)$$

are well defined for $t \le T$ and

$$V(t) = x + \int_0^t X(u) \cdot dS(u) + \int_0^t r(u)(V(u) - S(u) \cdot X(u))du$$

The market is said to be complete if, for every contingent claim Z paying out at time T, there exists a self-financing trading strategy (x, V, X) such that

$$V(T) = x + \int_0^T X(u)dS(u) + \int_0^T r(u)(V(u) - S(u) \cdot X(u))du = Z$$

with probability 1.

(x, V, X) is called an arbitrage if $x \leq 0$, $V(T) \geq 0$, and $V(T) > 0$ with positive probability. The market admits no arbitrage if there are no such arbitrage strategies.

In fact, the definition of no arbitrage above is too restrictive in continuous time, as we will see in Example 2.3 and Section 2.4. For now, however, we will stick to the restrictive definition, which works fine in discrete-time cases and certainly illustrates the concept of arbitrage well.

The integrals are to be interpreted as

$$\int_0^t X(u) \cdot dS(u) = \sum_{i=1}^N \int_0^t X_i(u)dS_i(u)$$

and $S(u) \cdot X(u)$ is just the usual scalar product between N-vectors. The integrals are Itō stochastic integrals, so we assume that S is a semimartingale (cf. (1.2)) that is continuous from the right with limits from the left. We will not go into detail about the Itō integral and when it is defined; we will only mention that we require X to be predictable with respect to the filtration and that (almost) every path is continuous from the right with limits from the left. Apart from this, finiteness of certain expectations involving X and S may be required for the integrals to be well defined. If we consider only continuous processes, it is enough to assume that X is adapted.

A self-financing trading strategy is a collection of the initial value x of the portfolio; the stochastic process X, which specifies the amount of the asset S that is part of the portfolio at any time; and V, which is just the value of the portfolio. As described above, for a self-financing trading strategy all changes in the holding of any asset must be financed by buying or selling other assets (including the money market). As we see in (2.1), if the total portfolio value at time t is $V(t)$ and we hold $X(t)$ assets, then the amount of money in the money market account is $V(t) - X(t) \cdot S(t)$, and our return over $[t, t + \Delta t]$ is approximately

$$X(t) \cdot (S(t + \Delta t) - S(t)) + r(t)(V(t) - X(t) \cdot S(t))\Delta t$$

So intuitively, it seems very reasonable to use (2.1) as our definition of a self-financing portfolio. More rigorously, for a portfolio where X is constant over $[t, t + \Delta t)$, we get

$$V(u) = X(t) \cdot S(u) + \exp\left(\int_t^u r(s)ds\right)(V(t) - S(t) \cdot X(t)) \qquad (2.2)$$

for $u \in [t, t + \Delta t]$. Now using the fact that

$$\exp\left(-\int_t^u r(s)ds\right)X(t) \cdot S(u) - X(t) \cdot S(t)$$

$$= \int_t^u \left(\exp\left(-\int_t^{\bar{u}} r(s)ds\right)X(t) \cdot dS(\bar{u})\right.$$

$$\left. - r(\bar{u})\exp\left(-\int_t^{\bar{u}} r(s)ds\right)X(t) \cdot S(\bar{u})d\bar{u}\right)$$

we see that the right-hand side of (2.2) equals

$$\exp\left(\int_t^u r(s)ds\right)\left\{V(t) + \int_t^u \left(\exp\left(-\int_t^{\bar{u}} r(s)ds\right)X(t) \cdot dS(\bar{u})\right.\right.$$

$$\left.\left. - r(\bar{u})\exp\left(-\int_t^{\bar{u}} r(s)ds\right)X(t) \cdot S(\bar{u})d\bar{u}\right)\right\}$$

Similarly,

$$\exp\left(-\int_t^u r(\bar{u})d\bar{u}\right)V(u) - V(t) =$$

$$\int_t^u \left(\exp\left(-\int_t^{\bar{u}} r(s)ds\right)(dV(\bar{u}) - r(\bar{u})V(\bar{u})d\bar{u})\right)$$

If we insert the expression for $V(t)$, we get

$$V(u) = \exp\left(\int_t^u r(s)ds\right)\left\{\exp\left(-\int_t^u r(\bar{u})d\bar{u}\right)V(u)\right.$$

$$- \int_t^u \left(\exp\left(-\int_t^{\bar{u}} r(s)ds\right)(dV(\bar{u}) - r(\bar{u})V(\bar{u})d\bar{u})\right)$$

$$+ \int_t^u \exp\left(-\int_t^{\bar{u}} r(s)ds\right)X(t) \cdot dS(\bar{u})$$

$$\left. - \int_t^u r(\bar{u})\exp\left(-\int_t^{\bar{u}} r(s)ds\right)X(t) \cdot S(\bar{u})d\bar{u}\right\}$$

which, of course is equivalent to

$$dV(u) = X(t) \cdot dS(u) + r(u)(V(u) - X(t) \cdot S(u))du$$

Hence, for trading strategies that involve only discrete-time trading, it is obvious that (2.1) is a good definition of a self-financing strategy. Letting $\Delta t \to 0$, a sequence of discrete-time self-financing strategies will tend to a strategy that satisfies (2.1), which is therefore our definition of a general self-financing strategy.

Note also that any x and sufficiently well-behaved X define a unique self-financing strategy by (2.2), and conversely, if $V = \{V(t); t \in [0, T]\}$ is the value of a self-financing strategy, then x and X are uniquely defined.

2.3 EXAMPLES

We now give a few very simple examples to illustrate the concepts.

EXAMPLE 2.1

Assume that there is only one asset, S, which stays constant during $[0, 1)$ and $[1, \infty)$ (this is really a one-period model). We assume that the asset price starts at $S(0)$ and that at time 1 the price can jump to a, b, or c with probabilities $p_a \in [0, 1]$, $p_b \in [0, 1]$, and $p_c = 1 - p_a - p_b \in [0, 1]$. Furthermore, we assume that $a < b < c$.

For simplicity let us assume (as we will in fact often do) that $r \equiv 0$. As probability space, we can use the set $\{a, b, c\}$, and we can define the process S on this probability space by

$$S(\omega, t) = \begin{cases} S(0) & \text{if } t < 1 \\ a & \text{if } t \geq 1 \text{ and } \omega = a \text{ (Figure 2.1)} \\ b & \text{if } t \geq 1 \text{ and } \omega = b \text{ (Figure 2.2)} \\ c & \text{if } t \geq 1 \text{ and } \omega = c \text{ (Figure 2.3)} \end{cases}$$

If $\mathbb{P}$ is the original probability measure on $\{a, b, c\}$, then a probability measure $\hat{\mathbb{P}}$ is equivalent to $\mathbb{P}$ if and only if

$$\forall \omega \in \{a, b, c\} : \mathbb{P}(\{\omega\}) = 0 \Leftrightarrow \hat{\mathbb{P}}(\{\omega\}) = 0$$

(continued)

EXAMPLE 2.1   (*continued*)

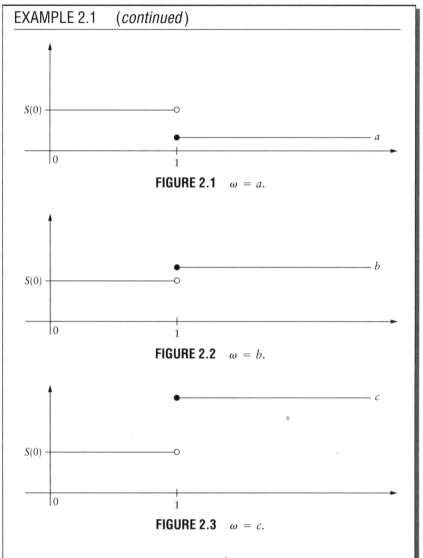

FIGURE 2.1 $\omega = a$.

FIGURE 2.2 $\omega = b$.

FIGURE 2.3 $\omega = c$.

Furthermore, S is a martingale under $\hat{\mathbb{P}}$ if and only if

$$a\hat{\mathbb{P}}(\{a\}) + b\hat{\mathbb{P}}(\{b\}) + c\hat{\mathbb{P}}(\{c\}) = S(0) \tag{2.3}$$

If we start by assuming that $p_a, p_b, p_c \neq 0$, an equivalent martingale measure must solve (2.3) with $\hat{\mathbb{P}}(\omega) \in (0, 1)$ for $\omega = a, b, c$. If $a \geq S(0)$, there is clearly no solution (recall $a < b < c$). In this case there is

(*continued*)

EXAMPLE 2.1   (*continued*)

also a clear arbitrage, because we can borrow $S(0)$ at time 0 and buy asset 1. At time 1, we then sell the stock and receive at least $S(0)$ (and strictly more than $S(0)$ with positive probability) and pay back the loan of $S(0)$. Similarly, if $c \le S(0)$, there is no martingale measure and an obvious arbitrage (this time we sell the stock at time 0 and buy it back at time 1).

On the other hand, if $a < S(0) < c$, there are infinitely many solutions for a martingale measure. In this case it is easy to show that there is no arbitrage in the model, because any portfolio is deterministic on $[0, 1)$, and in fact, for any self-financing trading strategy with initial value less than or equal to 0,

$$V(t) = X(t)S(0) + (V(t) - X(t)S(0)) \le 0, \qquad t \in [0, 1)$$

So we hold $X(t)$ in stock and $-X(t)S(0)$ in the money market. Define $x = \lim_{t \to 1-} X(t)$. Then we clearly need $x \ne 0$ if there is to be a positive probability of positive value of the portfolio at time 1. On the other hand, because $a < S(0) < c$, and because $p_a, p_c \ne 0$ no matter what nonzero amount of stock we hold, there is a positive probability of a negative portfolio value at time 1. On the other hand, the market is incomplete, as we easily see by noting that the value of any portfolio at time 1 is $xS(1) + y$ (where x is the amount of stock that is held at time 1 and y the amount of money in the money market account). Obviously, such a portfolio value cannot replicate $1_{S(\lambda) = a}$ (the indicator function).

Now let us assume that $p_b = 0$ and the two other probabilities are positive. As before, if $a \ge S(0)$ or $c \le S(0)$, there is no martingale measure (and there is arbitrage). But now, if $a < S(0) < c$, there is exactly one equivalent martingale measure. Again, it is easy to show there is no arbitrage, and now we can also easily show that the market is complete. In fact, completeness can be shown if we can show that any $\mathscr{F}_1$-measurable random variable can be replicated by a static portfolio set up at time 0. But a $\mathscr{F}_1$-measurable random variable is simply $Z = F(S(1))$ for some function on $\{a, c\}$. If x denotes the amount of stock and y the amount of cash we hold at time 1, then, to replicate Z, x and y must satisfy

$$\begin{cases} ax + y = F(a) \\ cx + y = F(c) \end{cases}$$

and because $a < c$, this set of equations has exactly one solution for any function F.

It is interesting to note that if we make the jump time stochastic in Example 2.1, it is not possible to achieve completeness *and* no arbitrage. This is because the randomness of the jump time in effect simply adds the possibility of a jump of size 0, and, as we saw in this example, we have completeness and no arbitrage if and only if there are only two possible jump sizes where one is strictly positive and the other strictly negative.

This also illustrates the fine line between completeness and no arbitrage. There has to be an equivalent martingale measure to avoid arbitrage, but the market is incomplete if there are more than one equivalent martingale measures. More informally, no arbitrage is ensured if we have sufficient randomness in the market, but too many sources of randomness make the market incomplete.

It is worth pointing out that the reason we cannot achieve no arbitrage and completeness when we introduce random jump times in Example 2.1 is that the stock has zero drift (actually, that the drift is the same as the money market rate of return). The point here is that by changing to an equivalent measure, we can change the jump intensity, but, of course, we cannot change the deterministic jump size. This is illustrated in the following example.

EXAMPLE 2.2

Let τ be exponentially distributed with parameter λ (i.e., $\mathbb{P}[\tau \leq t] = 1 - e^{-\lambda t}$) and define

$$
S(t) = \begin{cases} e^{\rho(t-1)}, & t < \min\{1, \tau\} \\ 0, & \tau \leq t \leq 1 \\ S(1)e^{r(t-1)}, & t > 1 \end{cases}
$$

Here r is the risk-free interest rate, which we assume is nonnegative and deterministic. This could be a model of a defaultable bond that matures at time $t = 1$, paying 1 if there has been no default before maturity and paying 0 in the case of default before maturity.

Clearly, if $\rho \leq r$, the market admits arbitrage (short-sell the bond and invest the proceeds in the money market).

On the other hand, if $\rho > r$, the market is arbitrage free. This is easy to see if we introduce $\tilde{\tau} = \min\{\tau, 1\}$ and note that we can show no arbitrage by showing that there is no self-financing trading strategy (x, V, X) with initial value $x = 0$ such that $V(\tilde{\tau}) \geq 0$ and $V(\tilde{\tau}) > 0$ with positive probability.

(continued)

EXAMPLE 2.2   (*continued*)

To have $V(\tilde{\tau}) \geq 0$, we must have

$$V(\tilde{\tau}-) - X(\tilde{\tau}-)S(\tilde{\tau}-) \geq 0$$

which in fact implies that

$$V(t) - X(t)S(t) \geq 0, \, t < \tau \qquad (2.4)$$

because the default can obviously happen at the next instance (or, more mathematically, for each $t < 1$, the σ-algebra on $\Omega_t = \{\omega \in \Omega \mid \tau(\omega) > t\}$ generated by $\chi_{\{\tau > t\}}S(t)$ is $\{\varnothing, \Omega_t\}$ and $\mathbb{P}[\tau \in [t, t + \delta]] > 0$ for all $\delta > 0$).

Because of (2.4) and the fact that (x, V, X) is self-financing with initial endowment $x = 0$,

$$\begin{aligned}
V(t) &= \int_0^t X(u)dS(u) + \int_0^t r(V(u) - X(u)S(u))du \\
&= \int_0^t \rho X(u)S(u)du + \int_0^t r(V(u) - X(u)S(u))du \\
&\leq \int_0^t (rV(u) + (\rho - r)V(u))du \\
&= \rho \int_0^t V(u)du
\end{aligned}$$

By Gronwall's lemma, $V(t) \leq 0$, and therefore $V \equiv 0$ and there is no arbitrage.

To show that the market is complete, we must show that any $\mathcal{F}_1$ measurable random variable Z can be replicated by a self-financing strategy. In this case, we can clearly write any such random variable as a (Borel measurable) function of τ, $Z = F(\tau)$. Because completeness can be shown by referring to representation theorems for martingales, as we shall see in the following, we will not rigorously prove completeness here. However, let us *assume* that the value of the contingent claim, which pays out Z at time 1, is uniquely determined as $V(t) = f(t, S(t))$ (which, of course, again means that the value depends on time to maturity and on whether default has happened). Let us assume that default has not happened at time t. Then the value of the derivative is $f(t, \exp(\rho(t - 1)))$. If we hold α stocks and β in the money market

(*continued*)

EXAMPLE 2.2 *(continued)*

account, the value of a portfolio consisting of the derivative and the α stocks and β in the money market account equals

$$\Pi(t) = f(t, e^{\rho(t-1)}) + \alpha e^{\rho(t-1)} + \beta$$

If there is no default in $[t, t + \Delta t]$, the value of the portfolio changes to

$$\Pi(t + \Delta t) = f(t + \Delta t, e^{\rho(t+\Delta t-1)}) + \alpha e^{\rho(t+\Delta t-1)} + \beta e^{r\Delta t}$$

and if there is a default, the value is

$$\Pi(t + \Delta t) = f(t + \Delta t, 0) + \beta e^{r\Delta t}$$

Clearly, by having

$$\alpha = (f(t + \Delta t, 0) - f(t + \Delta t, e^{\rho(t+\Delta t-1)})) / \exp(-\rho(t + \Delta t - 1))$$

the value of the portfolio at $t + \Delta t$ does not depend on the occurrence of default. In this special (and trivial) case, where the value of the claim depends only on the occurrence or nonoccurrence of default, we can statically hedge the claim. However, it is also clear that even if the default value of the claim is not in fact $f(t + \Delta t, 0)$ but depends on the actual time (in $[t, t + \Delta t]$) of default, by making Δt sufficiently small we can make the uncertainty as small as we like (provided of course, the default value is smooth with respect to the time of default). So, by approximating default times with discrete time, we can replicate the claim.

We end this section of examples with the classical diffusions:

EXAMPLE 2.3

Assume $W = (W_1, \ldots, W_K) = (W_1(t), \ldots, W_K(t))$ is a K-dimensional Brownian motion, and assume $\{\mathcal{F}_t\}$ is the completion of the σ-algebra generated by W. If $b : [0, \infty) \times \mathbb{R}^N \rightarrow \mathbb{R}^K$ and $\sigma : [0, \infty) \times \mathbb{R}^N \rightarrow \mathbb{R}^{N \otimes K}$ are bounded, Borel measurable, and Lipschitz continuous with respect to the space parameter, then we can define the traded assets as the

(continued)

EXAMPLE 2.3   (*continued*)

---

unique solution of the stochastic differential equation

$$dS_i(t) = b_i(t, S(t))S_i(t)dt + \sum_{j=1}^{K} \sigma_{i,j}(t, S(t))S_i(t)dW_j(t)$$

with given initial conditions.

If $S_i(0) > 0$, then there is a random variable ξ (actually a $\{\mathcal{F}_t\}$ stopping time) such that $S_i(t) > 0$ for all $t \in [0, \xi)$. For such t, we can use Itō's formula on $\ln S_i(t)$ to obtain

$$d(\ln S_i(t)) = \left(b_i(t, S(t)) - \frac{1}{2} \sum_{j=1}^{K} \sigma_{i,j}^2(t, S(t)) \right) dt$$

$$+ \sum_{j=1}^{K} \sigma_{i,j}(t, S(t))dW_j(t), \qquad 0 \le t \le \xi$$

From the classical existence-uniqueness results (cf. [68] or [103]), we know that S does not explode in finite time, so, of course, $\ln S_i(t)$ cannot reach $+\infty$ in finite time. More precisely,

$$\lim_{n \to \infty} \left(\inf \{t; \ln S_i(t) > n\} \right) = \infty \quad \text{a.e.}$$

On the other hand, $\tilde{b}(t, x) = b(t, e^x)$ and $\tilde{\sigma}(t, x) = \sigma(t, e^x)$ are globally Lipschitz on $x \in (-\infty, 0]$, and we therefore also have

$$\lim_{n \to \infty} \left(\inf \{t; \ln S_i(t) < -n\} \right) = \infty \quad \text{a.e.}$$

by the usual existence-uniqueness results. Hence, $\ln S_i(t)$ does not explode in finite time, and we therefore conclude that $S_i(t) > 0$ for all t.

Because of Girsanov's theorem, in this framework the existence and uniqueness of an equivalent martingale measure are determined by the existence and uniqueness of progressively measurable solutions $\theta(t)$ of the equation

$$\sigma(t, S(t))\theta(t) = \underline{r}(t) - b(t, S(t)), t \le T \tag{2.5}$$

(continued)

EXAMPLE 2.3   (*continued*)

where $\underline{r}(t)$ is the N-vector with $r_i(t) = r(t)$ (the instantaneous interest rate), T is our time horizon, and θ must satisfy

$$\int_0^T \|\theta(s)\|^2 ds < \infty \tag{2.6}$$

and

$$\hat{\mathbb{E}}\left[\exp\left(\int_0^T \theta(t) \cdot dW(t) - \frac{1}{2}\int_0^T \|\theta(t)\|^2 dt\right)\right] = 1 \tag{2.7}$$

where $\|v\| = \sqrt{v_1^2 + \cdots + v_N^2}$ is the usual norm in $\mathbb{R}^N$.

For (2.5) to have a solution, the matrices $\sigma(t,x)$ and $[\sigma(t,x) \mid \underline{r}(t) - b(t,x)]$ (σ with $\underline{r}(t) - b(t,x)$ as an added column) must have the same rank (almost everywhere with respect to Lebesgue measure and the distribution of S). If $N \leq K$ (i.e., there are fewer traded assets S than sources of randomness W) there are clearly solutions to (2.5) if $\text{rank}(\sigma(t,x)) = N$. In fact, the space of solutions is in some sense $K - N$ dimensional. On the other hand, if $N > K$ (more assets than sources of randomness), there is in general no solution.

Hence, if we ignore the technical conditions (2.6) and (2.7), in general we have a $K - N$ dimensional space of equivalent martingale measures if $N \leq K$ and no equivalent martingale measure if $N > K$. Using the results in Section 2.4, we can translate this into no arbitrage and completeness, and we see that to avoid arbitrage we need at least as many sources of randomness as traded assets ($K \geq N$), and for completeness we need as many traded assets as sources of randomness. Finally, only if the number of traded assets is the same as the number of sources of randomness can we possibly have no arbitrage *and* completeness. In fact, we have a complete market with no arbitrage in this situation as soon as the matrix σ is sufficiently regular:

$$\xi^T \sigma(t,x)\xi \geq \delta \|\xi\|^2$$

for some $\delta > 0$.

2.4   MARTINGALE MEASURES, COMPLETENESS, AND NO ARBITRAGE

In discrete-time models, the relationship between martingale measures and completeness and no arbitrage is completely unambiguous:

THEOREM 2.1

Let $(\Omega, \mathscr{F}, \mathbb{P})$ be a probability space, and let $\{\mathscr{F}_n; n = 1, \ldots, k\}$ be a filtration in $\mathscr{F}$. Let $S = (S_1, \ldots, S_N)$ be a vector of N semimartingales with respect to $(\mathbb{P}, \{\mathscr{F}_n\})$. The market consisting of the money market account and S as the traded assets is complete and admits no arbitrage if and only if there is a unique equivalent martingale measure.

In fact, under the assumptions given, the market is arbitrage free if and only if there exists an equivalent martingale measure. The market is then complete if and only if the martingale measure is unique. If there is no equivalent martingale measure (equivalently, the market admits arbitrage), the market can be both complete and incomplete. This last assertion is obvious because we can take an arbitrage-free, complete market and add an extra tradeable asset that is *not* a martingale under the martingale measure. That way, there is no equivalent martingale measure in the new market, but, of course, the market is still complete. Or we can take a market with no equivalent martingale measure and add (in a direct sum manner) an independent and incomplete set of traded assets. Because the two sets of traded assets are independent, the lack of a martingale measure in one set and the incompleteness in the other persist in the total set, which is therefore an incomplete market with no equivalent martingale measure.

Things are slightly more complex in continuous time, because arbitrage needs to be defined more carefully. In fact, as mentioned before, the definition given in (2.2) is too restrictive in continuous time. The problem is that it is actually possible to generate something out of nothing if we have infinitely many rehedges. This is well known from roulette, where the doubling strategy in principle wins every time: Play one unit on red. If red comes up, pocket the one-unit profit; else, place a bet of two units on red. Continue this doubling strategy until red comes up. If red first comes up at the nth play, the total profit is

$$-(1 + 2 + \cdots + 2^{n-1}) + 2^n = -\frac{2^n - 1}{2 - 1} + 2^n = 1$$

In other words, this doubling strategy yields a profit of 1 no matter when red comes up the first time, and red *will* come up at some time, with probability 1. The only problem is that this strategy requires unlimited funds to carry out, and therefore it is a type of strategy that should be ruled out when we determine whether there is arbitrage.

Following Delbaen and Schachermayer [32], we can define

DEFINITION 2.3

A self-financing trading strategy (x, V, X) is called admissible if there is a number $K \in \mathbb{R}$ such that $V(t) \geq K \, \forall t$ with probability 1.

and the concept of *no free lunch with vanishing risk*: The market admits free lunch with vanishing risk if there is a sequence of self-financing admissible trading strategies $(0, V_n, X_n)$ on $[0, T]$ such that the negative parts $V_n^-(T)$ tend to 0 uniformly and $V_n(T) \to V \in [0, \infty]$ with $V > 0$ with positive probability.

The result of Delbaen and Schachermayer is the following equivalence between the existence of an equivalent martingale measure and no free lunch with vanishing risk:

THEOREM 2.2

Let $(\Omega, \mathscr{F}, \mathbb{P})$ be a probability space with a filtration $\{\mathscr{F}_t\}$ and let $S = (S_1, \ldots, S_N)$ be a vector of semimartingales. The market consisting of the money market and S admits no free lunch with vanishing risk if and only if there is an equivalent martingale measure.

We can compare this result with the result from Shiryaev [112], that the market in Theorem 2.2 is complete if there is a *unique* martingale measure, to obtain a result that is very similar to the result in discrete-time markets:

THEOREM 2.3

The market in Theorem 2.2 is complete and admits no free lunch with vanishing risk if and only if there is a unique martingale measure.

2.5 COMPLETING THE MARKET

Hopefully, the examples and results in the last two sections have illustrated the interesting relationship between equivalent martingale measures and the concepts of no arbitrage and completeness. The rest of this chapter is devoted to completeness, which in practice seems to be of much greater importance in derivatives pricing than no arbitrage, for the very simple reason that a model that admits arbitrage would have to be discarded as a sensible mark-to-market tool. Arbitrage in the model would allow internal arbitrage, so that fictitious profits and losses could be created. Hence, the model has to be arbitrage free. As we will see below, the models that are used will generally be specified such that no arbitrage is ensured. On the other hand, it is a fact of nature that real markets are incomplete, so it is important to realize how to handle incompleteness.

As we will see below, there is incompleteness that can be rectified, and there is incompleteness with which the trader has to live. In equity markets, stochastic volatility models are prime examples of markets that are *a priori* incomplete but which can be made complete by adding more traded assets:

EXAMPLE 2.4

In the Heston model (cf. [61]), the asset is given by

$$dS(t) = \mu(t)S(t)dt + \sqrt{v(t)}dW^S(t)$$

where the volatility $\sqrt{v(t)}$ satisfies

$$dv(t) = \kappa(\theta - v(t))dt + \sigma\sqrt{v(t)}dW^v(t) \qquad (2.8)$$

Here μ is some progressively measurable process such that there is a solution to the equation, κ, θ, and σ are nonnegative, and W^S and W^v are Brownian motions with correlation ρ. We also assume that the short rate $r = r(t)$ is deterministic.

It is quite obvious that the market is incomplete (except if $\rho = \pm 1$) even if we use the filtration generated by S alone. But it is also fairly clear that the market "should" be complete if we add another adequate traded asset on top of S.

In interest rate products a similar type of incompleteness occurs when only the interest rate process is specified. The market is not complete before at least one traded asset (which "depends" on the rate) is introduced. Of course, for derivatives on interest rates, the traded bonds are obvious assets to include in the model.

EXAMPLE 2.5

In the Hull-White interest rate model, the short rate is given by the stochastic differential equation

$$dr(t) = (a(t) - b(t)r(t))dt + \sigma(t)dW(t)$$

where a, b, σ are deterministic functions. To make the market complete, we need at least one more traded asset than the money market.

It is worth pointing out that in these more complicated models, it makes a difference under which measure we specify the processes, because we do not specify the dynamics of all the traded instruments directly. Rather, we specify (market-unobservable) processes, which we must fit to the market. Depending on what the purpose of the model is, we might want to model the market directly in the martingale measure or in the real-world measure. For instance, if we have made statistical analyses (which take place in the real-world measure) to show that the volatility does indeed satisfy an equation like (2.8), we must clearly use the Heston model of Example 2.4 in the real-world measure. Such models, however, are much better suited for "prediction," or statistically arbitraging possible market imperfections, than for mark-to-market models. For mark-to-market models, we always work in the martingale measure to avoid arbitrage, and we therefore model in this measure directly.

To show the impact of the measure we use for the model, let us introduce (highly artificially and only for the sake of argument) a traded asset X given by

$$dX(t) = r(t)dt + \alpha d(W^v(t) - \rho W^S(t))$$

into the Heston model (the process $\tilde{W} := W^v - \rho W^S$ is independent of W^S, so we can make a change of measure that changes the drift of W^S without affecting the drift of $\tilde{W}$). Now assuming that the short rate and μ in Example 2.4 are sufficiently well behaved (for instance measurable and bounded), there is a unique martingale measure (provided v remains positive, i.e., up to some positive stopping time), so the market is arbitrage free and complete, and prices are calculated as expectations under the martingale measure of the discounted payout. Now under the risk-neutral measure, we are replacing $dW^S(t)$ by

$$d\tilde{W}^S(t) + (r(t) - \mu(t))/\sqrt{v(t)}dt$$

where $\tilde{W}^S$ is a Brownian motion under the martingale measure.

Hence, under the martingale measure, the stochastic volatility is given by

$$dv(t) = \kappa(\theta - v(t))dt + \sigma\sqrt{v(t)}d\tilde{W}^v(t) + \sigma\rho(r(t) - \mu(t))dt$$

The μ function is not observable, so we have in effect made the model much more complicated by changing the measure, because we have replaced the time-independent $\kappa\theta$ by a stochastic process. If the model is used for pricing and hedging derivatives, it is certainly much more natural to model in the martingale measure and impose the right (risk-neutral) drift on the traded assets from the beginning. That way, the model will automatically be free of arbitrage and we avoid a lot of technical problems related to the strict positiveness of the short volatility $\sqrt{v}$ and the boundedness of μ. In the remainder of this chapter, we will always model directly in a martingale measure. Note also that we are not losing any generality by modeling in a martingale measure, because we can always enhance the model in the martingale measure.

Now let us return to the Heston model and the problem of making it complete. First of all, we are modeling under a martingale measure, so

$$\mu(t) = r(t) - d(t)$$

where d is the dividend yield of S. In Example 2.4, we conjectured that the market would be complete if there were one more traded asset. Now, clearly, by this we mean an asset that is linearly independent of S. In many ways, it would be convenient if we could just use the short volatility $\sqrt{v}$ itself, but that is certainly not traded. But if we assume there is a nonlinear option on S that is traded, this option would probably complete the market. More specifically, let us assume that there is a call option on S, with strike K and maturity T, that is actively traded, so that at any time t we have a reliable market price $V(t)$. Now, because we are working in the martingale measure $\hat{\mathbb{P}}$, we must have

$$
\begin{aligned}
V(t) &= \hat{\mathbb{E}}[e^{-\int_t^T r(s)ds} V(T) \mid \mathscr{F}_t] \\
&= e^{-\int_t^T r(s)ds} \hat{\mathbb{E}}[\max\{S(T) - K, 0\} \mid \mathscr{F}_t]
\end{aligned}
\tag{2.9}
$$

where $\{\mathscr{F}_t\}$ is the σ-algebra generated by v and S. In practice, we then use the knowledge of $V(t)$ today to determine the values of the parameters in the model (of course, we normally have several market instruments with which to calibrate the parameters). In terms of completeness of the market consisting of the traded assets S and V, it turns out that $V(t)$ is a smooth function of S and v (again, refer to [61]). Using Itō's formula, it is then not difficult to show the completeness.

As we have just seen, a market can in some cases be completed by adding more traded instruments. In general, we need as many traded instruments as we have sources of randomness. The term "source of randomness" is not very well defined, which is one of the reasons equivalent martingale measures are useful. As long as there are more than one equivalent martingale measures, we need more traded instruments to make the market complete. We now state this (in a Hilbert space setup) in terms of the dimension of the orthogonal complement of a "stable" space generated by the set of traded instruments.

For simplicity, we consider a market given by a filtered probability space $(\Omega, \mathcal{F}, \mathbb{P}, \{\mathcal{F}_t\})$ and traded instruments $S = (S_1, \ldots, S_N)$. We assume that there is at least one martingale measure, and for simplicity (and without loss of generality) we assume that $\mathbb{P}$ is already a martingale measure and that interest rates are 0. Consider a fixed time horizon T, and restrict the claims we want to be able to replicate to $\mathcal{L}^2(\mathcal{F}_T)$ claims. Lastly, we consider only traded assets S_i such that $S_i(T) \in \mathcal{L}^2(\mathcal{F}_T)$. Note that S_i are all martingales, and if we define

$$\mathcal{H}^2 = \{X \text{ martingale}; \sup_{t \leq T} |X(t)| \in \mathcal{L}^2\}$$

then $S_i \in \mathcal{H}^2$ (see [44]). Every (signed) martingale measure can be represented by its density D, and we will consider only measures with $D \in \mathcal{L}^2(\mathcal{F}_T)$. For such D, we have

$$\mathbb{E}[(S_i(\tau) - S_i(0))D] = 0 \qquad (2.10)$$

for any stopping time $\tau \leq T$. Define the set of random variables

$$\mathcal{K} := \{S_i(\tau) - S_i(0); \tau \text{ stopping time}, i = 1, \ldots, N\} \qquad (2.11)$$

and let $\mathcal{K}^\perp$ denote the set of $D \in \mathcal{L}^2(\mathcal{F}_T)$ such that (2.10) holds for all $i = 1, \ldots, n$. Because $\mathcal{K}$ is a stable subset (in Elliott's sense, cf. [44]), the converse also holds: namely, if $D \in \mathcal{K}^\perp$ in the sense that $\mathbb{E}[DK] = 0$ for all $K \in \mathcal{K}$, then the signed measure with density D is a martingale measure. So the traditional positive probability measures that are equivalent martingale measures as well simply consist of the convex cone

$$\mathcal{M}_{EQ} := \{D \in \mathcal{K}^\perp; \mathbb{E}[D] = 1, D > 0\}$$

We want to give conditions for $\mathcal{M}_{EQ} = \{1\}$ and also provide a relation between the size of $\mathcal{M}_{EQ}$, or simply the dimension of $\mathcal{K}^\perp$, and the number of traded assets needed to complete the market (and a complete market is exactly equivalent to $\mathcal{M}_{EQ} = \{1\}$). It is easy to see that if $\mathcal{K}^\perp$ is a one-dimensional vector space, then $\mathcal{K}^\perp = \{C; C \in \mathbb{R}\}$ (because by assumption $1 \in \mathcal{K}^\perp$), which again implies $\mathcal{M}_{EQ} = \{1\}$. Alternatively, we can show this by noting that $\mathcal{K}^\perp = \{C; C \in \mathbb{R}\}$ implies that $\mathcal{K}$ spans $\mathcal{L}_0^2$ (the space of random variables in $\mathcal{L}^2$ with mean 0), which by definition means that the market is complete. But now we can easily prove the converse, that $\mathcal{M}_{EQ} = \{1\}$ implies that $\mathcal{K}^\perp$ is a one-dimensional vector space, because by Theorem 2.3, if $\mathcal{M}_{EQ} = \{1\}$, then the market is complete, and therefore $\mathcal{K}^\perp = \{C; C \in \mathbb{R}\}$.

EXAMPLE 2.6

Consider a probability space $(\Omega, \mathscr{F}, \mathbb{P})$ with a d-dimensional Brownian motion $W = (W_1, \ldots, W_d)$ and consider the filtration $\{\mathscr{F}_t\}$ generated by W (as always, the completed filtration). Also assume that $\mathscr{F} = \mathscr{F}_\infty$. By the Brownian representation theorem, for any $Z \in \mathscr{L}^2(\mathscr{F}_T)$ with zero mean, there is a progressively measurable process $\xi = (\xi_1, \ldots, \xi_d)$ with

$$\sum_{n=1}^{d} \int_0^T \mathbb{E}[\xi_n(t)^2]dt < \infty$$

such that

$$Z = \sum_{n=1}^{d} \int_0^T \xi_n(t)dW_n(t)$$

However, we can approximate any stochastic integral with respect to W by a stochastic integral with respect to a simple process

$$\tilde{\xi}_n(t, \omega) = \sum_{i=1}^{\infty} \alpha_{i,n} \chi_{\{(t,\omega); \tau_{i,n}(\omega) \le t < \tau_{i+1,n}(\omega)\}}$$

where for each n, $\{\tau_{i,n}\}_{i=1}^{\infty}$ is an increasing sequence of stopping times. This shows that

$$\mathscr{K} := \{W_i^\tau; \tau \text{ stopping time}, i = 1, \ldots, d\}$$

is a total set in $\mathscr{L}_0^2$. So it is possible to make the market complete by adding d tradeable assets. On the other hand, it is obvious that the market cannot be made complete by adding fewer than d traded assets. This confirms our result from Example 2.3.

In a Hilbert space setup as just described, we know that any $Z \in \mathscr{L}^2$ can be written as $Z = X + Y$ where $X \in \mathscr{K}$ and $Y \in \mathscr{K}^\perp$. Hence, $\dim(\mathscr{L}^2) = \dim(\mathscr{K}) + \dim(\mathscr{K}^\perp)$. Unfortunately, both sides are often ∞, so although we clearly have a simple relationship between the dimension of the space of martingale measures ($\sim \mathscr{K}^\perp$) and the dimension of the space of simple tradeable assets ($\sim \mathscr{K}$), we can easily have a situation where the formula above does not immediately tell how many traded assets are needed based on the dimension of the space of martingale measures. The issue is further complicated by the fact that the space

$$\{S(\tau) - S(0); \tau \text{ stopping time}\}$$

is in general infinite-dimensional, even when S is a one-dimensional process. This is indeed the case in Example 2.6. The next example, on the other hand, is purely finite-dimensional.

EXAMPLE 2.7

(Cf. Example 2.1) Let $\Omega = \{x_1, \ldots, x_n\}$ and assume that $\mathbb{P}$ is a probability measure on the σ-algebra $\mathcal{G}$ of all subsets of Ω such that $p_i := \mathbb{P}(\{x_i\}) \neq 0$. We want to consider a one-period market with zero interest rate that is complete. Of course, to define martingales, we need a filtration, and, as in Example 2.1, we consider

$$\mathcal{F}_t = \begin{cases} \{\varnothing, \Omega\}, & t < 1 \\ \mathcal{G}, & t \geq 1 \end{cases}$$

An adapted process is of the form

$$X(t, \omega) = \begin{cases} c, & t < 1 \\ f(\omega), & t \geq 1 \end{cases}$$

where c is any constant and f is any function on Ω. We note that

$$\text{span } \{X(\tau) - X(0); \tau \text{ stopping time}\} = \text{span } \{X(1) - X(0)\}$$

for any adapted process X. So the space $\mathcal{H}$ as defined in (2.11) is at most N-dimensional if there are N traded assets. We know that the market is complete if $\mathcal{H}^{\perp} = \text{span}\{1\}$. Also $\dim(\mathcal{L}^2(\mathcal{F}_T)) = n$ for $T \geq 1$. So we must have

$$\dim(\mathcal{H}) \geq \dim(\mathcal{L}^2(\mathcal{F}_T)) - 1 = n - 1$$

for the market to be complete. We can easily find $n - 1$ linearly independent adapted martingales to use as the set of traded instruments, and we therefore see—as expected—that the market can be made complete if we add $n - 1$ traded instruments to the money market instrument; if there are fewer than $n - 1$ tradeable instruments (plus the money market), the market is incomplete.

2.6   PRICING IN INCOMPLETE MARKETS

As we saw above, in many cases, the dimension of the space of equivalent martingale measures is small enough to allow us to complete the market by including more market instruments. In fact, for the Heston model for instance, there are often many more liquidly traded market instruments (call and put options) than are needed to make the Heston model complete. However, it is also quite clear that many models cannot be completed. The simplest cases are markets in which a key traded asset is allowed to jump with infinitely many positive jumps. For instance, a more reasonable model of a defaultable bond (Example 2.2) would probably be to make the bond pay some amount different from 0 in the case of default. More precisely, the bond still pays 1 if there is no default but pays an amount X in the case of default, where X is a random variable whose value is known only at the default time. If X has a continuous distribution (or can take infinitely many values), then we need infinitely many traded assets to make the market complete.

Similarly, in an equity model it seems reasonable to allow occasional jumps (with continuous jump size distribution) in the price of the key assets.

Even in the Black-Scholes world we could argue that in reality the markets are incomplete, for the simple reason that hedging takes place in discrete time and has a cost associated with it (transaction costs). So in real trading situations, updates of the hedges are done whenever the market has moved enough to make it necessary to change the hedge. Of course, other strategies are allowed, but in any case, it is quite clear that the completeness of the market is lost because of the discrete-time hedging. So it is obvious that even if one does not use the most complicated and sophisticated models, the problem of incompleteness needs to be addressed.

In a complete market, derivatives can be exactly replicated, and there is no need for risk preferences in the pricing and hedging, because there is no risk. In incomplete markets, on the other hand, risk preferences of the individual investor become crucial. Furthermore, we can no longer ignore the real-world measure. For instance, we could have a derivative with a corresponding hedging strategy that in some cases leads to positive P/L and in other cases to negative but bounded P/L. The probability of a loss is then of great importance, but the relevant probability is the real-world probability and not the risk-neutral one.

Assume that Z is a derivative paying out at time T (i.e., Z is $\mathscr{F}_T$-measurable), and let (x, V, X) be a self-financing strategy. If we sell the option for the amount x and hedge it using the strategy (x, V, X), our profit or loss at maturity equals

$$P_{x,V} = V(T) - Z$$

If U is our utility function, then we would want to maximize the expectation $\mathbb{E}[U(P_{x,V})]$ (under real-world measure $\mathbb{P}$). However, for most reasonable utility functions, this expectation tends to infinity as $x \to \infty$, and it is in any case obvious that we have to introduce some penalty on high values of x, simply because x is the price at which we want to sell the option and we can clearly not sell the option at any price. Hence in general the pricing problem becomes

$$U^*(x) = \sup_V \mathbb{E}[U(P_{x,V})], \qquad x \in \mathbb{R} \tag{2.12}$$

and

$$x^*(u) = \inf \{x; U^*(x) \geq u\}, \qquad u \in \mathbb{R} \tag{2.13}$$

So $U^*(x)$ is the maximum expected utility we can achieve by selling the option for x and hedging it with a self-financing strategy up to maturity, and $x^*(u)$ is the minimum initial endowment with which we can achieve a utility at least as great as u.

For pricing there is an argument for using $u = U(0)$ as the minimum expected utility we are willing to accept from selling the option. Indeed, we can achieve utility $U(0)$ by *not* selling the option, and if we can have a larger expected utility than $U(0)$ from selling the option, we should clearly do so if the concept of maximizing utility is to make any sense. Of course, if the infimum in (2.13) cannot be attained, we can use any $u > U(0)$ but not $U(0)$ itself.

As previously mentioned, in a complete and arbitrage-free market, there is a unique (x, V, X) such that $P_{x,V} = 0$ with probability 1, and trading the derivative at any other price than x would create an arbitrage. It is therefore nonsensical to price options in complete and arbitrage-free markets using utility functions. On the other hand, because we need utility functions in incomplete markets, it would be desirable if a specific utility approach being used in an incomplete market "converges" to the right price if the market is completed.

Before we address this issue, we give a few examples of commonly used utility functions. Generally, to reflect risk aversion and the very natural sentiment that more wealth is always better, utility functions are concave and increasing functions from $\mathbb{R}$ into $\mathbb{R}$, but neither property is needed (indeed, people playing the lottery or at casinos clearly have *convex* or *decreasing* utility functions).

■ Exponential utility:

$$U(x) = 1 - \exp(-\gamma x), \gamma > 0$$

■ Exponential utility with penalty:

$$U(x) = \begin{cases} -\infty, & x < 0 \\ 1 - \exp(-\gamma x), & x \geq 0 \end{cases}$$

■ Polynomial utility (normally $0 < \alpha < 1$):

$$U(x) = \begin{cases} -\infty, & x < 0 \\ x^\alpha, & x \geq 0 \end{cases}$$

■ Logarithmic utility:

$$U(x) = \begin{cases} -\infty, & x < 0 \\ \log(x), & x \geq 0 \end{cases}$$

The three last utility functions attach an infinite penalty to a loss, effectively reducing acceptable P/L's to those for which there is zero probability of a loss. By considering $U(x + c)$ instead of $U(x)$, we can introduce utility functions that rule out losses of more than c (this could be appropriate if a loss greater than c would lead to bankruptcy).

Another approach to pricing in incomplete markets is the *variance-optimal* method, in which we determine the price such that the square of the P/L is minimized:

$$\text{Minimize } \mathbb{E}[(P_{x,V})^2] \text{ over all self-financing } (x, V, X) \qquad (2.14)$$

To some extent this corresponds to the foregoing utility maximization, with $U(x) = -x^2$, but there is an important difference in that this function attaches the same utility to profits and losses, so we can include the initial endowment x in the maximization and do not need to pick the smallest x that achieves some utility. Despite the obvious drawback of penalizing profits, the variance-optimal method has received much attention in the literature (cf. [109]), and in most practical situations variance-optimal pricing (perhaps in combination with some other utility maximization) is a sensible and much used way of hedging, if not pricing.

Finally, let us mention *quantile* and *efficient* hedging as described in [47] and [48]. For quantile hedging, the aim is to minimize the probability that there is going to be a loss. In other words, the aim is to minimize $\mathbb{P}[V(T) < Z]$. The strategy that minimizes $\mathbb{P}[V(T) < Z]$ maximizes

$$\mathbb{P}[V(T) \geq Z] = \mathbb{E}[1_{\{V(T)-Z \geq 0\}}] = \mathbb{E}[1_{\{P_{x,V} \geq 0\}}]$$

So the utility function is simply $U(x) = 1_{[0,\infty)}(x)$, which is increasing but not concave.

More general forms of quantile and efficient hedging also take the size of the actual loss into account. A special case of efficient hedging covered in [48] is the minimization of $\mathbb{E}[(Z - V(T))^+]$. Because

$$\mathbb{E}[(Z - V(T))^+] = \mathbb{E}[(V(T) - Z)^-] = \mathbb{E}[P_{x,V}^-]$$

this corresponds to maximizing the utility function $U(x) = \min\{x, 0\}$, which is both increasing and concave.

Returning to the general framework, let us consider a simple setup in which a stock has Black-Scholes dynamics, but the stock can be traded only today and at maturity T,

$$S(t) = S(0) \exp\left(\sigma W(T) + (r - \frac{\sigma^2}{2})T\right)$$

Assume that we want to find a price at which we are willing to sell a call option with strike K on S with maturity T. So at time T, we have to pay

$$\max\{S(T) - K, 0\}$$

If x denotes our premium and δ is the amount of stock we buy today, then our total P/L at maturity equals

$$P_{x,\delta} = \delta S(T) + (x - \delta S(0))e^{rT} - \max\{S(T) - K, 0\}$$

If we use either of the utility functions that attach $-\infty$ to $(-\infty, 0)$, we see that

$$\mathbb{E}[U(P_{x,\delta})] = -\infty$$

for all $x < S(0)$. Also $\mathbb{E}[U(P_{S(0),1})] > -\infty$, and because U is increasing with any of these utility functions, our price of the call option is at least $S(0)$. In reality we cannot expect anybody to be willing to pay $S(0)$ for this call, because the customer could just as well buy the stock itself and receive a higher payout on the stock than on the option. Even in a market where the customer was for some reason barred from buying the stock at all, the customer would want a product with a higher payout for the premium of $S(0)$.

In fact, for any utility function which sets an upper limit on the acceptable loss (i.e., $P_{x,\delta} \geq c$), the optimal hedge involves having

$$\delta \geq 1 \quad \text{and} \quad x \geq ce^{-rT} + \delta S(0)$$

that is, a substantial premium and a massive "overhedge" to avoid the possibility of a great loss due to excessive upward moves in the stock.

This certainly seems extremely risk-averse for a seller of options, and utility functions of this form are probably very rare for derivative traders.

A utility function as the exponential utility is more reasonable, because it allows for some real risk. Delbaen et al. [31] treated the exponential utility in great detail and showed that $U^*(x)$ in Equation (2.12) can be calculated as

$$1 - \exp\left(-\inf_Q\left\{H(Q|\mathbb{P}) + \gamma x - \mathbb{E}_Q[\gamma Z]\right\}\right)$$

where

$$H(Q|\mathbb{P}) = \mathbb{E}_\mathbb{P}\left[\frac{dQ}{d\mathbb{P}} \log \frac{dQ}{d\mathbb{P}}\right]$$

is the entropy of Q with respect to $\mathbb{P}$, and the infimum is over all probability measures $Q \ll \mathbb{P}$ such that $H(Q|\mathbb{P}) < \infty$. For details and examples, we refer to [31] and the references therein.

Let us now briefly revisit the question of when pricing of options in the utility function framework produces the same price in a complete market as the correct no-arbitrage price. In fact, the answer to this problem is extremely simple if the utility pricing is done in the martingale measure.

THEOREM 2.4

Assume that a market consisting of $S = (S_1, \ldots, S_N)$ with filtration $\{\mathscr{F}_t\}$ has a unique martingale measure, $\mathbb{Q}$, and that S and the interest rate process r are independent. Let Z be $\mathscr{F}_T$-measurable with $\mathbb{E}_\mathbb{Q}|Z| < \infty$. As above, define for any self-financing strategy (x, V, X), the profit $P_{x,V}$ of hedging Z by (x, V, X). Let $U : \mathbb{R} \to \mathbb{R}$ be a strictly increasing and concave function and define

$$x^* = \inf\{x; U^*(x) \geq U(0)\}$$

where

$$U^*(x) = \sup_V \mathbb{E}_\mathbb{Q}[U(P_{x,V})]$$

is defined as in (2.12) only under the martingale measure.

Then

$$x^* = \mathbb{E}_\mathbb{Q}\left[\exp\left(-\int_0^T r(s)ds\right) Z\right]$$

In other words, x^* agrees with the usual no-arbitrage price of Z.

PROOF

If we define

$$\hat{x} = \mathbb{E}_\mathbb{Q}\left[\exp\left(-\int_0^T r(s)ds\right)Z\right] = \mathbb{E}_\mathbb{Q}[Z]\exp\left(-\int_0^T r(s)ds\right)$$

then we know that we can achieve $P_{\hat{x},\hat{V}} \equiv 0$ for some self-financing strategy $(\hat{x}, \hat{V}, \hat{X})$, because the market is complete according to Theorem 2.3. So we have

$$U^*(\hat{x}) \geq U(0) \qquad\qquad (2.15)$$

Now for any self-financing strategy (x, V, X),

$$\mathbb{E}_\mathbb{Q}\left[\exp\left(-\int_0^t r(s)ds\right)V(t)\right] = x$$

so

$$\mathbb{E}_\mathbb{Q}[P_{x,V}] = \mathbb{E}_\mathbb{Q}[V(T) - Z] < 0$$

for any self-financing strategy (x, V, X) with $x < \hat{x}$. Now, because the utility is concave and increasing,

$$\mathbb{E}_\mathbb{Q}[U(P_{x,V})] \leq U\big(\mathbb{E}_\mathbb{Q}[P_{x,V}]\big) < U(0), \qquad x < \hat{x}$$

by Jensen's inequality. So $U^*(x) < U(0)$ if $x < \hat{x}$, and therefore $x^* \geq \hat{x}$. Combining this with Equation (2.15), we conclude that $x^* = \hat{x}$.

As mentioned previously, the right measure in incomplete markets when maximizing utility is the real-world measure, not the martingale measure. In incomplete markets, in fact, if there is one martingale measure, there are several, so we simply cannot consider *the* martingale measure in incomplete markets. We could therefore ask what the real impact of Theorem 2.4 is. Even if we let incomplete markets converge to a complete market (in some sense), there is no reason to expect the real-world measures to converge to the martingale measure. If our tradeable assets deflated are not martingales under the real measure, it is unreasonable to expect them to be martingales in the complete-market limit. In other words, utility pricing will not in general agree with no-arbitrage pricing.

2.7 VARIANCE-OPTIMAL PRICING AND HEDGING

As we saw in Equation (2.14), for variance-optimal pricing and hedging, we minimize the variance of the P/L. Of course, in Equation (2.14) we are actually minimizing the square of the P/L, but it is obvious that for any self-financing strategy (x, V, X), the strategy $(\tilde{x}, \tilde{V}, X)$ where

$$\tilde{x} = x - \mathbb{E}[V(T) - Z]e^{-r(T-t)}$$

satisfies

$$\tilde{V}(T) = V(T) - \mathbb{E}[V(T) - Z]$$

and therefore

$$\mathbb{E}[(P_{\tilde{x},\tilde{V}})^2] = \mathbb{E}[(P_{x,V} - \mathbb{E}[V(T) - Z])^2] = \mathbb{E}[(P_{x,V} - \mathbb{E}[P_{x,V}])^2]$$
$$= \mathbb{E}[(P_{x,V})^2] - (\mathbb{E}[P_{x,V}])^2 \leq \mathbb{E}[(P_{x,V})^2] \qquad (2.16)$$

So the minimization in Equation (2.14) automatically ensures that $\mathbb{E}[P_{x,V}] = 0$, and we are therefore minimizing the variance of the P/L. It might seem nonsensical to penalize profits as well as losses when pricing an option. However, as we saw, we *always* need to penalize profits in order to avoid the price of the option going to infinity. For the usual utility function approach, we are in effect doing this by minimizing overprices that achieve a certain minimum expected utility.

Regarding the equivalence of the variance-optimal approach and the usual no-arbitrage pricing in complete markets, the situation is much better than for general utility functions. In fact, variance-optimal pricing always agrees with the no-arbitrage price in complete markets.

In practice, as we have mentioned before, real markets are incomplete simply because hedging is done discretely in time and the day-to-day hedging is done in such a way that the variance of the P/L is minimal. In fact, in many cases the price of an option is calculated as the sum of a spread that the trader feels is appropriate for the specific type of deal (this spread obviously depends on the riskiness of the deal) and the usual "Black-Scholes" price calculated as if the market were complete without transaction costs and with continuous trading. The spread can then be considered as a kind of reserve, and the hedging is done in a way that approximately minimizes the variance of the remaining P/L between rehedges (namely, the portfolio is kept delta-, and, if possible, gamma- and vega-, neutral).

The variance-optimal pricing approach has received much attention in the literature. The key result is that the price of any option equals the expected value of the discounted payout under the so-called variance-optimal measure, which is a signed martingale measure.

DEFINITION 2.4

A signed L^2 martingale measure is a signed measure Q with $Q(\Omega) = 1$, $Q \ll \mathbb{P}$,

$$\frac{dQ}{d\mathbb{P}} \in L^2(\Omega, \mathscr{F}, P)$$

and

$$\mathbb{E}\left[\frac{dQ}{d\mathbb{P}} e^{-\int_s^t r(u)du} S(t) \,\Big|\, \mathscr{F}_s\right] = \mathbb{E}\left[\frac{dQ}{d\mathbb{P}} \,\Big|\, \mathscr{F}_s\right] S(s)$$

A variance-optimal martingale measure is any signed L^2 martingale measure that minimizes

$$\mathbb{E}\left[\left(\frac{dQ}{d\mathbb{P}} - \mathbb{E}\left[\frac{dQ}{d\mathbb{P}}\right]\right)^2\right] = \mathbb{E}\left[\left(\frac{dQ}{d\mathbb{P}}\right)^2\right] - 1$$

over all signed L^2 martingale measures.

Note that the variance-optimal martingale measure in general depends on the original measure $\mathbb{P}$. This is very easy to see if we note that $\mathbb{P}$ itself will always be the variance-optimal martingale measure provided it is a martingale measure. Of course, this result confirms that in a complete market there can be only one equivalent (positive) martingale measure. Furthermore, it is worth pointing out that although the actual variance-optimal measure depends on the original measure, it does not follow that all variance-optimal prices will differ depending on the original measure. Specifically, any contingent claim that can be replicated will be priced exactly the same with variance-optimal pricing no matter what the original measure is.

In [109], it is shown that

THEOREM 2.5

Assume that the minimum in Equation (2.14) is attained by the self-financing strategy $(\hat{x}, \hat{V}, \hat{X})$ and that there is a signed L^2 martingale measure. Then there is a variance-optimal martingale measure, and for any variance-optimal martingale measure $\hat{\mathbb{P}}$,

$$\hat{x} = \hat{\mathbb{E}}[Z]$$

In [109], it is shown that the variance-optimal measure is in general a *signed* measure, but, of course, in many cases it will in fact be a real probability measure. Theorem 2.5 and the discussion preceding it also illustrate how important the measure under which we do the minimization is to the variance-optimal pricing in incomplete markets. On the other hand, we have better convergence properties for variance-optimal pricing than for the utility function approach, as the following example illustrates:

EXAMPLE 2.8

Consider the simple diffusion setup as in Example 2.3 with a K-dimensional Brownian motion $W = (W_1, \ldots, W_K)$ under the real-world measure $\mathbb{P}$. Assume that the interest rate is 0 and define the K processes

$$dS_k(t) = b_k S_k(t)dt + S_k(t)\sum_{n=1}^{k} \sigma_{k,n}dW_n(t) \qquad (2.17)$$

where for simplicity we assume that the b_k are constants and σ is a regular $K \times K$ matrix.

We can now consider a sequence of markets $\mathcal{M}_n$ where $\mathcal{M}_n$ has $S_1, \ldots, S_n$ as the only traded instruments. Clearly $\mathcal{M}_K$ is complete and $\mathcal{M}_n$ is incomplete for $n < K$. If we define $\mathcal{F}_t^k$ as the smallest σ-algebra that includes $\mathcal{F}_t^{W_1}, \ldots, \mathcal{F}_t^{W_k}$, then it is clear that in the market $\mathcal{M}_n$ we can replicate every claim that is $\mathcal{F}_t^n$-measurable. Note that with the processes as defined in Equation (2.17), these claims are exactly the claims that can be represented as (measurable) functions of the prices of $S_1, \ldots, S_n$. For every such claim, the variance-optimal price is therefore equal to the risk-neutral price. So as we consider the increasing sequence of markets

$$\mathcal{M}_1, \mathcal{M}_2, \ldots, \mathcal{M}_K$$

increasing subsets of the set of all contingent claims will have the same value if we price using variance-optimal pricing as if we price risk neutrally in the complete market $\mathcal{M}_K$.

2.8   SUPER HEDGING AND QUANTILE HEDGING

In this last section on incomplete markets we mention super hedging and the interesting relation to the results obtained in [47] and [48] on quantile and efficient hedging.

Super hedging and pricing consists of finding a minimum price x^* such that there is an admissible trading strategy (x^*, V^*, X^*) with $V(T) - Z \geq 0$ with probability 1. It is quite obvious that super hedging and pricing can be described in terms of the utility function

$$U(x) = \begin{cases} -\infty & \text{if } x < 0 \\ 1 & \text{if } x \geq 0 \end{cases}$$

So, as described in Section 2.6, the price will often be much higher than any buyer of the option would be willing to pay. Nevertheless, the results that can be obtained for super hedging turn out to be very useful in other contexts such as quantile hedging. For details on super hedging see [43] and [67]. A main result is that if we define

$$\bar{V}(t) = \text{ess sup } \hat{\mathbb{E}}[Z \mid \mathscr{F}_t], \qquad t \in [0, T]$$

where the supremum is taken over all equivalent martingale measures, then $\bar{V}$ is the smallest process that satisfies $\bar{V}(T) \geq Z$ and is a supermartingale in *all* the equivalent martingale measures. Furthermore, there is a unique decomposition

$$\bar{V}(t) = \bar{V}(0) + \int_0^t X(s)dS(s) - C(t) \tag{2.18}$$

where $(\bar{V}(0), \bar{V} + C, X)$ is an admissible trading strategy and C is increasing and measurable with respect to the optional σ-algebra (for details on the decomposition see [46] or [74]). Regarding the optional σ-algebra and optional processes, which are concepts from the general theory of stochastic processes, we mention only that optional processes have certain measurability properties that are stronger than those of progressively measurable processes but weaker than those of predictable processes. In other words, an optional process is progressively measurable but not necessarily predictable. For further details, see the description of predictable processes in Chapter 1 and the references therein.

$\bar{V}(t)$ is the super hedging price of the derivative at time t, and C_t then describes the total amount of money that can be taken out of the hedge portfolio at time t due to the performance during $[0, t]$. At maturity, the total P/L is

$$C(T) + \bar{V}(T) - Z$$

(which is by construction nonnegative).

As in [47], we define a randomized test as a random variable φ that satisfies $0 \leq \varphi \leq 1$ and is $\mathscr{F}_T$-measurable. Consider a price $x_0 \leq \bar{V}(0)$. Then it is shown in [47] that

THEOREM 2.6

There exists a randomized test $\tilde{\varphi}$ such that

$$\mathbb{E}[\tilde{\varphi}] = \sup \mathbb{E}[\varphi]$$

where the supremum is over all randomized tests φ such that

$$\hat{\mathbb{E}}[\varphi Z] \leq x_0$$

for all equivalent martingale measures $\hat{\mathbb{P}}$. Denote

$$\tilde{V}(t) = \text{ess sup } \hat{\mathbb{E}}[\tilde{\varphi} Z \mid \mathscr{F}_t], \qquad t \in [0, T]$$

where the supremum is over all equivalent martingale measures, and let

$$\tilde{V}(t) = \tilde{V}(0) + \int_0^t \tilde{X}(s)dS(s) - \tilde{C}(t)$$

be the optional decomposition of $\tilde{V}$ as defined in Equation (2.18). Then the admissible trading strategy $(x_0, \tilde{V} + C, \tilde{X})$ maximizes

$$\mathbb{E}\left[1_{\{V(T) \geq Z\}} + \frac{V(T)}{Z} 1_{\{V(T) < Z\}}\right]$$

over all admissible trading strategies (x, V, X) with $x \leq x_0$. Furthermore,

$$\mathbb{E}\left[1_{\{\tilde{V}(T) \geq Z\}} + \frac{\tilde{V}(T)}{Z} 1_{\{\tilde{V}(T) < Z\}}\right] = \mathbb{E}[\tilde{\varphi}]$$

The expected success ratio

$$R_{x,V} = \mathbb{E}\left[1_{\{V(T) \geq Z\}} + \frac{V(T)}{Z} 1_{\{V(T) < Z\}}\right]$$

for a given trading strategy (x, V, X) is always going to be a number greater than the success probability $\mathbb{P}[V(T) \geq Z]$ and less than or equal to 1. So the success ratio does not provide us with the actual success probability, but it is clear that it provides us with certain upper and lower bounds for the success probability.

Now consider the problem of finding the minimum price at which we can find an admissible trading strategy that achieves a certain success ratio. In other words, for a given $\varepsilon > 0$, we want to determine

$$\inf \left\{ x; \mathbb{E} \left[1_{\{V(T) \geq Z\}} + \frac{V(T)}{Z} 1_{\{V(T) < Z\}} \right] \geq 1 - \varepsilon \right\} \qquad (2.19)$$

where the infimum is over all admissible trading strategies (x, V, X). As before, and again following [47], it is easy to see that this problem reduces to finding a randomized test $\tilde{\varphi}$ such that

$$\inf \sup \hat{\mathbb{E}}[\varphi Z] = \sup \hat{\mathbb{E}}[\tilde{\varphi} Z]$$

where the supremum is over all equivalent martingale measures and the infimum is over all randomized tests φ with

$$\mathbb{E}[\varphi] \geq 1 - \varepsilon$$

We end this section by an example of quantile hedging in a specific setup (for more details, we refer to [90]):

EXAMPLE 2.9

We consider an option Z maturing at time T, and we assume that the initial capital available for hedging is v_0. The underlying asset solves

$$dS(t) = S(t)(\mu dt + \sigma(t) dW(t))$$

where W is a Brownian motion under the original probability measure $\mathbb{P}$, μ is constant, and

$$\sigma(t) = \begin{cases} \sigma_0, & 0 \leq t < t_0 \\ \eta, & t_0 \leq t \leq T \end{cases}$$

Here t_0 is known, σ_0 is a constant, and η is a random variable with known distribution ν, which is assumed independent of W.

(continued)

EXAMPLE 2.9 *(continued)*

We let $\alpha^\eta(s, y)$ denote the maximal probability of having $V(T) \geq Z$ conditional on η, $S(t_0) = s$, and $V(t_0) = y$, and we define

$$\alpha(s, y) = \int \alpha^\eta(s, y) \nu(d\eta)$$

It is now clear that to maximize the probability of success, we need to maximize

$$\mathbb{E}[\alpha(S(t_0), Y)]$$

over all $\mathcal{F}_{t_0}$-measurable random variables that satisfy

$$e^{-rt_0}\hat{\mathbb{E}}[Y] \leq v_0$$

where $\hat{\mathbb{E}}$ is expectation under the risk-neutral measure.

If the optimal random variable $\tilde{Y}$ exists, we must simply hedge $\tilde{Y}$ in the Black-Scholes world up to time t_0, and after that it is easy to determine the best hedge of Z given $S(t_0)$, η, and $V(t_0)(=\tilde{Y})$.

As in [90], we consider an option with payoff

$$Z = 1_{S(t_0)-w \leq S(T) \leq S(t_0)+w}$$

and we assume that the volatility η is uniformly distributed on $[\sigma_0 - \iota, \sigma_0 + \iota]$. In other words,

$$\nu(dx) = \frac{1}{2\iota}1_{\sigma_0-\iota \leq x \leq \sigma_0+\iota}dx$$

In this case, the optimal $\tilde{Y}$ can be expressed as

$$\tilde{Y} = \tilde{g}(S(t_0))$$

and the function $\tilde{g}$ can be determined numerically as shown in Figure 2.4 for different levels of uncertainty.

The actual parameters are $\sigma_0 = 20\%$, $\mu = 5\%$, $T = 1$, $t_0 = 6$ months, interest rate $r = 3\%$, and $w = 10\% \cdot S(0)$. The available initial value v_0 used for the calculations is the Black-Scholes value of the option when the volatility stays at $\sigma_0 = 20\%$ throughout the deal. Hence, as $\iota \to 0$, the model converges to Black-Scholes, and $\tilde{g}$ for $\iota = 0$ is simply the Black-Scholes value of the option at time t_0.

(continued)

EXAMPLE 2.9   (*continued*)

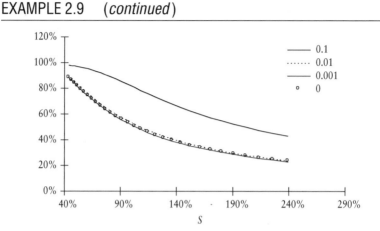

FIGURE 2.4   The optimal function to hedge for different values of ι.

Lastly, we choose $L > 0$ and consider hedging Z by hedging $g(S(t_0))$ up to t_0, where g is of the form

$$g(s) = \sum_{i=1}^{n} a_i 1_{\{S(0)-iL \le s \le S(0)+iL\}}$$

We can then compare the success probabilities for different initial values v_0 of initial capital and for different numbers n of available options for hedging. For $L = 10\% \cdot S(0)$, the results are shown in Figure 2.5.

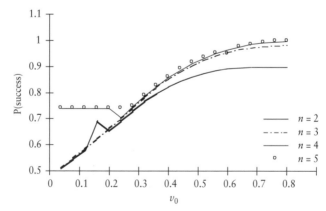

FIGURE 2.5   The success probability for different initial values and different number of available options for hedging.

CHAPTER 3

Financial Modeling with Lévy Processes

I n the preceding chapter, we examined a situation in which the market was incomplete and not all contingent claims could be duplicated by a riskless portfolio. As mentioned there, this situation arises in particular in the context of the *Bond/Stock* market as defined in Shiryaev [112], when the risky asset may have jumps of a stochastic size at random times. In this chapter, we study in more detail one such situation, that arises when the price process is modeled as the exponential of a Lévy process. Indeed, except in the case of the Brownian motion with drift, a Lévy process has random jumps at random times. However, we stress that the presence of jumps does not systematically yield an incomplete market (see [34], [65]).

In this chapter, we will not apply the techniques mentioned in the previous chapter to deal with incomplete markets, but we will adopt a more practical approach. In fact, in practice, the market in the world of equities does not only consist of a riskless bond and a risky stock, but some options also have enough liquidity to have negligible transaction costs and to be used in hedging strategies. This observation, among others, has given rise in the last years to a growing interest in Lévy processes and their use for financial modeling applications. In [79], Leblanc and Yor give a theoretical argument in favor of considering Lévy processes instead of the usual diffusions. Many empirical studies have been done on the relevance of some types of Lévy processes and their performance as a modeling tool: see [98], [101]; on the other hand, much progress has been made in the understanding of these processes and the financial interpretation attached to them. In particular, we shall see that they provide an ad hoc framework to define a stochastic clock, linked to the actual realization of transactions. We will mainly be concerned with the pricing of derivative products in the context of models involving Lévy processes and we will not study hedging strategies, but we will take the approach of risk-neutral valuation.

We first introduce Lévy processes and their main properties, the setting being the one introduced in Chapter 1, before showing how to use them in practical modeling issues. In particular, we study a model involving both the jump features of Lévy processes and stochastic volatility.

3.1   A PRIMER ON LÉVY PROCESSES

The goal of this section is to gather the most important facts about Lévy processes, with short proofs or no proof at all. We will limit ourselves to those properties that are relevant to the main concern of this book: modeling equity derivatives. We will study changes of measure that preserve the Lévy property of the paths, and will give two very important examples of Lévy processes.

The interested reader is referred to the masterful books of Bertoin [7] or Sato [108] for more details and information.

Here and in the remainder of this chapter, we assume the settings of Chapter 1. All properties of X are implicitly understood with respect to the filtration generated by X, denoted by $\mathcal{F}_t$.

First Properties

One property of Brownian motion is that its increments are independent and time-homogeneous. Lévy processes retain this property from the Brownian motion, but in general do not have necessarily continuous paths.

DEFINITION 3.1

A process X taking values in $\mathbb{R}^d$ is called a *Lévy process* if:

1. It has almost surely right-continuous paths.
2. Its increments are independent and time-homogeneous, i.e., for all $t > s$, the distribution of $X_t - X_s$ depends only on $t - s$ and is independent of $(X_u, u \leq s)$.

In all this chapter, X will be a Lévy process, started at 0, unless otherwise specified. Since we have for all $n \geq 1$

$$X_1 = (X_1 - X_{1-1/n}) + \cdots + (X_{2/n} - X_{1/n}) + X_{1/n}$$

we see that X_1 can be expressed as the sum of n independent random variables with common law (the law of $X_{1/n}$), that is, the law of X_1 is infinitely divisible. From this it follows that the characteristic function of X_1 has a Lévy-Khintchine representation:

THEOREM 3.1

The characteristic function of X_1 can be written

$$\mathbb{E}[e^{i\langle u, X_1 \rangle}] = e^{-\phi(u)}, \quad u \in \mathbb{R}^d \tag{3.1}$$

where ϕ has the following Lévy-Khintchine representation

$$\phi(u) = i\langle a, u \rangle + \frac{1}{2}Q(u) - \int (e^{i\langle u, x \rangle} - 1 - i\langle u, x \rangle 1_{|x| \le 1})\nu(dx) \tag{3.2}$$

where a is a constant vector in $\mathbb{R}^d$, Q is a nonnegative quadratic form, and ν is a Radon measure on $\mathbb{R}^d \backslash \{0\}$, such that $\int (|x|^2 \wedge 1)\nu(dx) < \infty$.

This theorem is a well-known result, the proof of which can be found in [45] or [80], for example. a is called the *drift* of the Lévy process X, Q is the *diffusion coefficient* and ν is the *Lévy measure*.

It is easy to prove, based on the infinite divisibility of the law of X_1 and the independence of the increments of X, that the characteristic function of X_t is given by

$$\mathbb{E}[e^{i\langle u, X_t \rangle}] = e^{-t\phi(u)}, \quad t \ge 0 \tag{3.3}$$

ϕ is called the *characteristic exponent* of the process X. The following theorem establishes a one-to-one correspondence between Lévy processes and characteristic functions having a representation as in (3.2).

THEOREM 3.2

Let a be a constant in $\mathbb{R}^d$, Q a non-negative quadratic form, and ν a Radon measure on $\mathbb{R}^d \backslash \{0\}$ such that $\int (|x|^2 \wedge 1)\nu(dx) < \infty$. Let

$$\phi(u) = i\langle a, u \rangle + \frac{1}{2}Q(u) - \int (e^{i\langle u, x \rangle} - 1 - i\langle u, x \rangle 1_{|x| \le 1})\nu(dx)$$

There exists a Lévy process X such that

$$\mathbb{E}[e^{i\langle u, X_1 \rangle}] = e^{-\phi(u)}$$

We provide a complete proof of this theorem, mostly following [7], since this gives some insight on a possible approximation of a Lévy process, a consideration of importance in practice.

PROOF

The proof consists of actually constructing an appropriate Lévy process. Let $X_t^{(1)} = -at + RW_t$ where W is a standard d-dimensional Brownian motion and $RR' = Q$ (R' denotes the transpose of R). The characteristic function of this process is well-known to be $\mathbb{E}[e^{i\langle u, X_t^{(1)}\rangle}] = e^{-\phi^{(1)}(u)}$, where

$$\phi^{(1)}(u) = i\langle a, u\rangle + \tfrac{1}{2}Q(u)$$

Consider the process $X_t^{(2)} = \sum_{k=1}^{N_t} Y_k$ where N is a Poisson process with intensity $\lambda := \int_{|x|>1} \nu(dx)$ and Y_k is a sequence of random variables pairwise independent, independent of N, and with common distribution

$$1_{|x|>1}\nu(dx)\big/\lambda$$

$X^{(2)}$ is then a compound Poisson process as defined in Example 3.2, and has characteristic function $e^{-\phi^{(2)}(u)}$, where

$$\phi^{(2)}(u) = -\int (e^{i\langle u,x\rangle} - 1)1_{|x|>1}\nu(dx)$$

For $\epsilon > 0$, denote by $Z^{(\epsilon,3)}$ the compound Poisson process with intensity $\lambda_\epsilon = \int_{\epsilon<|x|<1} \nu(dx)$ and distribution $1_{\epsilon<|x|<1}\nu(dx)/\lambda_\epsilon$. In order to be able to get a limit process as $\epsilon \downarrow 0$, we need to compensate $Z^{(\epsilon,3)}$; hence, we define the martingale

$$X_t^{(\epsilon,3)} = Z_t^{(\epsilon,3)} - t\int x1_{\epsilon<|x|<1}\nu(dx)$$

On the other hand, $X_1^{(\epsilon,3)}$ has characteristic function $e^{-\phi^{(\epsilon,3)}(u)}$, with

$$\phi^{(\epsilon,3)}(u) = -\int (e^{i\langle u,x\rangle} - 1 - i\langle u,x\rangle)1_{\epsilon<|x|<1}\nu(dx)$$

It can be shown, using Doob's maximal inequality for martingales (see [27], [100], [103]), that $X^{(\epsilon,3)}$ converges in L^2 to a process $X^{(3)}$ as $\epsilon \downarrow 0$. Because ν integrates x^2 in a neighborhood of 0 and

$e^{iux} - 1 - iux \sim -u^2x^2/2$ for x near 0, we deduce that $\phi^{(\epsilon,3)}(u)$ converges pointwise as $\epsilon \downarrow 0$ to a function

$$\phi^{(3)}(u) = -\int (e^{i\langle u,x\rangle} - 1 - i\langle u,x\rangle)1_{|x|<1}\nu(dx)$$

It follows that $X^{(3)}$ has the characteristic exponent $e^{-\phi^{(3)}(u)}$. Now each of the processes $X^{(1)}$, $X^{(2)}$, $X^{(3)}$ is a Lévy process, and they are independent of one another. Hence $X = X^{(1)} + X^{(2)} + X^{(3)}$ is a Lévy process as well, whose Lévy exponent is given by $\phi^{(1)} + \phi^{(2)} + \phi^{(3)}$.

At this point, we can already explain why a Lévy process is suitable for financial modeling. In fact, the independence of the increments yields the strong Markov property (see [7]), while the proof of Theorem 3.2 shows that X is a semimartingale. In fact any Lévy process can be represented as $X = X^{(1)} + X^{(2)} + X^{(3)}$ as above, with each of $X^{(1)}$, $X^{(2)}$, $X^{(3)}$ a semimartingale.

In the next example, we identify the characteristics of Brownian motion and Poisson process, already studied in Chapter 1 from the viewpoint of stochastic calculus.

EXAMPLE 3.1 (BROWNIAN MOTION-POISSON PROCESS)

The Brownian motion with drift is a continuous Lévy process. It is well known that the characteristic exponent of the Brownian motion with variance parameter σ^2 and drift b is given by $-uib + u^2\sigma^2/2$. In that case, the characteristic exponent has drift b, diffusion parameter σ, and zero Lévy measure. From Theorems 3.1 and 3.2, we see that the only Lévy process with continuous paths is (up to a multiplicative constant) a Brownian motion with drift.

Let us now turn to the Poisson process; we give here another definition (equivalent to the definition in Chapter 1). Let $(V_n, n \geq 1)$ a sequence of independent random variables with a common exponential distribution of parameter λ. Let $T_n = V_1 + \cdots + V_n$. The process $N_t = \sum_{k \geq 1} 1_{T_k \leq t}$ (with the convention that $N_t = 0$ if $T_1 > t$) is called a Poisson process with intensity λ. The characteristic function of N_1 is $e^{-(\lambda - \lambda e^{iu})}$, so the characteristic exponent is given by

$$\phi(u) = \lambda - \lambda e^{iu} = \int (1 - e^{iux})\lambda\delta_1(dx)$$

The Poisson process has zero drift and diffusion coefficient, and its Lévy measure is $\lambda\delta_1$.

The next example generalizes Poisson processes: The jump times are the same, but the jump sizes are allowed to be random. The processes $X^{(2)}$ and $X^{(\epsilon,3)}$ in the proof of Theorem 3.2 are of this type.

EXAMPLE 3.2 (COMPOUND POISSON PROCESS)

Let N be a Poisson process with intensity λ and Y_i a sequence of independent variables that have the same distribution μ on $\mathbb{R}^d$, which furthermore are independent of N. The time-changed random walk

$$P_t = \sum_{k=1}^{N_t} Y_k$$

(where, by convention, $P_t = 0$ if $N_t = 0$) is called a compound Poisson process with intensity λ and distribution μ.

The characteristic function of P_1 is easily computed as $\exp[-\lambda(1 - \phi^Y(u))]$, where $\phi^Y(u) = \int e^{iux}\mu(dx)$ is the characteristic function of the Y_k. Hence the characteristic exponent is

$$\phi(u) = \int (1 - e^{iux})\lambda\mu(dx)$$

so the compound Poisson process has zero drift and diffusion coefficient, and its Lévy measure is $\nu(dx) = \lambda\mu(dx)$.

Compound Poisson processes are of great importance, since it follows from the proof of Theorem 3.2 that any Lévy process can be approximated by such a process; see also [108]. This fact will be used in the discussion of simulation of a Lévy process.

We now proceed to give two formulas that are very useful in the applications. They allow us to compute the expectation of some functionals of a Lévy process. For more details, see [7] or [103].

PROPOSITION 3.1 (COMPENSATION FORMULA)

Let X be a $\mathbb{R}^d$-valued Lévy process with Lévy measure ν, and f a predictable function, i.e., $f : \Omega \times \mathbb{R}_+ \times \mathbb{R}^d \to \mathbb{R}$ is $\mathcal{P} \otimes \mathcal{B}^d$-measurable. Then

$$\mathbb{E}\left[\sum_{s\geq 0} f(\omega, s, \Delta X_s)1_{\Delta X(s)\neq 0}\right] = \mathbb{E}\left[\int_0^\infty ds \int \nu(dx)f(\omega, s, x)\right] \quad (3.4)$$

In the special case where f is deterministic, the right-hand side of (3.4) is simply

$$\int_0^\infty ds \int \nu(dx) f(s, x)$$

and this gives a means of computing the expectation on the left-hand side.

PROOF

Equation (3.4) is easily obtained for functions f of the form

$$f(\omega, s, x) = g(\omega, s) h(x)$$

where g is a simple predictable process

$$g(\omega, s) = \sum_{i=1}^n H_i(\omega) 1_{t_i < s}$$

where H_i is $\mathcal{F}_{t_i}$-measurable, and h is a simple Borel function

$$h(x) = \sum_{j=1}^m a_j 1_{x_j \le x < x_{j+1}}$$

A standard monotone class argument (see [27] or [103]) yields the result for general f.

As a corollary of the compensation formula above, we obtain

PROPOSITION 3.2 (EXPONENTIAL FORMULA)

Let X be a Lévy process with Lévy measure ν. For all t and all complex-valued Borel functions $f(s, x)$ such that $\int_0^t ds \int |1 - e^{f(s,x)}| \nu(dx) < \infty$, we have

$$\mathbb{E}\left[\exp\left(\sum_{s \le t} f(s, \Delta X_s) 1_{\Delta X(s) \ne 0}\right)\right] = \exp\left(-\int_0^t ds \int (1 - e^{f(s,x)}) \nu(dx)\right) \quad (3.5)$$

Beware that, contrary to the compensation formula, the function f in (3.5) above cannot be replaced by a predictable function (i.e., f cannot depend explicitly on ω).

Measure Changes

Recall from Chapter 2 that if we model the asset price under the historical measure, we need to go to an equivalent martingale measure in order to compute the price of derivatives as expectations. Because Lévy processes have jumps, the market that contains bonds and one stock, modeled as the exponential of a Lévy process, is in general incomplete, and there may be several equivalent martingale measures (see Chapter 2).

Denote by $\mathbb{P}$ the historical probability. We give here two examples of a change of measure that allow us to define a probability $\mathbb{Q}$, equivalent to $\mathbb{P}$, such that X is still a Lévy process under $\mathbb{Q}$. This is quite an important fact, since going to an equivalent martingale measure should change the distribution of the asset price (reflecting the market risk-aversion), but not the intrinsic structure of the dynamics which in the case of Lévy processes consists of the independence of the increments.

Esscher transforms   Let $u \in \mathbb{R}^d$ and assume that $\mathbb{E}[e^{\langle u, X_t \rangle}] < \infty$ for some (and then for all) t. The process $M_t = e^{\langle u, X_t \rangle + t\phi(-iu)}$ is then a strictly positive, uniformly integrable martingale such that $\mathbb{E}[M_t] = 1$. Hence, as in Chapter 1, we can define a new probability measure by the formula

$$\mathbb{P}^u|_{\mathscr{F}_t} = M_t \cdot \mathbb{P}|_{\mathscr{F}_t}$$

$\mathbb{P}^u$ is called the *Esscher transform* of $\mathbb{P}$. The following result shows the effect of changing the measure from $\mathbb{P}$ to $\mathbb{P}^u$ on the properties of X.

THEOREM 3.3

Let X be a Lévy process under $\mathbb{P}$, with drift a, diffusion coefficient $Q = RR'$, and Lévy measure ν. Suppose $\mathbb{E}[e^{\langle u, X_1 \rangle}] < \infty$ and define $\mathbb{P}^u$ as above. Then under $\mathbb{P}^u$, X is a Lévy process, with drift a^u, diffusion coefficient Q^u, and Lévy measure ν^u given by

$$a^u = a + Ru + \int_{|x| \leq 1} x(e^{\langle u, x \rangle} - 1)\nu(dx) \tag{3.6a}$$

$$Q^u = Q \tag{3.6b}$$

$$\nu^u(dx) = e^{\langle u, x \rangle}\nu(dx) \tag{3.6c}$$

Moreover, the characteristic exponent of X under $\mathbb{P}^u$ is given by

$$\phi^u(v) = \phi(v - iu) - \phi(-iu) \tag{3.7}$$

PROOF

Let us first prove (3.7). We have

$$\mathbb{E}^u\left[e^{i\langle v, X_t\rangle}\right] = \mathbb{E}\left[M_t e^{i\langle v, X_t\rangle}\right]$$

$$= \mathbb{E}\left[e^{i\langle v, X_t\rangle + \langle u, X_t\rangle}\right] e^{t\phi(-iu)}$$

$$= e^{-t(\phi(v-iu) - \phi(-iu))}$$

$$= e^{-t\phi^u(v)}$$

and (3.7) follows. Using this and writing ϕ in its Lévy-Khintchine form (3.2) yields (see [108] or [112] for details)

$$\phi^u(v) = i\langle a^u, v\rangle + \frac{1}{2}Q(v) - \int (e^{i\langle v, x\rangle} - 1 - i\langle v, x\rangle 1_{|x|\leq 1})v^u(dx)$$

which is the Lévy-Khintchine formula for ϕ^u.

Esscher transforms have been introduced in finance in [21], and their use in the context of Lévy processes is hinted at in [10]; such transforms can be applied to processes more general than Lévy processes (see [66]): The change in the characteristics of X given by the Theorem 3.3 is a particular example of a change of local characteristics of a semimartingale under an absolutely continuous change of measure (see [63]).

Entropy   In the situation of incomplete markets, various criteria exist to select the pricing measure among the equivalent martingale measures. The choice of an Esscher transform described above is more like a structural choice, since the structure of the paths of the Lévy process X is not very much changed under the change of measure. Other criteria, such as those described in Chapter 2, make reference to the historical measure and the strategy used to choose an equivalent martingale measure to minimize some distance to the original measure. The entropy is one such distance. Recall from Chapter 2 the

DEFINITION 3.2

Let $\mathbb{P}$ and $\mathbb{P}'$ be two probability measures with $\mathbb{P}' \ll \mathbb{P}$. The relative entropy of $\mathbb{P}'$ with respect to $\mathbb{P}$ is defined as

$$H(\mathbb{P}'|\mathbb{P}) = \int \log\left(\frac{d\mathbb{P}'}{d\mathbb{P}}\right) d\mathbb{P}' \tag{3.8}$$

Any probability measure $\mathbb{P}'$ that satisfies

1. $e^{-rt}S_t$ is a $\mathbb{P}'$-martingale.
2. For any measure $\mathbb{Q}$ under which $e^{-rt}S_t$ is a martingale, $H(\mathbb{P}'|\mathbb{P}) \le H(\mathbb{Q}|\mathbb{P})$.

is called a *minimal entropy martingale measure (MEMM)* for S.

In his paper [87], Miyahara has obtained a sufficient condition for the MEMM to exist. We cite his result here:

THEOREM 3.4

Assume that

$$\int_{|x|<1} |x|\nu(dx) < \infty$$

and that there exists a constant β such that

$$a + \left(\frac{1}{2} + \beta\right)\sigma^2 + \int (e^x - 1)\exp(\beta(e^x - 1))\nu(dx) = 0 \tag{3.9}$$

Then the formula

$$\mathbb{P}^*|_{\mathscr{F}_t} = \exp\left[\beta\sigma W_t - \frac{\beta^2\sigma^2}{2}t \right. \tag{3.10}$$
$$\left. + \int_0^t\int \beta(e^x - 1)\mu(ds, dx) - \int_0^t ds \int (\exp(\beta(e^x - 1)) - 1)\nu(dx)\right] \cdot \mathbb{P}|_{\mathscr{F}_t}$$

defines a probability measure $\mathbb{P}^*$ which is a MEMM of S. Moreover X remains a Lévy process under $\mathbb{P}^*$, under which its characteristic exponent is

$$\phi^*(u) = ia^*u + \frac{\sigma^{*2}}{2}u^2 - \int (e^{iux} - 1 - iux1_{|x| \le 1})\nu^*(dx)$$

where

$$a^* = a + \beta\sigma^2 \qquad\qquad (3.11)$$

$$\sigma^* = \sigma \qquad\qquad (3.12)$$

$$\nu^*(dx) = \exp(\beta(e^x - 1))\nu(dx) \qquad\qquad (3.13)$$

This result is another example of a change of local characteristics of a semimartingale under a change of measure, as developed in [63].

The use of Theorems 3.3 and 3.4 will become clear in Section 3.2. In particular, the Esscher transform will prove to be a useful tool to derive the price of European options.

Notice that similar to the case of diffusion processes, the diffusion coefficient is not changed by either of the transformations above.

Subordination

We introduce in this section the notion of a subordinated Lévy process, which is the core of a number of the models we study later. We first need to introduce some special kinds of Lévy processes.

DEFINITION 3.3

A real-valued Lévy process is called a *subordinator* if it has almost surely nondecreasing paths.

Clearly, a subordinator cannot have a Brownian component, for otherwise it could not have monotone paths. Instead of the characteristic exponent ϕ of a subordinator, one often uses the *Laplace* exponent ψ, defined by

$$\mathbb{E}[e^{-\lambda X_t}] = e^{-t\psi(\lambda)}, \quad \lambda \ge 0$$

The Lévy-Khintchine formula holds for the Laplace exponent under the form

$$\psi(\lambda) = a\lambda + \int (1 - e^{-\lambda x})\nu(dx)$$

where a is again called the drift and ν is the Lévy measure. Obviously the support of the Lévy measure must be contained in $(0, \infty)$ in order that the process have only positive jumps. Subordinators have many interesting properties, described in, for example, [7] and [8], although we will use them in this book only as appropriate time-change functions.

The Poisson process is an obvious example of a subordinator. The following example is less trivial and will be used in the Variance-Gamma (VG) model (see Section 3.3).

EXAMPLE 3.3 (GAMMA PROCESS)

The *Gamma process* is defined to be the Lévy process γ whose increments $\gamma(t + h) - \gamma(t)$ have the Gamma distribution with parameter h:

$$\frac{dx}{\Gamma(h)} e^{-x} x^{h-1}, \quad x > 0$$

The characteristic function of X_1 can be computed as

$$\int_0^\infty e^{-(1-iu)x} dx = \frac{1}{1 - iu}$$

which shows that the characteristic exponent of γ is

$$\phi(u) = \ln(1 - iu)$$

By the Frullani integral, the Lévy-Khintchine representation of ϕ is

$$\phi(u) = \int_0^\infty (1 - e^{iux}) \frac{e^{-x}}{x} dx$$

so the Gamma process is a pure jump process with no drift, and Lévy measure $\frac{e^{-x}}{x} dx$. Unlike the Poisson process, its Lévy measure is not bounded and hence its paths are not of finite variation; the small jumps of the Gamma process have an infinite rate of arrival.

The following subordinators will play a central role in Section 3.3 where we describe the Normal Inverse Gaussian (NIG) and Carr-Geman-Madan-Yor (CGMY) models, which involve time-changed Brownian motions.

EXAMPLE 3.4 (HITTING TIMES OF BROWNIAN MOTION)

Let W be a standard Brownian motion, and set $T_x = \inf\{t, W_t = x\}$ for $x > 0$. A standard martingale argument (see next section) shows that the Laplace transform of T_x is given by

$$\mathbb{E}[e^{-\lambda T_x}] = e^{-x\sqrt{2\lambda}}$$

From the equality

$$\frac{1}{\sqrt{2\lambda}} = \frac{1}{\sqrt{2}\Gamma(1/2)} \int_0^\infty e^{-\lambda y} \frac{dy}{\sqrt{y}}$$

we obtain the Lévy-Khintchine decomposition for T_x in the form

$$\sqrt{2\lambda} = \int_0^\infty (1 - e^{-\lambda x})\nu(dx)$$

where the Lévy measure $\nu(dx)$ is given by

$$\nu(dx) = \frac{1}{\sqrt{2}\Gamma(1/2)} \frac{dx}{x^{3/2}}, \quad x > 0$$

That (T_x) is a Lévy process follows from the Markov property of W. Since its paths are increasing, it is a subordinator with no drift and Lévy measure ν.

By making use of the Girsanov theorem, we see that if $W^{(\mu)}$ is a Brownian motion with drift μ, then $T_x^{(\mu)} \equiv \inf\{t, W_t^{(\mu)} = x\}$ is again a subordinator, the Laplace transform of which is given by

$$\mathbb{E}[e^{-\lambda T_x^{(\mu)}}] = e^{-x(\sqrt{2\lambda+\mu^2}-\mu)}$$

On the other hand, the law of $T^{(\mu)}$ is equal to the law of T under the Esscher transform of $\mathbb{P}$ defined by the density process

$$\exp\left(-\frac{\mu^2}{2}T_x + \mu x\right), x > 0$$

It is remarkable that the Laplace exponent takes the form $C\lambda^{1/2}$ in the example above. This example can be generalized by allowing values other than $1/2$ in the expression of the Laplace exponent; the resulting subordinators are described in the following example.

EXAMPLE 3.5 (STABLE SUBORDINATORS)

Given $\alpha \in (0, 1)$, there exists a subordinator whose Laplace exponent can be written

$$\psi(\lambda) = C\lambda^\alpha \tag{3.14}$$

where C is a positive constant. From the formula

$$\lambda^\alpha = \frac{\alpha}{\Gamma(1-\alpha)} \int_0^\infty (1 - e^{-\lambda x}) x^{-1-\alpha} dx$$

valid for $0 < \alpha < 1$, we deduce that the corresponding Lévy measure is given by

$$\nu(dx) = \frac{C\alpha}{\Gamma(1-\alpha)} \frac{dx}{x^{1+\alpha}}$$

We now turn to the definition of a subordinated Lévy process, a notion that goes back to Bochner [14].

DEFINITION 3.4

Let Z be a subordinator and Y an independent Lévy process. The process X defined by

$$X_t = Y_{Z_t}$$

is called a *subordinated Lévy process*.

A subordinated Lévy process is then a Lévy process, evaluated not in calendar time, but according to a random clock specified by the subordinator. Although a subordinated Lévy process could be studied directly as a Lévy process, it may be simpler to regard it as a time-changed process, especially if the two processes involved are well known. The correspondence is given by the following:

THEOREM 3.5

Let Z be a subordinator with drift β and Lévy measure ρ and Y an independent Lévy process with characteristic exponent

$$\phi^Y(u) = i\langle a^Y, u\rangle + \frac{1}{2}Q^Y(u) - \int (e^{i\langle u, x\rangle} - 1 - i\langle u, x\rangle 1_{|x| \le 1})\nu^Y(dx)$$

Set $X_t = Y_{Z_t}$. Then X is a Lévy process, whose characteristic exponent is given by

$$\phi(u) = i\langle a, u \rangle + \frac{1}{2} Q(u) - \int (e^{i\langle u, x \rangle} - 1 - i\langle u, x \rangle 1_{|x| \leq 1}) \nu(dx)$$

where

$$a = \beta a^Y + \int \rho(ds) \int_{|x| \leq 1} x \mathbb{P}[Y_s \in dx] \qquad (3.15)$$

$$Q = \beta Q^Y \qquad (3.16)$$

$$\nu(dx) = \beta \nu^Y(dx) + \int \rho(ds) \mathbb{P}[Y_s \in dx] \qquad (3.17)$$

PROOF

Write first

$$\mathbb{E}\left[e^{i\langle u, X_t \rangle}\right] = \mathbb{E}\left[e^{i\langle u, Y_{Z_t} \rangle}\right] = \mathbb{E}\left[e^{-Z_t \phi^Y(u)}\right]$$

By writing the Lévy-Khintchine formula for ϕ^Y and for Z, the Lévy-Khintchine formula for X appears, and its characteristics can be read directly. See [108, Theorems 33.1 and 33.2] for details.

EXAMPLE 3.6 (COMPOUND POISSON PROCESS)

The compound Poisson process studied in Example 3.2 is a simple case of a subordinated Lévy process. Retaining the notation in Example 3.2, the random walk

$$S_n = \sum_{i=1}^{n} Y_i$$

has independent and stationary increments Y_i. The compound Poisson process $P_t = S_{N_t}$ can be seen as a subordinated process, where S_n plays the role of the subordinated process, and N is the subordinator without drift and Lévy measure $\lambda \delta_1(dx)$.

(continued)

EXAMPLE 3.6 (COMPOUND POISSON PROCESS)   (*continued*)

Applying the results of Theorem 3.5, we obtain that P is a Lévy process with no gaussian component, drift equal to

$$a = \int \lambda \delta_1(ds) \int_{|x| \leq 1} x \mathbb{P}[S_s \in dx] = \int_{|x| \leq 1} x \mathbb{P}[S_1 \in dx] = \mathbb{E}[Y1_{|Y| \leq 1}]$$

and Lévy measure

$$\nu(dx) = \int \lambda \delta_1(dx) \mathbb{P}[S_s \in dx] = \lambda \mathbb{P}[S_1 \in dx]$$

So we recover the results of Example 3.2, where the drift was incorporated into the integral. The compound Poisson process lies at the heart of the Merton model studied in Section 3.3.

Subordinated Lévy processes form a wide class of processes that are admissible candidates for modeling the price process of an asset. We will study a couple of models where the stock price process is a subordinated Brownian motion—see Section 3.3.

Lévy Processes with No Positive Jumps

Other kinds of Lévy processes which are very interesting are those whose jumps are all negative. The Lévy process X and related quantities then have quite simple properties.

Because the Lévy measure has support contained in $(-\infty, 0)$, we can define the Laplace exponent ψ of X by the formula

$$\mathbb{E}[e^{uX_t}] = e^{t\psi(u)}, \quad u \geq 0$$

The Laplace exponent is related to the Lévy exponent by $\psi(u) = -\phi(-iu)$. It is possible to perform Esscher transforms as described earlier. The martingale property of $e^{uX_t - t\psi(u)}$ also yields a simple determination of the law of first hitting times. Let $T(x) = \inf\{t : X_t > x\}$ for $x > 0$; $T(x)$ is a stopping time in the natural filtration of X. Since X has no positive jumps, it holds that $X_{T(x)} = x$ $\mathbb{P}$ almost surely. Doob's optional sampling theorem applied at the finite stopping time $t \wedge T(x)$ yields

$$\mathbb{E}[e^{uX_{t \wedge T(x)} - (t \wedge T(x))\psi(u)}] = 1$$

and letting t tend to ∞, we obtain

$$\mathbb{E}[e^{ux - T(x)\psi(u)} 1_{T(x)<\infty}] = 1$$

One can prove that ψ is a nonpositive, one-to-one function of u, for u greater than a value $\Phi(0) \geq 0$; denoting by Φ its inverse, we get the Laplace transform of $T(x)$:

$$\mathbb{E}[e^{-uT(x)} 1_{T(x)<\infty}] = e^{-x\Phi(u)}, \quad u > 0 \tag{3.18}$$

EXAMPLE 3.7

Consider a compound Poisson process with drift $b > 0$

$$P_t = \sum_{k=1}^{N_t} Y_k + bt$$

where the Poisson process N has intensity λ and the Y_k are i.i.d. with common distribution μ carried by $(-\infty, 0)$. Hence all the jumps of P are negative. For $u > 0$, we have easily from the exponential formula:

$$\mathbb{E}[e^{uP_t}] = \exp\{-\lambda t(1 - \mathbb{E}[e^{uY_1}]) + but\}$$

so that $\psi(u) = bu - \lambda(1 - \mathbb{E}[e^{uY_1}]) = bu - \int_{-\infty}^{0}(1 - e^{uy})\lambda\mu(dy)$. Suppose that $-Y_1$ has an exponential distribution with parameter $a > 0$, so that $\mu(dy) = ae^{ay}1_{y<0}dy$, then

$$\psi(u) = bu - \frac{\lambda u}{a + u}, \qquad \Phi(v) = \frac{\lambda + v - ab + \sqrt{(\lambda + v - ab)^2 + 4abv}}{2b}$$

According to (3.18), $\mathbb{P}[T(x) = \infty] > 0$ if and only if

$$\Phi(0) = \frac{\lambda - ab + |\lambda - ab|}{2b} > 0$$

The following counterexample shows that the preceding analysis does not hold if the jumps are positive.

EXAMPLE 3.8

Let N be a Poisson process with intensity λ. All the jumps of N are of size 1, and $T(x)$ coincides with the time τ_n of the n-th jump of N, n

(continued)

EXAMPLE 3.8   (*continued*)

being the smallest integer strictly greater than x. It is well known that τ_n has a Gamma distribution with parameters (n, λ)

$$\mathbb{E}[e^{-\mu \tau_n}] = \left(\frac{\lambda}{\lambda + \mu}\right)^n$$

Hence,

$$\mathbb{E}[e^{-\mu T(x)}] = \left(\frac{\lambda}{\lambda + \mu}\right)^n, \qquad \forall x \in [n-1, n)$$

whereas an—unjustified!—application of the above results would give

$$\mathbb{E}[e^{-\mu T(x)}] = \left(1 + \frac{\mu}{\lambda}\right)^{-x}$$

As a consequence of the above result for the first hitting times process $T(x)$, we can easily obtain the distribution of the supremum of a Lévy process X, taken at particular random times. Let $S_t = \sup_{s \leq t} X_s$, and τ be a variable independent of X, having an exponential distribution with parameter θ. Then

$$\mathbb{P}[S_\tau \geq x] = \int_0^\infty \theta e^{-\theta t} \mathbb{P}[S_t \geq x] dt$$

$$= \int_0^\infty \theta e^{-\theta t} \mathbb{P}[T(x) \leq t] dt$$

$$= \mathbb{E}[e^{-\theta T(x)}] = e^{-x \Phi(-\theta)}$$

The law of $T(x)$ is much more difficult to determine in the case when X may have positive jumps because in most situations a fixed level is crossed by a jump, and $X_{T(x)} \neq x$; however, some results are given in [102] in the special case of stable processes, and more recently in [73] for some particular jump diffusion processes.

3.2   MODELING WITH LÉVY PROCESSES

After introducing Lévy processes, we describe a general class of models involving Lévy processes. We carry out the classical program of arbitrage valuation, for which all the necessary technical tools have been introduced in the previous section. Specific examples will be treated more precisely in the next section.

Model Framework

We model the price process of a security S as the exponential of a Lévy process:

$$S_t = S_0 e^{X_t}$$

where X is a Lévy process started at 0 under $\mathbb{P}$. In this setting we explain how to value derivative products by following the steps given in Chapter 2. We neglect the financial risk related to interest rates, assuming the latter only have an impact on the time value at a constant rate. Precisely, we suppose that interests are compounded continuously at a constant rate r.

The flow of information is supposed to be $(\mathcal{F}_t)$, the natural filtration of X, which coincides with the natural filtration of the price process S. We—as usual—assume absence of arbitrage in the market (see Chapter 2, and [60], [32]). Recall the steps needed to define an admissible pricing rule:

1. Choose an equivalent martingale measure for S, $\hat{\mathbb{P}}$.
2. The price p of a contingent claim paying out at time T, modeled as an $\mathcal{F}_T$-measurable random variable H, is defined as the expected value under $\hat{\mathbb{P}}$ of its actualized payoff: $p = \hat{\mathbb{E}}[e^{-rT}H]$.

The Choice of a Pricing Measure

The first step in the valuation of an option is the choice of the pricing rule, that is, the choice of an equivalent martingale measure. In the Black-Scholes model, or more generally in complete models, there is only one equivalent, risk-neutral measure and one does not have a choice to make. In incomplete markets, we have a wide family of equivalent risk-neutral measures to choose from; see Chapter 2.

In case the hypotheses in Theorem 3.3 are fulfilled, we can use Esscher transforms to define an equivalent probability measure under which X remains a Lévy process. In order for the Esscher transform $\mathbb{P}^u$ to be a martingale measure, it is required that $e^{-rt}S_t = S_0 e^{-rt+X_t}$ be a martingale under $\mathbb{P}^u$. Let $e^{t\psi(u)} = \mathbb{E}[e^{uX_t}]$ under the original measure $\mathbb{P}$; then the process $e^{uX_t - t\psi(u)}$ is a $\mathbb{P}$-martingale. The Laplace exponent of X under the measure $\mathbb{P}^u$ is given by

$$\psi^u(v) = \psi(v + u) - \psi(u)$$

and $e^{\nu X_t - t\psi^u(\nu)}$ is a $\mathbb{P}^u$-martingale for all ν. Hence it is a necessary condition that $r = \psi^u(1)$ for $\mathbb{P}^u$ to be a martingale measure. Therefore, there exists, at most, one possible pricing rule defined as an Esscher transform.

If one does not wish to make the structural assumption that leads to choosing the pricing rule as an Esscher transform of the original measure, another possible choice is the minimization of the relative entropy. In order to do so, it is sufficient that the related results of Section 3.1 be applicable. X remains a Lévy process under the new measure, but the behavior of its jumps is drastically changed.

In practice, the original measure is irrelevant for option pricing, as is the way the pricing measure has been deduced from it—see Chapter 2. In fact, all one is interested in is the structure of the Lévy process X under the pricing measure and the modeling assumptions are usually about this point. The model parameters are calibrated to fit observed option prices, under the restriction that $e^{-rt}S_t$ be a martingale. Often, as above, the change of measure is defined by one or several parameters; these are implicitly calibrated together with the actual parameters of the model; see Section 3.4. Hence, we consider that $\mathbb{P}$ is already a martingale measure, and also is our pricing measure, whatever way it would have been obtained from the real-world measure.

European Options Pricing

Once the pricing rule (i.e., the pricing probability measure) has been chosen, prices are defined as the expected value of their actualized payoff. In the case of Lévy processes, European options can be priced efficiently, using a technique based on the characteristic exponent, which we now explain.

We first recall a useful result on Fourier inversion. Let Z be a real random variable with distribution function F and characteristic function ϕ:

$$\phi(u) = \int e^{iux} F(dx)$$

Then the following formula holds for all x (see [80] or [114]):

$$F(x) = \frac{1}{2} + \frac{1}{2\pi} \int_{\mathbb{R}} \frac{e^{iux}\phi(-u) - e^{-iux}\phi(u)}{iu} du \qquad (3.19)$$

Assume that a contingent claim has a payoff at time T given by $h(S_T)$ and the pricing probability is $\mathbb{P}$, under which X is a Lévy process. Let ϕ be the characteristic exponent of X under $\mathbb{P}$, that is

$$\mathbb{E}\left[e^{iuX_t}\right] = e^{-t\phi(u)}, \qquad u \in \mathbb{R}$$

Upon defining $\tilde{h}(x) = h(\log(x/S_0))$, we can write the price of this option as

$$p = e^{-rT}\mathbb{E}\left[\tilde{h}(X_T)\right]$$

Denoting by F_T the distribution function of X_T under $\mathbb{P}$, this expression is equal to

$$e^{-rT}\int \tilde{h}(x)F_T(dx)$$

where F_T can be retrieved from the characteristic exponent of X:

$$F_T(x) = \frac{1}{2} + \frac{1}{2\pi}\int_{\mathbb{R}} \frac{e^{iux - T\phi(-u)} - e^{-iux - T\phi(u)}}{iu}du$$

Suppose that $\int |e^{-T\phi(u)}|du < \infty$ so that Lebesgue theorem applies and F_T is differentiable; then there exists the density

$$f_T(x) = F_T'(x) = \frac{1}{\pi}\int_{\mathbb{R}} \mathfrak{R}\left(e^{-iux - T\phi(u)}\right)du$$

($\mathfrak{R}(z)$ denotes the real part of the complex number z), and the option is worth

$$p = e^{-rT}\int \tilde{h}(x)f_T(x)dx$$

In any case, the value of p can be obtained by performing a numerical integration procedure. However, the analysis can be carried further in some cases, as shown in the next example.

EXAMPLE 3.9

Consider the case of a put option with strike price K and maturity T, the payoff of which is given by $h(S_T)$, where $h(x) = (K - x)^+$. In that case, it is in fact possible to go one step further if we make the additional assumption that $\mathbb{E}\left[e^{X_T}\right] < \infty$. Define a new probability measure as the Esscher transform of $\mathbb{P}$:

$$\mathbb{P}^S\big|_{\mathcal{F}_t} = e^{X_t - t\phi(-i)} \cdot \mathbb{P}\big|_{\mathcal{F}_t}$$

(continued)

EXAMPLE 3.9 *(continued)*

Let p be the price of the put option:

$$
\begin{aligned}
e^{rT}p &= \mathbb{E}\left[(K - S_T)^+\right] = \mathbb{E}\left[(K - S_T)1_{K > S_T}\right] \\
&= K\mathbb{P}\left[S_T < K\right] - \mathbb{E}\left[S_T 1_{S_T < K}\right]
\end{aligned}
$$

The last expectation can be expressed as $S_0 \mathbb{P}^S(S_T < K)$. In terms of the Lévy process X, the price is then

$$
e^{rT}p = K\mathbb{P}\left[X_T < k\right] - S_0 \mathbb{P}^S[X_T < k] \tag{3.20}
$$

where $k = \log(K/S_0)$. Let ϕ^S be the Lévy exponent of X under $\mathbb{P}^S$; then we have

$$
\begin{aligned}
e^{rT}p = K&\left(\frac{1}{2} + \frac{1}{2\pi}\int_{\mathbb{R}} \frac{e^{iuk - T\phi(-u)} - e^{-iuk - T\phi(u)}}{iu} du\right) \\
&- S_0\left(\frac{1}{2} + \frac{1}{2\pi}\int_{\mathbb{R}} \frac{e^{iuk - T\phi^S(-u)} - e^{-iuk - T\phi^S(u)}}{iu} du\right)
\end{aligned}
$$

Going to the probability $\mathbb{P}^S$ is a technique known as the *change of numéraire*, introduced in [42]. This can be generalized to other payoffs, provided one can find appropriate probability measures $\mathbb{Q}_i$ such that the price can be expressed in terms of $\mathbb{Q}_i(\mathscr{E})$, $\mathscr{E}$ being the exercise set (i.e, the different states of the world when the option is to be exercised).

3.3 PRODUCTS AND MODELS

We give a more detailed treatment of a few popular examples. We first describe some products for which pricing can be done efficiently with Lévy processes, before considering some particular models.

Exotic Products

Exotic products can be priced within the framework we have just introduced, by using numerical methods that will be described later. However, for some of them, a more explicit solution is available, that can spare the use of heavy numerics. We give two examples here: perpetuities and barrier options.

Perpetuities and perpetual options   Both perpetuities and perpetual options
have infinite maturity.

Perpetuities give a lifelong return, linked to a security whose price may
be modeled, as explained at the beginning of Section 3.3. The determination
of their price is linked to the study of exponential functionals

$$A_\infty = \int_0^\infty S_s ds = S_0 \int_0^\infty e^{X(s)} ds$$

for a suitable process X. A_∞ represents the aggregated returns given by a
stock with S as a price process. The distribution of A_∞ has received a lot of
attention in the last few years; see [23], [24], [37], and [57], [92], [93], [94],
[95] in relation to ruin theory.

Specifically, if $X_t = 2\mu t + \sigma W_t$ (a Brownian motion with drift), then
$1/A_\infty$ is distributed as a Gamma variable with shape parameter $\frac{\mu}{\sigma^2}$ and scale
parameter $\frac{\sigma^2}{2}$, that is, it has a density

$$\frac{1}{\Gamma(\mu/\sigma^2)} \left(\frac{2x}{\sigma^2}\right)^{\mu/\sigma^2 - 1} e^{-2x/\sigma^2}, \quad x > 0$$

(see [24], [37], [57], [93]). If X is a compound Poisson process defined by

$$X_t = -\sum_{i=1}^{N_t} S_i$$

where N is a Poisson process with intensity λ, and S_i are independent with
an exponential distribution with parameter α, then A_∞ is distributed as a
Gamma variable with shape parameter $1 + \alpha$ and scale parameter λ; if X
has a drift, specified by

$$X_t = rt - \sum_{i=1}^{N_t} S_i \qquad (r > 0)$$

then A_∞ has a Beta distribution $B_2(1 + \alpha, \frac{\alpha}{r}(\frac{\lambda}{\alpha} - r))$. See [57] for more details
and more results in the same vein.

This exponential functional is also related to Asian options, which can
be seen as European options on an artificial underlying, whose price at
time t is

$$A_t := \int_0^t S_s ds$$

When X is a Brownian motion, Geman and Yor [53] derive explicit formulas for the Laplace transform of the price of an Asian option, that is,

$$\int_0^\infty e^{-qt} \mathbb{E}(A_t - K)^+ dt$$

Unfortunately, for a general Lévy process, few explicit formulae are known (see however [23], [24]).

Perpetual options are American-style options that offer their holder the right to exercise any time. They then pay off $(S_\tau - K)^+$ or $(K - S_\tau)^+$, where τ is the (optimal) exercise time. The problem of valuing perpetual American options with Lévy processes has been examined in [17], [55], and [56].

Specifically, consider the case of the perpetual American put option, which pays out $(K - S_\tau)^+$ at any time τ when the holder of the option decides to exercise the option. Because the decision to exercise must be made from the information in the market, τ must be a stopping time, and the value of the option is, according to the standard risk-neutral valuation rules:

$$\sup_\tau \mathbb{E}\left[e^{-r\tau}(K - S_\tau)^+\right]$$

Gerber and Shiu, see [55] and [56], argue that attention can be restricted to those stopping times of the form

$$\tau = \tau_L = \inf\{t, S_t \le L\}$$

so that the problem can be restated as

$$\max_L V(S_0, L)$$

where $V(S_0, L) = \mathbb{E}\left[e^{-r\tau_L}(K - S_{\tau_L})^+\right]$. In the case when X has no negative jumps, $S_{\tau_L} = L$ and all that remains to do is to apply formula (3.18) to obtain the price of the perpetual American put option as

$$\sup_L V(S_0, L) = \sup_L (K - L)^+ e^{-\ln(L/S_0)\Phi(-r)}$$

where Φ is the reciprocal function of the Laplace exponent of X, as in [55]. The maximization problem above can easily be solved explicitly, and we have

$$\tilde{L} = \arg\max_L V(S_0, L) = -K\frac{\Phi(-r)}{1 - \Phi(-r)} \tag{3.21a}$$

$$V(S_0, \tilde{L}) = \frac{K}{1 - \Phi(-r)}\left[-\frac{K\Phi(-r)}{S_0(1 - \Phi(-r))}\right]^{-\Phi(-r)} \tag{3.21b}$$

If X has negative jumps, the following result is obtained in [56] in a particular case. Suppose that $X = ct + Z_t$ is a compound Poisson process with drift c, with intensity λ, and jump distribution $p(x)$, $x \leq 0$. Let

$$g(y) = \frac{d}{dy} \int_0^\infty e^{-rt} \mathbb{P}\left[\ln(L/S_0) - X_{\tau_L} \in dy, \tau_L \in dt\right]$$

the *discounted probability that S will ever fall below the level L* as it is called in [56]. In the special case when X is a compound Poisson process with drift, g can be computed as

$$g(y) = \frac{\lambda}{c} e^y \int_y^\infty e^{-x} p(x) dx$$

Then $W(x, L) = V(Le^x, L)$ satisfies the equation

$$W(x, L) = \int_0^x W(x - y, L) g(y) dy + \int_x^\infty (K - Le^{x-y})^+ g(y) dy$$

The perpetual American call option can be treated in a similar way. Equations similar to (3.12a, 3.12b) are obtained when X has no positive jumps, while if X has positive jumps, the same study as just discussed can be done.

In [17], results are obtained that cover a broader range of Lévy processes, by means of advanced analysis techniques. However, they do not cover the Variance-Gamma model examined in the next section, and the price of the perpetual American put option is characterized as the solution to a variational problem far less explicit that the one studied here.

More generally, results are currently obtained concerning the optimal stopping of processes with jumps—for example, see [88], opening the way to the valuation of American options.

Barrier options Barrier options are among the most popular of exotic derivatives. In the case of geometric Brownian Motion, their pricing has been extensively studied by a number of authors, for example, [54], [75], [97], from both a theoretical and a numerical point of view. We explain how this work can be repeated in the case where we use a Lévy process in place of the Brownian motion to model the underlying price process.

We focus on the case of an Up-and-In barrier Call option, whose payoff is defined to be

$$(S_T - K)^+ 1_{\sup_{t \leq T} S_t > H}$$

where K is the strike price and H is the barrier level. We suppose $S_0 < H$ and $H > K$. Denote by τ the first instant when S crosses the level H. Recall that $S_t = S_0 e^{X_t}$, so that τ can also be written as

$$\tau = \inf\{t, X_t > h\}, \qquad h = \ln(H/S_0)$$

Suppose that X has no positive jumps, then we have $X_\tau = h$ almost surely From Section 3.1, we know that the Laplace transform of τ is given by

$$\mathbb{E}\left[e^{-u\tau} 1_{\tau < \infty}\right] = e^{-h\Phi(-u)}$$

where Φ is the inverse bijection of the Laplace exponent of X.

The option expires worthless if $\tau > T$; its price is therefore

$$e^{-rT} S_0 \mathbb{E}\left[1_{\tau \leq T}(e^{X_T} - e^k)^+\right]$$

where $k = \ln(K/S_0)$. This can be written, using conditional expectations:

$$S_0 \mathbb{E}\left[1_{\tau \leq T}(e^{X_T} - e^k)^+\right] = S_0 \mathbb{E}\left[\mathbb{E}[1_{\tau \leq T}(e^{X_T} - e^k)^+ | \mathcal{F}_\tau]\right]$$

$$= S_0 \mathbb{E}\left[1_{\tau \leq T} e^{X_\tau} \mathbb{E}[(e^{X_T - X_\tau} - e^k)^+ | \mathcal{F}_\tau]\right]$$

Because X is a strong Markov process, the conditional expectation $\mathbb{E}\left[(e^{X_T - X_\tau} - e^k)^+ | \mathcal{F}_\tau\right]$ can be interpreted as the price of a call option with strike price K and maturity $T - \tau$ when the spot price is 1. How to price such an option has been explained in Section 3.2, and we denote by $C(\tau, X_\tau)$ this quantity. It remains to compute $S_0 \mathbb{E}\left[1_{\tau \leq T} e^{X_\tau} C(\tau, X_\tau)\right]$; however, because $X_\tau = h$ almost surely this reduces to

$$S_0 e^h \mathbb{E}\left[1_{\tau \leq T} C(\tau, h)\right] = S_0 e^h \int_0^T C(t, h) dF(t)$$

where F denotes the distribution function of τ (under $\mathbb{P}$), that can be retrieved from its Laplace transform by

$$F(t) = \frac{1}{2} + \frac{1}{2\pi} \int_0^\infty \frac{e^{-iut} e^{-h\Phi(-iu)} - e^{iut} e^{-h\Phi(iu)}}{iu} du$$

When X has positive jumps, the barrier is crossed by a jump with positive probability; the preceding analysis applies identically, except for the fact that one cannot replace X_τ with h in the conditional expectation. Hence the final formula for the price of the Up-and-In call option in this case is

$$e^{-rT} S_0 \mathbb{E}\left[1_{\tau \le T} e^{X_\tau} C(\tau, X_\tau) \right]$$

This can be computed numerically using Monte Carlo simulation; analytical computations require the joint law of the pair (τ, X_τ). This law is known via its Laplace transform, given by the Pecherskii-Rogozin identity (see [91], [96]). More precisely, it is possible to show that

$$\int_0^\infty e^{-qh} \mathbb{E}[e^{-\alpha\tau - \beta(X_\tau - h)}] dh = \frac{1}{q - \beta} \left\{ 1 - \frac{\kappa(\alpha, \beta)}{\kappa(\alpha, q)} \right\}$$

where the function κ is given by

$$\kappa(\alpha, \beta) = \exp\left\{ -\int_0^\infty dt \int_0^\infty \frac{1}{t} (e^{-t} - e^{-\alpha t - \beta x}) \mathbb{P}(X_t \in dx) \right\}$$

Hence, it is in principle possible to retrieve the joint law of (τ, X_τ); however, this method demands a very high computational effort. The pricing problem for barrier options under Lévy processes has been studied from another viewpoint in [17].

Some Particular Models

We now describe some particular models that depart from the Brownian motion and the Poisson process. Using these models, we will see (Section 3.4) what can be achieved in terms of the replication of the implied volatility surface observed in the market. Discontinuous paths are of interest because the implied volatility for short dated options has a very steep skew, as observed in today's equities and index markets. Figure 3.1 shows the density of the distribution of the log-price one year from now for some of the models studied here, as well as the Gaussian distribution (Black-Scholes model) for comparison.

For all the distributions in Figure 3.1, the martingale restriction is satisfied; moreover, they all have the same "volatility" (see later). We observe already that the different curves "JD" (Jump Diffusion), "NIG" (Normal Inverse Gaussian), and "VG" (Variance Gamma) have fatter tails than the Gaussian distribution that corresponds to the Black-Scholes model [13]; they obviously also have different skewness and kurtosis. These features are

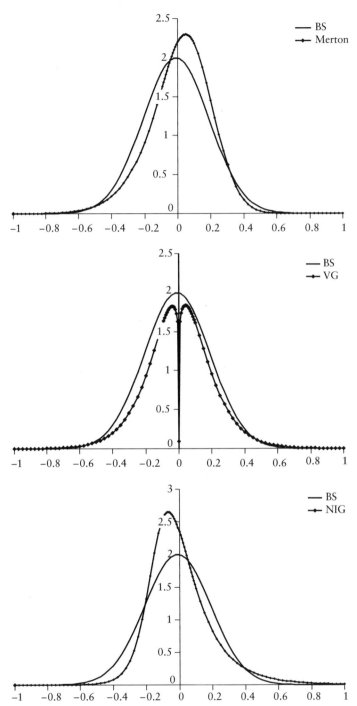

FIGURE 3.1 Density of $\ln(S_T/S_0)$ for $T = 1$ year for different models, compared to the Gaussian density (Black-Scholes model).

in accordance with observations made on empirical densities obtained from market data.

Martingale restriction As mentioned earlier, we build our models directly under a risk-neutral measure; the parameters are determined by calibrating the model to option prices, as explained in Section 3.4. Under such a measure, the no-arbitrage assumption requires that discounted asset prices $e^{-rt}S_t$ are martingales. Since we suppose that $S_t = S_0 e^{X_t}$ for some Lévy process X, this amounts to demand that

$$
\begin{aligned}
1 &= \mathbb{E}[e^{-rt+X_t}] \\
&= e^{-rt-t\phi(-i)}
\end{aligned}
$$

By the Lévy-Khintchine formula, this is equivalent to

$$
r + a - \frac{1}{2}\sigma^2 - \int (e^x - 1 - x 1_{|x| \le 1}) \nu(dx) = 0 \tag{3.22}
$$

where a, σ, and ν are the drift, diffusion coefficient, and Lévy measure of X. Equation (3.22) is called martingale restriction, as it imposes a restriction on the parameters of the model.

Volatility When the price process of an asset S is defined as $S_t = S_0 e^{X_t}$ for a Lévy process X, its variability is due to the structure of X. In order to facilitate the comparison with the Black-Scholes model, we define a *volatility* parameter in this framework. A natural choice is the conditional quadratic variation of the logarithm of the asset price: let $s_t = \ln(S_t/S_0) \equiv X_t$, and

$$
v_t^2 = \frac{d\langle s, s \rangle_t}{dt} = \frac{d\langle X, X \rangle_t}{dt} \tag{3.23}
$$

It can be checked that, if $\int x^2 \nu(dx) < \infty$, which is the case for the models we study, then

$$
\langle X, X \rangle_t = t\left(\sigma^2 + \int x^2 \nu(dx)\right)
$$

for all t, hence the volatility parameter v_t is in fact constant in time, and equal to

$$
v = \sqrt{\sigma^2 + \int x^2 \nu(dx)} \tag{3.24}
$$

See [25] for a similar discussion. Note that in the case of the Black-Scholes model, the volatility is σ as expected.

A simple jump-diffusion model   Consider a model that consists of a Black-Scholes diffusion, to which is added a pure jump random process: The asset price process is supposed to be driven by

$$S_t = S_0 e^{X_t} \tag{3.25}$$

under a risk-neutral probability measure $\mathbb{P}$ that we assume to be our pricing measure. Under $\mathbb{P}$, X is the Lévy process given by

$$X_t = \mu t + \sigma W_t + \log(1 + \zeta) N_t \tag{3.26}$$

Here, W is a standard Brownian motion and N is an independent Poisson process with constant intensity λ. Since we model directly under a risk-neutral measure $\mathbb{P}$, we need to choose μ so that $e^{-rt} S_t$ is a $\mathbb{P}$-martingale—that is, we must have

$$\mu = r - \frac{\sigma^2}{2} - \lambda \zeta$$

This model, already studied in [19], is a simple and natural extension of the Black-Scholes model; it is also a particular case of the model studied in [6]. Indeed, the price process S is solution of the stochastic differential equation (SDE)

$$\frac{dS_t}{S_{t-}} = r dt + \sigma dW_t + \zeta d\bar{N}_t \tag{3.27}$$

which is the Black-Scholes SDE with an additional term $\zeta d\bar{N}_t$, where $\bar{N}$ is the compensated Poisson process $\bar{N}_t = N_t - \lambda t$.

The method, described in Example 3.9, to price European options is of course available, but due to the simple structure of the Lévy process X, a more efficient way can be discussed. We will write the price of a European contingent claim as a series; only the first few terms are needed for acceptable accuracy.

We wish to compute the price of the payoff $h(S_T)$ occuring at time T. Note that conditionally on $N_T = n$, X is a Gaussian variable with variance $\sigma^2/2$ and mean $r_n T - \sigma^2 T/2$ where $r_n T = \mu T + n \log(1 + \zeta)$; hence S_T is a log-normal variable. The "conditional price," given $N_T = n$, is therefore given by a Black-Scholes formula (that is, a formula that would hold in the Black-Scholes model), with input parameters r_n as the interest rate and σ as

TABLE 3.1 Convergence of the series (3.28)

n	$e^{(r_n-r)T}BS_n$	Weight $e^{-\lambda T}(\lambda T)^n/n!$	Partial Sum
0	11.66757	0.90458	10.5543
1	2.72888	0.0907	10.80189
2	0.32691	0.004547	10.80338
4	0.017854	0.00015	10.80338
5	3.8×10^{-6}	3.8×10^{-6}	10.80338
6	1.4×10^{-8}	7.6×10^{-8}	10.80338

In this example, $h(x) = (x - K)^+$, where the strike K is at the money. Maturity is 1 year, interest rate is 5 percent. The parameters used are $\lambda = 0.1$, $\zeta = -0.1813$. The true price is 10.80338% of spot.

the volatility; denote this by $BS_n(h)$. The (unconditional) price is obtained by taking into account the law of N_T, which is a Poisson variable with parameter λT, by virtue of the rule of chained expectations: We obtain that the price of the European option with payoff $h(S_T)$ is given by

$$e^{-rT} \sum_{n=0}^{\infty} e^{-\lambda T} \frac{(\lambda T)^n}{n!} e^{r_n T} BS_n(h) \tag{3.28}$$

Numerically, only a few terms are needed to achieve a correct accuracy. Table 3.1 shows that this method is quite efficient in that the convergence is very fast.

Merton's model revisited   The jump-diffusion model is a simple extension of the Black-Scholes model. However, it lacks flexibility because the size of the jumps is fixed. Hence we now study the model pioneered by Merton [86]. This model is as follows. Let W be a standard Brownian motion and N an independent Poisson process with intensity λ. Let also P be a compound Poisson process

$$P_t = \sum_{i=1}^{N_t} U_i \tag{3.29}$$

where the U_i are given by

$$U_i = \exp(\gamma + \delta \varepsilon_i) - 1$$

the ε_i being independent standard Gaussian variables, also independent of W and N. The stock price is modeled as the solution of the SDE

$$\frac{dS_t}{S_{t-}} = \mu dt + \sigma dW_t + dP_t$$

There is an explicit expression for S in terms of the driving processes (see [76]):

$$S_t = S_0 \exp\left\{ (\mu - \frac{\sigma^2}{2})t + \sigma W_t \right\} \prod_{i=1}^{N_t} (U_i + 1)$$
$$= S_0 \exp(X_t)$$

where X is the Lévy process

$$X_t = (\mu - \frac{\sigma^2}{2})t + \sigma W_t + \sum_{i=1}^{N_t} (\gamma + \delta \varepsilon_i) \tag{3.30}$$

Notice that this model extends the jump-diffusion model, since upon setting $\delta = 0$ and $\gamma = \ln(1 + \zeta)$, Equations (3.26) and (3.30) are the same. In order that $e^{-rt}S_t$ be a martingale, we choose $\mu = r - \lambda(e^{\gamma + \delta^2/2} - 1)$.

The method described in Example 3.9 can be used to price European options. However, as already noticed regarding the jump-diffusion model, a more efficient method can be used to derive the price of European options. Assume we wish to value a contingent claim that pays out $h(S_T)$ at time T. Then the same reasoning as with the jump-diffusion model holds: conditional on $N_T = n$, X_T is a Gaussian variable with mean $\mu_n T = (\mu - \sigma^2/2)T + n\gamma$ and variance $\sigma_n^2 T = \sigma^2 T + n\delta^2$; the price of the option is then given by

$$e^{-rT} \sum_{n=0}^{\infty} e^{-\lambda T} \frac{(\lambda T)^n}{n!} e^{r_n T} BS_n(h) \tag{3.31}$$

where $BS_n(h)$ is the price of the option in the Black-Scholes model if the interest rate is $r_n T = \mu T + n(\gamma + \delta^2/2)$ and the volatility is σ_n. The results given in Table 3.2 show that only a few terms of the above series are actually necessary to achieve a good accuracy.

To conclude on the jump-diffusion models we note that the variance-optimal hedging strategy described in Chapter 2 can be computed in the Merton model, see [76].

We next turn to models based on the concept of subordination (see Section 3.1). In fact, an empirical study by Ané and Geman in [1] shows that the logarithms of stock returns are Gaussian, provided they are considered

TABLE 3.2 Convergence of the series (3.31)

n	$e^{(r_n-r)T}BS_n$	Weight $e^{-\lambda T}(\lambda T)^n/n!$	Partial Sum
0	11.63949	0.90458	10.52897
1	3.53830	0.0907	10.84992
2	0.87303	0.004547	10.853888
4	0.18586	0.00015	10.853917
5	0.03566	3.8×10^{-6}	10.853917
6	0.00635	7.6×10^{-8}	10.853917

In this example, $h(x) = (x - K)^+$, where the strike K is at the money. Maturity is 1 year, interest rate is 5 percent. The parameters used are $\lambda = 0.1$, $\gamma = -20$ percent and $\delta = 10$ percent. The true price is 10.853917 percent of spot.

in an appropriate time scale described by the "activity," that is, the number of trades in the stock. Also, motivated by the fact that price moves have a minimal value given by the tick in the market, pure jump models are investigated. Because the stock returns are lognormal in the appropriate time scale, it makes sense to consider the Brownian motion as the basic subordinated process. The time change—the new clock—is then chosen in a specific way to keep the model tractable.

The models presented below show the renewed interest in models in which the time is not "absolute." Such models have already been considered by Mandelbrot [83]; however, although his model was suitable for the purpose of statistical studies on the prices processes, it did not fit in the framework of arbitrage theory since it failed to produce semimartingales.

The NIG and GH model The *Normal Inverse Gaussian (NIG) model* was introduced by Barndorff-Nielsen [4] and studied in [98], [101]. Let W and W' be two independent standard Brownian motions and let $\alpha, \delta > 0$, $\mu, \beta \in \mathbb{R}$, with $\alpha^2 \geq \beta^2$. Set

$$T_t = \inf \{u > 0 : W_u + u \sqrt{\alpha^2 - \beta^2} = \delta t\}$$

the (scaled) process of first hitting times for a Brownian motion with drift $\sqrt{\alpha^2 - \beta^2}$, and define a Lévy process by the formula

$$X_t = \mu t + W'_{T_t} + \beta T_t \qquad (3.32)$$

The distribution of X_1 is then denoted $NIG(\alpha, \beta, \mu, \delta)$; this is a mean-variance mixture of Gaussian variables, where the mixture is driven by the law of T_1. The Lévy exponent of X is given by

$$\phi_{NIG}(u) = \delta\left(\sqrt{(u - i\beta)^2 + \alpha^2} - \sqrt{\alpha^2 - \beta^2}\right) - iu\mu$$

From this we see that e^{-rt+X_t} is a martingale if $\alpha \geq |1 + \beta|$ and

$$\mu - \delta\left(\sqrt{\alpha^2 - (1 + \beta)^2} - \sqrt{\alpha^2 - \beta^2}\right) = r$$

X_1 has a density given by:

$$f_{NIG}(x) = \frac{\alpha e^{\delta\sqrt{\alpha^2 - \beta^2} - \beta\mu}}{\pi} \frac{K_1\left(\alpha\delta\sqrt{1 + \left(\frac{x-\mu}{\delta}\right)^2}\right)}{\sqrt{1 + \left(\frac{x-\mu}{\delta}\right)^2}} e^{\beta x}$$

where K_1 is the modified Bessel function of the second kind (see [78]). Here μ is a location parameter, whereas δ is a scale parameter. As shown in [4], the mean and variance of the NIG distribution depend on α and β only through the ratio β/α; these have on the other hand an effect on the skewness and kurtosis. Furthermore, it is shown in [4] that the $NIG(\alpha, \beta, \mu, \delta)$ process has no diffusion component, the Lévy measure is

$$\nu_{NIG}(dx) = \frac{\alpha\delta}{\pi|x|}K_1(\alpha|x|)e^{\beta x}dx$$

and the drift coefficient

$$a_{NIG} = \mu + \frac{2\alpha\delta}{\pi}\int_0^1 \sinh(\beta x)K_1(\alpha x)dx$$

A good feature of the NIG model is that the distribution of X_t is known for every time t: X_t has distribution $NIG(\alpha, \beta, \mu t, \delta t)$. Hence this model could be used to price European options without the need to invert the characteristic exponent via Equation (3.19); it could also be considered for applications using Monte Carlo techniques. To conclude, note that if $\beta = 0$, and $\alpha \to +\infty$ with $\delta = \sigma^2\alpha$, we recover the Gaussian distribution with mean μ and variance σ^2.

The NIG model can be generalized by considering Lévy processes with the characteristic exponent of the form

$$\phi(u) = iu\left(\mu + \frac{\beta\delta^2 K_{\lambda+1}(\delta\sqrt{\alpha^2 - \beta^2})}{K_\lambda(\delta\sqrt{\alpha^2 - \beta^2})}\right) + \int (e^{iux} - 1 - iux)g(x)dx$$

where K_λ is the modified Bessel function of the second kind of index ν and the Lévy density g is given by

$$g(x) = \frac{e^{\beta x}}{|x|}\left(\int_0^\infty \frac{e^{-2\sqrt{2y+\alpha^2}|x|}}{\pi^2 y\left(J_{|\lambda|}^2(\delta\sqrt{(2y)}) + Y_{|\lambda|}^2(\delta\sqrt{2y})\right)}dy + \lambda e^{-\alpha|x|}1_{\lambda\geq 0}\right)$$

Such models, called *generalized hyperbolic models* (GH), have been introduced by Barndorff-Nielsen, who has shown that the Lévy process above can be represented as a subordinated Brownian motion. Their financial applications have been considered in [39], [40], [98], [101]. The law of X_1 is still known explicitly, but, contrary to the NIG model, the law of X_t is not known for $t \neq 1$; however, approximations have been developed in [101] that allow us to consider this model for applications.

The Variance Gamma and CGMY models The *Variance Gamma (VG) model*, introduced by [81] and [82], is another example where the logarithm of the asset price is a time-changed Brownian motion. Consider a Brownian motion W and an independent Gamma process γ with variance parameter $\nu > 0$. The Variance Gamma process is the Lévy process

$$X_t = \theta\gamma_t + \sigma W_{\gamma_t}$$

with $\theta \in \mathbb{R}$ and $\sigma > 0$. Note that for every $t > 0$, we have $\text{Var}(X_t) = \gamma_t$ conditionally on the stochastic clock γ, which explains the name. Theorem 3.5 applies and we deduce that X has no Gaussian component, no drift, and Lévy measure

$$\nu^{VG}(dx) = \frac{1}{\nu|x|}\exp\left(\frac{\theta}{\sigma^2}x - \sqrt{\frac{2}{\nu} + \frac{\theta^2}{\sigma^2}}|x|\right)dx$$

The Lévy measure is symmetric with respect to the origin if $\theta = 0$; otherwise θ introduces skewness in the distribution. On the other hand, the characteristic function of X_t is given by

$$\mathbb{E}[e^{iuX_t}] = \left(\frac{1}{1 - i\theta\nu u + \frac{\sigma^2\nu}{2}u^2}\right)^{\frac{t}{\nu}}$$

This formula shows that e^{-rt+X_t} is a martingale if

$$r + \frac{1}{\nu}\log\left(1 - \theta\nu - \sigma^2\nu/2\right) = 0$$

In this framework, European options can be valued by the method described above by Fourier inversion, and the fast Fourier transform algorithm (see Section 3.5).

The CGMY (Carr-Geman-Madan-Yor) model generalizes the Variance Gamma model and is defined and studied in [25], [50], [51]; its Lévy measure has a density given by

$$
k(x) = \begin{cases} \dfrac{C}{x^{Y+1}} e^{-Mx} & x > 0 \\ \dfrac{C}{|x|^{Y+1}} e^{Gx} & x < 0 \end{cases}
$$

with $C > 0$, $M \geq 0$, $G \geq 0$ and $Y < 2$, $Y \notin Z$; the CGMY model mixes stable subordinators with time-changed Brownian motion. The characteristic function of X_1 is

$$
\mathbb{E}[e^{iuX_1}] = e^{-C\Gamma(-Y)((M-iu)^Y - M^Y + (G+iu)^Y - G^Y)}
$$

so that the Lévy exponent is

$$
\phi(u) = C\Gamma(-Y)((M - iu)^Y - M^Y + (G + iu)^Y - G^Y) \qquad (3.33)
$$

C is the overall level of activity (hence variability) of the process; G and M control the importance of large negative and positive moves; at last, Y controls finer properties of the process: As shown in [25], if $Y < 0$, the process has finite activity (that is, finitely many jumps in any closed time interval). If $0 < Y < 1$, the process has infinite activity, but still has finite variation. If $1 < Y < 2$, it has infinite activity and variation. It is also shown in [51] that if $Y > -1$, the CGMY model can be interpreted in terms of Brownian motion.

Note that on setting $Y = 0$ and $M = G$, the CGMY process is nothing but the Variance Gamma process, whereas if $Y = -1$, we get the difference of two independent compound Poisson processes with exponentially distributed jumps.

Equation (3.33) shows that e^{-rt+X_t} is a martingale if

$$
r + C\Gamma(-Y)[(M - 1)^Y - M^Y + (G + 1)^Y - G^Y] = 0
$$

A Brownian component can easily be added to the CGMY process; ϕ is simply changed to

$$
\phi_e(u) = C\Gamma(-Y)((M - iu)^Y - M^Y + (G + iu)^Y - G^Y) + \frac{\sigma^2 u^2}{2}
$$

Such a process is called extended CGMY (CGMYe) in [25]. Suppose the stock price process is a CGMYe process under the (risk-neutral) pricing measure. Statistical tests are reported in [25], that show that the diffusion component is sometimes significant.

The last two families of models we have just examined build on the empirical observation made in [1] that the returns of asset have a Gaussian distribution when measured in an appropriate time scale; both these families then consistently define the log-price process as a time-changed Brownian motion. However, the time-change is chosen *a priori*, as the hitting times of Brownian motion for the NIG model or as a Gamma process for the Variance Gamma process. Also of interest is the question of discovering the time scale from market observations: This has been partly addressed in [50]. We present in Table 3.3 a summary of the properties of the different models studied.

The last sections of this chapter are devoted to practical, day-to-day applications of the theory and models described above. We first make more

TABLE 3.3   Characteristics of different models involving Lévy processes

Model	Parameters	Martingale Constraint	Squared Volatility
JD	$\sigma > 0$ $\lambda > 0$ $\zeta > -1$	$\mu = r - \frac{\sigma^2}{2} - \lambda\zeta$	$\sigma^2 + \lambda(\ln(1 + \zeta))^2$
Merton	$\sigma > 0$ $\lambda > 0$ $\gamma \in \mathbb{R}$ $\delta > 0$	$\mu = r - \sigma^2/2$ $-\lambda(e^{\gamma + \delta^2/2} - 1)$	$\sigma^2 + \lambda(\gamma^2 + \delta^2)$
NIG	$\alpha \geq 0$ $\beta \in \mathbb{R}$ $\mu \in \mathbb{R}$ $\delta > 0$	$\mu - \delta\left(\sqrt{\alpha^2 - (1 + \beta)^2}\right.$ $\left. - \sqrt{\alpha^2 - \beta^2}\right) = r$	$\frac{\delta\alpha^2}{(\alpha^2 - \beta^2)^{3/2}}$
VG	$\theta \in \mathbb{R}$ $\sigma > 0$ $\nu > 0$	$\frac{1}{\nu} \ln \frac{1}{1 - \theta\nu - \frac{\sigma^2\nu}{2}} = r$	$\sigma^2 + \nu\theta^2$
CGMY	$C > 0$ $G \geq 0$ $M \geq 0$ $Y < 2, Y \notin \mathbb{Z}$	$C\Gamma(-Y)[(M - 1)^Y - M^Y$ $+(G + 1)^Y - G^Y]$ $-\sigma^2/2 = r$	$C\Gamma(2 - Y)(M^{Y-2} + G^{Y-2})$

precise the statement at the beginning of this section that only the structure of the process under the pricing measure is important, and we show how this pricing measure is selected based on the information available in the market. Then we briefly discuss numerical methods for Lévy processes, that may be required in case no analytical formula is known. We conclude by the study of a concrete example that embeds a Lévy process but also a stochastic volatility feature. This model is used for the valuation of exotic products that depend heavily on volatility structure.

3.4 MODEL CALIBRATION AND SMILE REPLICATION

One of the reasons that models with jumps, such as those presented in the previous section, are more and more investigated is the failure of continuous paths models to reproduce the implied volatility skew in a fully satisfactory way, especially in the equities and index markets on a short-term scale. In the previous section, we had assumed that we modeled "directly under a risk-neutral probability measure," chosen as a pricing measure. How are the parameters chosen in practice? The amount of data available on the market allows one, as noticed earlier, to regard some options as basic instruments; therefore, from a modeling point of view, these options give us input data rather than being an output of computations. This is especially true of options traded on listed markets.

However, the no-arbitrage hypothesis should still hold globally; hence all options prices whether or not observed in the market must be obtained as the expectation of their discounted payoff for the model under consideration. Just like the "martingale restriction" described at the beginning of this section, this imposes restrictions on the (risk-neutral) parameters, and gives us a way to derive the parameters to be used for the purpose of pricing exotic options consistently with market observations.

Let us now describe this more precisely. In practice, the available data consist of the quotes of European call and put options. At a given time, denote by $(p_{mkt}(K_i, T_i), i = 1, \ldots, N)$ a set of prices of European call and put options with strikes K_i and maturities T_i, observed on the market. On the other hand, the model under consideration takes a set of parameters θ as an input, and issues as an output a set of prices $(p_{mod}(\theta; K_i, T_i), i = 1, \ldots, N)$ for the options above. So our goal is to equalize the observations $p_{mkt}(K_i, T_i)$ and the model output $p_{mod}(K_i, T_i)$. This is not possible in practice because

- There are usually more observations than parameters entering the model, hence more constraints than degrees of freedom.
- The observations are not perfect, that is, are subject to a kind of "error measurement"; the quotes observed are not pure risk-neutral

prices since they take into account market imperfections such as transaction costs, operational margin, etc. Moreover, one does not really observe one quote, but rather the bid and ask quotes.

Since it is not possible to achieve the ideal goal of equalizing market observations and model output, we content ourselves with a more modest one: to minimize the gap between those. Such minimization will provide us with a set of parameters which is in some sense the most sensible set to use, given the situation observed in the market. To actually obtain these optimal parameters, we solve numerically the optimization problem:

$$\min_{\theta} \sum_{i=1}^{N} w_i f\left(p_{mod}(\theta; K_i, T_i), p_{mkt}(K_i, T_i)\right)$$

where $f(x, y)$ is a distance between x and y (for instance $f(x, y) = (x - y)^2$) and w_i are suitable weights.

Figures 3.2 and 3.3 show typical implied volatility surfaces obtained from the Merton and CGMY models. The implied volatilities obtained from

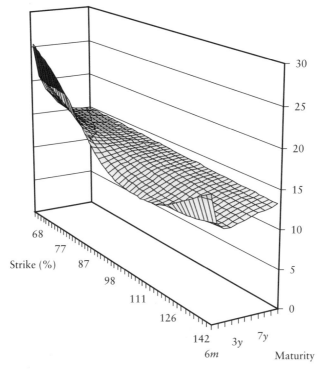

FIGURE 3.2   Implied volatilities from the Merton model. Parameters used were $\sigma = 10$ percent, $\lambda = 0.1$, $\gamma = -20$ percent, $\delta = 20$ percent.

the Merton model exhibit a strong skew for very short maturities, quite similar to the observations in the market for certain indices (see Figure 3.4). However, the skew decays extremely rapidly as maturity increases, which makes it impossible to use this model to calibrate the entire volatility surface.

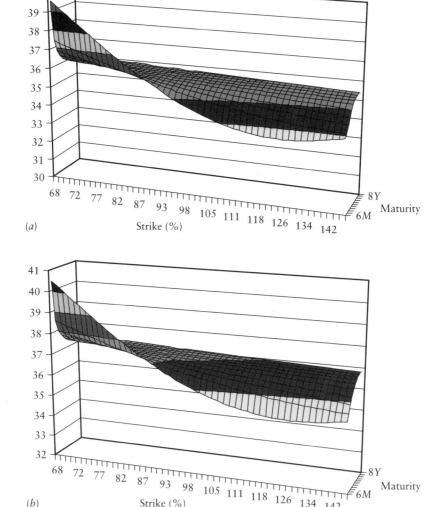

FIGURE 3.3 Implied volatility for the CGMY model, with (b, d) and without (a, c) diffusion component. Parameters used: a, b: $C = 0.5$, $G = 4.5$, $M = 9$, $Y = 0.9$; c, d: $C = 1$, $G = 4.5$, $M = 4.5$, $Y = -0.4$. A diffusion component, when present is taken equal to 10 percent.

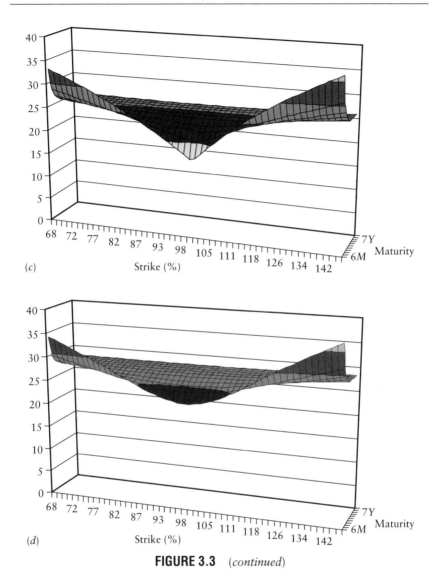

FIGURE 3.3 (*continued*)

The philosophy of the CGMY model is to model the log-returns in very short time. In terms of replicating the observed volatility surface, this model performs quite well for options with short maturities, but the "smile effect" (precisely the fact that options of different strikes are priced at different volatilities) disappears quite fast as the maturity increases (Figure 3.3). This behavior of the implied volatility surface is similar to that of many models with jumps. The addition of a constant diffusion component merely

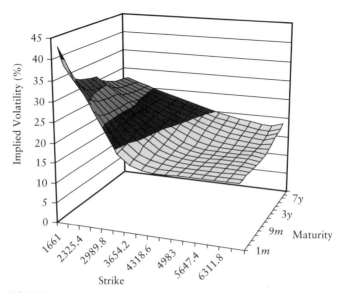

FIGURE 3.4   ETR implied volatility on 01.31.2001. Spot = 3322.

yields an increase in the global level of volatility; because it is constant, it introduces no time structure and no strike structure.

Figure 3.4 shows the implied volatility surface for the ETR2 index on January 31, 2001. Following are the results of the calibration procedure just described, as applied to the models studied in the previous section. It can be seen that the smile can be very well approximated for single maturity $(T_i = T \, \forall i)$ and that the approximation is best for very short maturities. It was in particular for these maturities that continuous paths models failed to stick to the smile.

For a very short maturity of one month, the Merton and CGMY models both outperform the Heston model, which is a continuous one, as shown in Figure 3.5.

However, the calibration gives very poor results as soon as different matutities come into play. This reflects the fact that the jump models we have considered, just like the standard Black-Scholes model, bring no term structure to asset prices. This is clear from the observation that the volatility parameter attached to our jump model is constant in time. On the contrary, continuous paths models such as diffusions, are known to produce such a term structure that can be fitted to the implied volatility surface term structure.

To illustrate this phenomenon, Figure 3.6 shows the results of the attempt to calibrate the Merton model to option data for several distinct

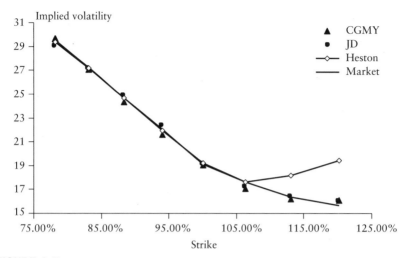

FIGURE 3.5 Calibration results for one-month maturity. All models were calibrated to the ETR2 index.

maturities: The model implied volatilities are unable to stick to the observed smiles. A trivial remedy would be to consider deterministic time-dependent parameters: computations could still be easily made by using the Markov property. But this would increase the number of parameters in the model, and it would not be very satisfactory to have to maintain one set of parameters per maturity.

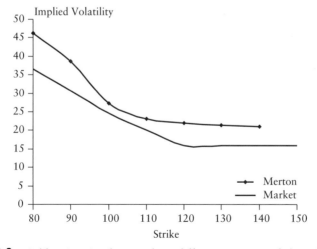

FIGURE 3.6 Calibration simultaneously to different maturities fails in the Merton model.

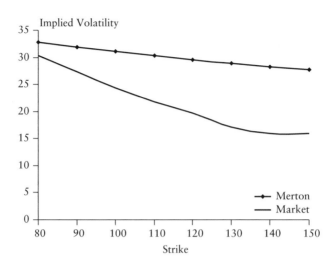

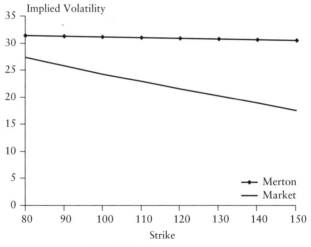

FIGURE 3.6   (*continued*)

It was already noticed in [4], [39], and [40], that pure jump models perform best when used to fit intraday data, that is, for instance, hour-by-hour returns. More and more such data are available from institutions specializing in financial information systems, and the databases are also more reliable. Hence these models become applicable to some activities such as intraday trading, which is a non-negligible part of the activity of a financial institution. On the other hand, continuous models such as diffusion processes were built on a view of a wider time scale, and perform well at this level. One reason is (as in the central limit theorem) that if many short-time increments are aggregated, the result tends to be so close to the one implied by a continuous process that it is not possible to make a distinction.

These observations justify the study in Section 3.6 of a model that incorporates both a diffusion and a jump component, thereby mixing their effects on the resulting implied volatility.

3.5   NUMERICAL METHODS FOR LÉVY PROCESSES

When options need to be priced that are not within the class of European options described in the Section 3.3 (this is most often the case), numerical methods have to be used. These methods are classical:

- Fast Fourier transform
- Monte Carlo simulation
- Numerical solving of integro differential equations

The last method will be described extensively in Chapter 4, which covers partial differential equations.

Fast Fourier Transform

The method described above and illustrated in Example 3.9 to evaluate European options requires the inversion of the Fourier transform by the integral (3.19). In general, there is no closed form expression for this integral, and the computation has to be done numerically.

The fast Fourier transform (FFT) is a well-known algorithm that reduces the computational cost of calculating a characteristic function. Carr and Madan [26] discuss a way to apply the FFT so that the output is directly the option prices, instead of calculating the probabilities in (3.19). Their method consists of multiplying the call price by a deterministic factor so that it becomes square integrable; the FFT can then be applied directly and yields the price after rescaling. Their method allows us, using a multidimensional version of the FFT algorithm, to obtain in one run a set of option prices for different strikes and maturities. In order for this method to be applicable, the characteristic exponent has to be known precisely, or numerical errors become significant. This is the only restriction; the method can be used for all the models described above, as well as for the one discussed in the last section.

Monte Carlo Simulation

The simulation of the continuous part of a Lévy process, which consists of a drift term and a Brownian motion, is well known (see [71]). Hence we will concentrate on the jump part. Due to the path structure of the jumps of some Lévy processes, it may not be possible to simulate them exactly; we will have to do an approximation.

Let $\epsilon > 0$, and the approximation consists in discarding the jumps of size less than ϵ, so that the jump part of the "truncated" Lévy process is a compound Poisson process. Precisely, suppose that we want to simulate the Lévy process X, whose characteristic exponent has the Lévy-Khintchine representation (3.2). Recall the construction we have made in the proof of Theorem 3.2. There, $X^{(1)}$ was a Brownian motion with drift, $X^{(2)}$ was a compound Poisson process that renders the "big" jumps of X, and $X^{(\epsilon,3)}$ is a martingale obtained by compensating the compound Poisson process $Z^{(\epsilon,3)}$. We have that $X^{(1)} + X^{(2)} + X^{(\epsilon,3)} \to X$ in L^2 as $\epsilon \to 0$. Our approximation is to simulate $X^{(1)} + X^{(2)} + X^{(\epsilon,3)}$ instead of X.

Simulation of a terminal variable   In order to price European options, we need only know the final value of the asset price, not the whole path. Let then T be the (fixed) terminal time, and suppose we want to simulate $S_T = S_0 e^{X_T}$. It is well known how to simulate a standard Gaussian variable $U^{(1)}$; a simulation of $X^{(1)}$ is then $X^{(1)} = -aT + R\sqrt{T}U^{(1)}$. Now let us turn to $X^{(2)}$, a compound Poisson process of intensity λ and distribution $\nu(dx)1_{|x|>1}$. Simulate first a Poisson variable $N^{(2)}$ with parameter λT (the number of jumps up to time T) and simulate then $N^{(2)}$ random variables $Y_1, \ldots, Y_{N^{(2)}}$ with distribution $\nu(dx)1_{|x|>1}$. A simulation of $X^{(2)}$ is then $X^{(2)} = Y_1 + \cdots + Y_{N^{(2)}}$. $Z^{(\epsilon,3)}$ is simulated in exactly the same way, and $X^{(\epsilon,3)}$ is then obtained by setting $X^{(\epsilon,3)} = Z^{(\epsilon,3)} - T\mathbb{E}[Z_1^{(\epsilon,3)}]$.

In the procedure above, the more we know analytically, the more time we can save in calculations.

Simulation of a path   When concerned with the pricing of path-dependent options, such as barrier options or Asian options, the sole knowledge of the terminal value of the underlying price is not enough, and we need to simulate the whole path. Because the increments of a Lévy process are independent, this is in principle a recursive application of the procedure just described to simulate terminal variables.

Denote again the time horizon by T and suppose that we wish to sample the path at equally spaced time points $\delta, 2\delta, \ldots, n\delta = T$. Because X is a Markov process, simulating $X_{k\delta}$ when $X_{(k-1)\delta}$ has already been simulated is the same as simulating (a new) X_δ and adding the result to $X_{(k-1)\delta}$. So what we need to do to simulate one path is to simulate n independent copies of X_δ; this can be done as just discussed. However when the time-step δ is small enough, we can make a further approximation. Indeed, it is well known that for $c > 0$ small enough, the distribution of a Poisson variable N with parameter c can be written as

$$\mathbb{P}(N = 0) \simeq 1 - c$$

$$\mathbb{P}(N = 1) \simeq c$$

$$\mathbb{P}(N > 1) = o(c)$$

Hence as a first-order approximation of the Poisson distribution we can use the Bernouilli distribution with parameter c. When δ is small enough, an alternative to simulate the jump part of $X^{(2)}$ is the following: Sample a random number U in $[0, 1]$; if $U \leq \lambda\delta$, then set $X^{(2)} = 0$, otherwise simulate a random variable Y with distribution $\nu(dx)1_{|x|>1}$ and set $X^{(2)} = Y$.

The same can be done for $Z^{(\epsilon,3)}$; it is then most desirable to know $\mathbb{E}[Z_1^{(\epsilon,3)}]$ explicitly, since we wish to set as before $X = X^{(1)} + X^{(2)} + X^{(\epsilon,3)}$, where $X^{(\epsilon,3)} = Z^{(\epsilon,3)} - \delta\mathbb{E}[Z_1^{(\epsilon,3)}]$.

More sophisticated simulation and other approximation methods are currently being developed; see for instance [3] or [106]. Note that, convergence is much slower than it is for the simulation of diffusion processes, due to the number of variates to simulate according to different distributions.

Finite Difference Methods

Since Lévy processes are homogeneous Markov processes, they can be associated with an infinitesimal generator. However, because the paths are not continuous, this operator is not a differential operator as is the case for diffusion processes. Specifically, the infinitesimal generator of a d-dimensional Lévy process X with Lévy-Khintchine representation (3.2) is given by (see [7])

$$\mathcal{A}f(x) = -\langle a, f'(x) \rangle + \frac{1}{2} \sum_{1 \leq i,j \leq d} Q_{ij} f_{ij}''(x)$$

$$+ \int (f(x+y) - f(x) - 1_{|y| \leq 1}\langle y, f'(x) \rangle)\nu(dy) \quad (3.34)$$

Consider a European call option: Its payoff is $C = (S_T - K)^+ = S_0(e^{X_T} - e^k)^+$. In the following we adopt the normalization $S_0 = 1$. Assume $r = 0$; the price of this option at time t is given by $C_t = \mathbb{E}[(e^{X_T} - e^k)^+|\mathcal{F}_t]$; since

X is a Markov process, this is a function of X_t: $C_t = C(X_t)$. Assume this function is smooth enough so that we can apply Itō's formula:

$$
\begin{aligned}
dC(X_t) &= C'(X_{t-})dX_t + \tfrac{1}{2}C''(X_t)d\langle X^c, X^c\rangle_t + \Delta C(X_t) - C'(X_{t-})\Delta X_t \\
&= C'(X_{t-})(adt + \sigma dB_t + \Delta X_t) + \tfrac{1}{2}C''(X_t)\sigma^2 dt \\
&\quad + C(X_{t-} + \Delta X_t) - C(X_{t-}) - C'(X_{t-})\Delta X_t \\
&= \text{martingale} + \left(aC'(X_{t-}) + \frac{\sigma^2}{2}C''(X_{t-})\right)dt \\
&\quad + \mathbb{E}\left[C(X_{t-} + \Delta X_t) - C(X_{t-}) - C'(X_{t-})\Delta X_t 1_{|\Delta X_t| \le 1}\big|\mathcal{F}_{t-}\right]dt \\
&= \text{martingale} + \mathcal{A}C(X_t)dt
\end{aligned}
$$

Because we neglected interest rates, the function $C(X_t)$ should be a martingale by the no-arbitrage assumption and hence the following necessary condition must be fulfilled

$$
\mathcal{A}C \equiv 0
$$

This integro-differential equation is the counterpart of the heat equation that has to be satisfied by the derivatives prices process in the Black-Scholes model. It is the same for all options: The payoff only changes the boundary conditions. This equation cannot be solved in general; however, it is possible to use finite difference methods to get a numerical solution.

3.6   A MODEL INVOLVING LÉVY PROCESSES

As a last application of the theory described above, we study a model that involves Lévy processes but also contains another component: stochastic volatility. This is also in a spirit to remedy the most obvious drawback of pure Lévy processes models: that the implied volatility smile exists only for very short maturities, and vanishes very quickly as the maturity increases.

In fact, we study here a model that combines the stochastic volatility feature from the Heston model [61] and jumps from the Merton model [86]. We thereby hope to be able to replicate the whole volatility surface.

We first recall the main facts about the stochastic volatility model we use (see [61]).

The two-dimensional SDE

$$
dv_t = \kappa(\theta - v_t)dt + \sigma\sqrt{v_t}dW_t^v \tag{3.35a}
$$

$$
dS_t = S_t\left[\left(r - \frac{v_t}{2}\right)dt + \sqrt{v_t}dW_t^S\right] \tag{3.35b}
$$

admits a unique strong solution, where W^v and W^S are two Brownian motions with constant correlation ρ. The process $\sqrt{v}$ plays the role of the volatility parameter in a Black-Scholes world.

Heston [61] has shown that the characteristic function of $s_t = \ln(S_t)$ can be computed as

$$\Theta^H(u) = \mathbb{E}\left[e^{ius_t}\right] = e^{C^H(t,u)+D^H(t,u)v_0+ius_0} \tag{3.36}$$

where C^H and D^H are deterministic functions of t and u. Moreover, arguing as in Example 3.9, a probability related to the *numéraire S* can be defined, under which the characteristic function of s_t has the same form as under $\hat{\mathbb{P}}$:

$$\Theta^{H,S}(u) = \mathbb{E}^S\left[e^{ius_t}\right] = e^{C^{H,S}(t,u)+D^{H,S}(t,u)v_0+ius_0} \tag{3.37}$$

Hence the method presented in Example 3.9 can be used to price European options, by inverting the characteristic function.

The model we study is a particular case of a general model described in [35]. However, contrary to this description, we do not take the path of Cox processes, but rather concentrate on a Poisson process style approach.

Let then W_S, W_v be Brownian motions with constant correlation ρ and let N_S, N_v be independent Poisson processes with respective intensities λ_S and λ_v, also independent of (W_S, W_v). Then, define P_S as in Equation (3.29):

$$P_S(t) = \sum_{i=1}^{N_S(t)} (e^{\gamma_S+\delta_S\varepsilon_i} - 1)$$

where $(\varepsilon_i, i \geq 0)$ is a sequence of independent, standard Gaussian random variables, also independent of W_S, W_v, N_S and N_v. Similarly, set

$$P_v(t) = \sum_{i=1}^{N_S(t)} \eta_i + \sum_{j=1}^{N_v(t)} \beta_j$$

where $(\beta_j, j \geq 0)$ is a sequence of independent, identically distributed random variables, also independent of W_S, W_v, N_S, N_v, and $(\varepsilon_i, i \geq 0)$. Moreover, we assume that β_1 satisfies

$$\mathbb{P}[\beta_1 \geq 0] = 1$$

The two-dimensional SDE

$$\frac{dS_t}{S_{t-}} = \mu dt + \sqrt{v_t}dW_S(t) + dP_S(t) \tag{3.38a}$$

$$dv_t = \kappa(\theta - v_t)dt + \sigma \sqrt{v_t}dW_v(t) + dP_v(t) \tag{3.38b}$$

admits a unique strong solution, and is a Markov process in its own filtration. As pointed out earlier, we model directly under a martingale measure. μ is accordingly chosen to be equal to

$$\mu = r - d - \lambda(e^{\gamma_S + \delta_S^2/2} - 1)$$

where r is the interest rate and d the dividend yield (supposed to be constant). The paths of this model can be described as follows. Let τ_i be the sequence of jump times of either N_S or N_v. From $t = 0$ to $t = \tau_1-$, the process (S, v) behaves as in the Heston model. If τ_1 is a jump time of N_S, both the paths of S and v are shifted by a random amount; if τ_1 is a jump time of N_v, only the path of v is shifted. From time τ_1 on, the process resumes a Heston dynamics with new initial values, until the next time τ_2 a jump occurs, and so on. Figure 3.7 shows a typical path of the model under consideration. It is possible to show that the characteristic function

$$\Theta(u) := \mathbb{E}[e^{ius_t}]$$

is equal to

$$\Theta(u) = \Theta^H(u)\Theta^{(2)}(u)\Theta^{(3)}(u) \tag{3.39}$$

where Θ^H is the characteristic function corresponding to the Heston model (no jumps), $\Theta^{(2)}$ and $\Theta^{(3)}$ take into account the jumps from N_S and N_v. Explicit expressions for these functions are quite intricate:

$$\Theta^{(2)}(u) = \exp\left[\lambda_S t\left(e^{iu\gamma_S - u^2\delta^2/2}\left(\frac{1}{t}\int_0^t \mathcal{L}_\eta(D^H(s, u))ds - 1\right)\right)\right] \tag{3.40}$$

$$\Theta^{(3)}(u) = \exp\left[\lambda_v t\left(\frac{1}{t}\int_0^t \mathcal{L}_\beta(D^H(s, u))ds - 1\right)\right]$$

Details on the computation of Θ can be found in [72]; $\mathcal{L}$ denotes the Laplace transform

$$\mathcal{L}_\omega(z) = \mathbb{E}[e^{z\omega}], \qquad z \in \mathbb{C}, \qquad \omega = \beta \text{ or } \eta$$

As highlighted in Example 3.9, a change of *numéraire* can be used in order to achieve the computation of European option prices; under the associated probability, the characteristic functions retain the same form (3.39) (see [72]). The price of European options can then be obtained by the method described earlier.

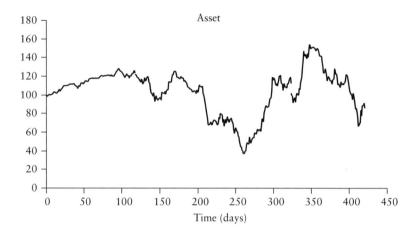

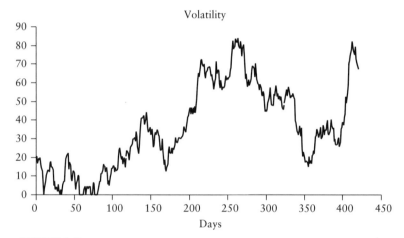

FIGURE 3.7   Path of the model described by Equations (3.38a), (3.38b).

As mentioned in [35], this model can be extended to a state-dependent intensity $\lambda(S, v)$. Similar models were studied in [5] and [110].

Figure 3.8 displays the absolute price errors in bps after calibration of the model we study to the whole volatility surface. As can be seen, apart from extreme strike values for very short maturities (values that are not really meaningful), the model is able to replicate overall the volatility surface. As a result of the calibration procedure, the jump in volatility is not significant. In fact, empirical studies show that a jump in the volatility (with this structure) has no real effect on the structure of the implied volatility surface; it simply shifts the overall level of volatility.

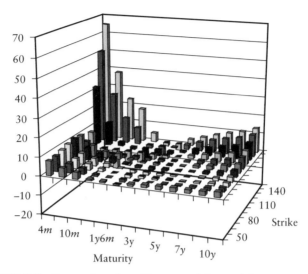

FIGURE 3.8   Errors (bps) by calibration of the model (3.38a, 3.38b).

The drawback is that this result was obtained by using a model that includes nine parameters, which is not really satisfactory because numerical optimization with nine degrees of freedom is very time consuming.

CHAPTER 4

Finite-Difference Methods for Multifactor Models

A common efficient approach to pricing complex financial derivatives is to numerically solve the appropriate parabolic differential equation (PDE) given by the Feynman-Kac theorem. The dimension of the PDE equals the number of independent stochastic factors involved. Multifactor models occur in different situations. A number of options have more than one underlying, such as options on baskets or outperformance options. In those cases, each underlying corresponds to one stochastic source each of which increases the dimensionality of the PDE. The other situation is that market parameters considered deterministic in the Black-Scholes theory are modeled as stochastic processes. Examples are the Vasicek model ([117]) for a stochastic interest short rate, and the Heston model ([61]) for a stochastic instantaneous volatility.

4.1 PRICING MODELS AND PDEs

In this section we give examples of pricing models and their related partial differential equations. We always first state the system of stochastic differential equations, and then give the corresponding partial differential equation used for option pricing in appropriate coordinates. The choice of coordinates is, however, arbitrary and here chosen in such a way as to make the coefficients of the equations look as simple as possible. For specific problems, there might be more appropriate choices of coordinates.

The relation between the stochastic processes and the partial differential equation is established by the *Feynman-Kac theorem*. Given a stochastic process $\mathbf{X}_t = (X_t^1, \ldots, X_t^d)$ satisfying the system of stochastic differential equations

$$dX_t^i = \mu_i(t, \mathbf{X}_t)\, dt + \sigma_i(t, \mathbf{X}_t)\, dW_t^i, \qquad i = 1, \ldots, d$$

and given a function $h(\mathbf{x})$, $\mathbf{x} = (x_1, \ldots, x_d)$, the theorem states that the function of expectation values

$$u(t, \mathbf{x}) = \mathbb{E}\left[h(\mathbf{X}_T) \,|\, \mathbf{X}_t = \mathbf{x} \right]$$

satisfies the PDE

$$u_t + \sum_{i=1}^{d} \mu_i u_{x_i} + \frac{1}{2} \sum_{i,j=1}^{d} \rho_{ij} \sigma_i \sigma_j u_{x_i, x_j} = 0$$

subject to the terminal condition

$$u(T, \mathbf{x}) = h(\mathbf{x})$$

where ρ_{ij} are the correlations

$$dW^i \, dW^j = \rho_{ij} \, dt$$

Multiasset Model

For options with multiple underlyings, such as outperformance or basket options, one needs a model for the joint dynamics of the asset prices. The general *multiasset model* considered here has the form

$$\frac{dS_t^i}{S_t^i} = (r - p_i) \, dt + \sigma_1(S_t^i, t) \, dW_t^i, \qquad i = 1, \ldots, d \qquad (4.1)$$

where $W^1, \ldots, W^d$ are Brownian motions correlated by $dW^i \, dW^j = \rho_{ij} \, dt$. After a change of variables

$$x_i = \log(S^i / S_0^i)$$

the corresponding PDE for the price $u(t, \mathbf{x})$ is

$$u_t + \frac{1}{2} \sum_{i=1}^{d} \sigma_i^2 u_{x_i x_i} + \sum_{i<j=1}^{d} \rho_{ij} \sigma_i \sigma_j u_{x_i x_j} + \sum_{i=1}^{d} \left(r - p_i - \frac{1}{2} \sigma_i^2 \right) u_{x_i} - ru = 0$$

Stock-Spread Model

A number of options have a payoff function depending on the quotient of two stock prices. An example is the relative outperformance option where the payoff is

$$P(S^1, S^2) = \max\left(0, \frac{S_T^1}{S_T^2} - K\right)$$

Denoting the quotient by $Z_t = S_t^1/S_t^2$ and applying Itō's formula, the two-dimensional version of system (4.1) can be shown to be equivalent to

$$\frac{dS_t^1}{S_t^1} = (r - p_1)\,dt + \sigma_1(S_t^1, t)\,dW_t^1$$

$$\frac{dZ_t}{Z_t} = (-p_1 + p_2 + \sigma_2^2 - \rho\sigma_1\sigma_2)\,dt + \tilde{\sigma}\,d\tilde{W}_t$$

where $\tilde{\sigma}$ is defined by

$$\tilde{\sigma}(S_t^1, Z_t, t)^2 = \sigma_1^2(S^1, t)^2 + \sigma_2(S^1/Z, t)^2 - 2\rho\sigma_1(S^1, t)\sigma_2(S^1/Z, t)$$

and the correlation between W_t^1 and $\tilde{W}_t$ is

$$\tilde{\rho} = \frac{\sigma_1 - \rho\sigma_2}{\tilde{\sigma}}$$

The corresponding pricing PDE after the change of coordinates

$$x = \log(S^1/S_0^1), \qquad y = \log(Z/Z_0)$$

is

$$u_t + \tfrac{1}{2}\sigma_1^2 u_{xx} + \tilde{\rho}\sigma_1\sigma_2 u_{xy} + \tfrac{1}{2}\sigma_2^2 u_{yy}$$

$$+ (r - p_1 - \tfrac{1}{2}\sigma_1^2)u_x + (-p_1 + p_2 + \sigma_2^2 - \rho\sigma_1\sigma_2 - \tfrac{1}{2}\tilde{\sigma}^2)u_y + ru = 0$$

with $\tilde{\sigma}$ and $\tilde{\rho}$ being defined above.

If σ_1 and σ_2 are constant, then the spread process Z_t is log-normal and any contingent claim depending only on Z can be priced in a one-factor model. The two-factor model is needed if a local volatility model is to be used.

The Vasicek Model

The *Vasicek model* is a one-factor model for the instantaneous interest rate process

$$dr_t = \left(\theta(t) - \lambda(t)r_t\right) dt + \sigma_r(t) \, dW^r$$

The two-dimensional pricing equation for an option on the asset S, that accounts for the stochastic interest rates is

$$u_t + \tfrac{1}{2}\sigma^2 u_{xx} + \rho\sigma_r\sigma u_{xr} + \tfrac{1}{2}\sigma_r^2 u_{rr}$$

$$+(r - p - \tfrac{1}{2}\sigma^2)u_x + (\theta - \lambda r)u_r + ru = 0 \qquad (4.2)$$

Here, ρ is the correlation between W_t^r and W_t and $x = \log(S/S_0)$.

The Heston Model

The Heston model is a two-factor model for the stock price and the instantaneous volatility process given by the system of SDEs

$$dS_t = (r_t - p_t)S_t \, dt + \sqrt{v_t}\, S_t \, dW_t^S \qquad (4.3)$$

$$dv_t = \kappa(\theta^2 - v_t) \, dt + \gamma \sqrt{v_t}\, dW_t^v \qquad (4.4)$$

The correlation between the two Brownian motions W_t^S and W_t^v is denoted by ρ. The two-dimensional pricing equation for an option on the asset S is

$$u_t + (r - p)S\, u_S + \kappa(\theta^2 - v)u_v$$

$$+\tfrac{1}{2}vS^2 \, u_{SS} + \rho v_t \gamma S\, u_{Sv} + \tfrac{1}{2}\gamma^2 v\, u_{vv} = ru \qquad (4.5)$$

4.2 THE PRICING PDE AND ITS DISCRETIZATION

The partial differential equations that arise in option pricing theory, in particular the equations from Section 4.1, become parabolic differential equations if the option price is written as a function of time to maturity $T - t$ instead of t. Since analytical and numerical properties of parabolic differential equations are extensively studied in literature, we adapt to their notation and consider first the abstract problem of numerical solutions of parabolic PDEs. All formulas can directly be applied to option pricing problems if t is interpreted as time to maturity. An initial condition at $t = 0$ of the parabolic equation then corresponds to a terminal condition at maturity T, which is the terminal payoff of the option.

In general, a parabolic partial differential equation (on a rectangular domain) can be written as

$$u_t = L[u], \qquad \text{in} \qquad t \in 0 < t < T, \mathbf{x} \in D \tag{4.6}$$

where $D = (a_1, b_1) \times \ldots \times (a_d, b_d) \subset \mathbb{R}^d$ is a d-dimensional rectangle and u_t denotes the partial derivative $(\partial u(t, \mathbf{x}))/(\partial t)$ with respect to (w. r. t.) the time variable t. The operator L is an elliptic differential operator defined by

$$L[u] \equiv \sum_{i=1}^{d} a_{ii} u_{x_i, x_i} + \sum_{i<j}^{d} a_{ij} u_{x_i, x_j} + \sum_{i=1}^{d} b_i u_{x_i} + cu \tag{4.7}$$

Subscripts u_{x_i} and u_{x_i, x_j} again denote first- and second-order partial derivatives w. r. t. the variables x_i and x_j. All coefficients $a_{ij}(t, \mathbf{x}), b_i(t, \mathbf{x})$, and $c(t, \mathbf{x})$ are defined on $[0, T] \times \overline{D}$. To get a well-defined unique solution to (4.6), it has to be complemented by additional conditions to be fulfilled on the boundary of the rectangle, and at an initial point of time $t = 0$. The full problem including boundary condition and initial condition is

$$u_t = L[u] \qquad \text{in} \qquad D \times (0, T)$$

$$u(0, \mathbf{x}) = u_0(\mathbf{x}) \qquad \text{in} \qquad D \tag{4.8}$$

$$B[u] \equiv \alpha u + \beta u_\nu = \gamma \qquad \text{on} \qquad \partial D$$

Here, u_ν denotes the (outer) normal derivative on the boundary of D. Under mild assumptions on the coefficients of equation (4.7), the above problem has a unique well-defined solution. Many problems in multifactor option pricing can be written in the form (4.6) with appropriate boundary and initial conditions.

Often the pricing problem involves an infinite domain that has to be replaced by a large enough finite rectangle for computational purposes. In those cases it might be appropriate to use a linearity boundary condition (cf. [115]). In two dimensions, this type of boundary condition is of the form $u_{xx} = 0$ on the left and right boundary, and $u_{yy} = 0$ on the upper and lower boundary. The mixed derivative term u_{xy} is also supposed to vanish on the boundary. Applying the differential equation on the (e. g., left and right) boundary then yields

$$u_t = a_{22} u_{yy} + b_1 u_x + b_2 u_y + cu \tag{4.9}$$

The conditions on the upper and lower boundaries are found similarly.

To discretize the PDE (4.6), the domain $[0, T] \times \overline{D}$ is represented by mesh points $(t_k, \mathbf{x}_{j_1,\ldots,j_d})$, where

$$\mathbf{x}_{j_1,\ldots,j_d} \equiv (x_{j_1}^1, \ldots, x_{j_d}^d) = (j_1 \Delta x_1, \ldots, j_d \Delta x_d)$$

and $t_k = k\Delta t$. The bounds for the indices are

$$0 \leq k \leq N_0 - 1$$
$$0 \leq j_\nu \leq N_\nu - 1 \qquad \nu = 1, \ldots, d$$

such that the total number of grid points is

$$N = \prod_{i=0}^{d} N_i$$

The finite difference solution on the mesh points is denoted by $u_{j_1,\ldots,j_d}^k$. The following difference operators (for simplification here only defined in two dimensions) will be used for notational convenience:

$$\delta_x^2 u_{ij} = u_{i+1,j} - 2u_{ij} + u_{i-1,j}$$
$$\delta_{xy} u_{ij} = u_{i+1,j+1} - u_{i+1,j-1} - u_{i-1,j+1} + u_{i-1,j-1}$$
$$D_x u_{ij} = u_{i+1} - u_{i-1}$$

Then the derivatives in the differential operator L can be approximated to second order in Δx_i as

$$(\Delta t)\frac{\partial u}{\partial x_i} \approx \frac{1}{2}\lambda_{x_i} D_{x_i} u$$

$$(\Delta t)\frac{\partial^2 u}{\partial x_i^2} \approx \mu_{x_i} \delta_{x_i}^2 u \qquad\qquad (4.10)$$

$$(\Delta t)\frac{\partial^2 u}{\partial x_i \partial x_j} \approx \frac{1}{4}\mu_{x_i x_j} \delta_{x_i x_j} u$$

where

$$\lambda_{x_i} = \frac{\Delta t}{\Delta x_i} \qquad \mu_{x_i} = \frac{\Delta t}{(\Delta x_i)^2}$$

$$\mu_{x_i x_j} = \frac{\Delta t}{(\Delta x_i)(\Delta x_j)}$$

Let $\mathbf{u}^k$ denote the vector of all mesh values $u^k_{j_1,\ldots,j_d}$ at time step k. The values $\mathbf{u}^0$ are known from the initial condition. The discretization of equation (4.6) approximates the derivatives by the appropriate difference quotients and is evaluated at all inner points of the domain D. The operator $(\Delta t)\, L[u]$ is approximated by the difference operator

$$(\mathbf{Mu}^k)_{j_1,\ldots,j_d}$$
$$= \left(\sum_{i=1}^{d} a_{ii} \mu_{x_i} \delta^2_{x_i} + \sum_{i<j}^{d} a_{ij} \mu_{x_i,x_j} \delta_{x_i,x_j} + \sum_{i=1}^{d} b_i \Lambda_{x_i} D_{x_i} + c \right) u^k_{j_1,\ldots,j_d}$$

The operator $\mathbf{M}$ can be seen as a matrix operating on the vector $\mathbf{u}^k$. For the boundary mesh points, the discretization of the boundary condition has to be employed. A straightforward implementation of the mixed boundary condition in (4.8), or the linearity boundary condition (4.9), is to take a one-sided difference approximation of the normal derivative u_ν. Another possibility is to use central differences, using a virtual mesh point outside the mesh. This point can be eliminated using the discretized differential equation on the boundary point.

4.3   EXPLICIT AND IMPLICIT SCHEMES

For simplification we will only consider inner points at the moment. The *explicit scheme* evaluates the differential operator at time step k and approximates the time derivative by a forward difference $(\mathbf{u}^{k+1} - \mathbf{u}^k)/(\Delta t)$. The discretized equation becomes

$$\mathbf{u}^{k+1} = \mathbf{u}^k + \mathbf{Mu}^k$$

Starting from the initial condition $\mathbf{u}^0$ one iteratively calculates the values for $\mathbf{u}^{k+1}$ using the values $\mathbf{u}^k$. Obviously this is easy to implement. The main problem is that the scheme becomes unstable if Δt is too large compared to $(\Delta x_i)^2$. For computations with high accuracy and thus a larger number of mesh points, the scheme becomes inefficient due to the extremely large number of time steps needed.

A more general approach is the θ-method, that evaluates the spacial difference operator at time steps k and $k + 1$ and interpolates:

$$\mathbf{u}^{k+1} = \mathbf{u}^k + \theta \mathbf{Mu}^{k+1} + (1 - \theta)\mathbf{Mu}^k$$

Collecting terms, this becomes

$$(1 - \theta M)\, u^{k+1} = \big(1 + (1 - \theta)M\big)u^k \qquad (4.11)$$

The special case $\theta = \frac{1}{2}$ is also called the Crank-Nicolson scheme. Its particular property is that the convergence is second order in Δt. Solving (4.11) for u^{k+1} involves solving a large system of linear equations, which has to be done for each time step. Since the coefficient matrix M is a very sparse matrix, that is, most of its entries are zero, it can only efficiently be solved using iterative solvers, such as successive overrelaxation (SOR) conjugate gradient (CG) methods.

4.4 THE ADI SCHEME

The alternating direction implicit (ADI) scheme is an unconditionally stable scheme that involves only solving tridiagonal linear systems. In contrast to implicit schemes, it is therefore not necessary to employ iterative schemes to solve large sparse linear systems. The idea is to use d partial steps per time step, each of which treats the derivatives w. r. t. one of the variables x_i implicit and the remaining derivatives explicit. Using the notation of Section 4.2, we define the following difference operators:

$$M_{x_1} = \mu_{x_1} a_{11} \delta^2_{x_1} + \tfrac{1}{2}\lambda_{x_1} b_i\, D_{x_1} + c\,\Delta t$$

$$M_{x_i} = \mu_{x_i} a_{ii} \delta^2_{x_i} + \tfrac{1}{2}\lambda_{x_i} b_i\, D_{x_i} \qquad \text{for } i > 1$$

$$M_{x_i x_j} = \tfrac{1}{4}\mu_{x_i x_j} a_{ij}\delta_{x_i x_j}$$

The ADI scheme used here is similar to the scheme in [29]:

$$(1 - \theta M_{x_1})u^{k+\frac{1}{d}} = \Big(1 + (1 - \theta)M_{x_1} + \textstyle\sum_{i=2}^{d} M_{x_i} + \sum_{i<j}^{d} M_{x_i x_j}\Big) u^k$$

$$(1 - \theta M_{x_2})u^{k+\frac{2}{d}} = u^{k+\frac{1}{d}} - \theta M_{x_2} u^k$$

$$\vdots \qquad\qquad \vdots$$

$$(1 - \theta M_{x_d})u^{k+1} = u^{k+\frac{d-1}{d}} - \theta M_{x_d} u^k \qquad (4.12)$$

In each fractional step, one of the spacial variables x_i is treated partially implicitly by the θ-method, whereas the other variables are treated explicitly. The mixed derivative terms are always treated explicitly. The accuracy of the scheme is $\mathcal{O}(\Delta t) + \mathcal{O}((\Delta x_i)^2)$ for all choices of θ. If no mixed derivatives are present, the accuracy is $\mathcal{O}((\Delta t)^2) + \mathcal{O}((\Delta x_i)^2)$ for $\theta = \frac{1}{2}$.

The accuracy in time for equations with mixed derivative terms can be improved by including an additional step to time-center the mixed derivative. The complete scheme is

$$(1 - \theta M_{x_1})\hat{u}^{k+\frac{1}{d}} = \left(1 + (1 - \theta)M_{x_1} + \sum_{i=2}^{d}M_{x_i} + \sum_{i<j}^{d}M_{x_i x_j}\right)u^k$$

$$(1 - \theta M_{x_2})\hat{u}^{k+\frac{2}{d}} = \hat{u}^{k+\frac{1}{d}} - \theta M_{x_2}u^k$$

$$\vdots \qquad\qquad \vdots$$

$$(1 - \theta M_{x_d})\hat{u}^{k+1} = \hat{u}^{k+\frac{d-1}{d}} - \theta M_{x_d}u^k$$

$$(1 - \theta M_{x_1})u^{k+\frac{1}{d}} = \left(1 + (1 - \theta)M_{x_1} + \sum_{i=2}^{d}M_{x_i}\right)u^k$$

$$\qquad\qquad\qquad + \frac{1}{2}\left(\sum_{i<j}^{d}M_{x_i x_j}\right)\left(u^k + \hat{u}^{k+1}\right)$$

$$(1 - \theta M_{x_2})u^{k+\frac{2}{d}} = u^{k+\frac{1}{d}} - \theta M_{x_2}u^k$$

$$\vdots \qquad\qquad \vdots$$

$$(1 - \theta M_{x_d})u^{k+1} = u^{k+\frac{d-1}{d}} - \theta M_{x_d}u^k \qquad\qquad (4.13)$$

The accuracy of the above scheme is $\mathbb{O}((\Delta t)^2) + \mathbb{O}((\Delta x_i)^2)$ for $\theta = \frac{1}{2}$. Sufficient conditions for unconditional stability are derived in [29] (for the case of constant coefficients and no drift terms). They are

$$\theta \geq \frac{1}{2} \qquad\qquad \text{for} \qquad d = 2, 3$$

$$\theta \geq \frac{(d - 1)^d}{2d^{d-1}} \qquad \text{for} \qquad d > 3$$

In particular, in two and three dimensions, the choice $\theta = \frac{1}{2}$ yields an unconditionally stable scheme of second order in space and time.

The implementation of the scheme is straightforward. Each of the fractional steps involves solving a tridiagonal linear system of as many equations and unknowns as there are mesh points. If N denotes the number of mesh points, the computational effort is of the order $\mathbb{O}(N)$. For the implementation, see [99].

The difference scheme above applies only for inner mesh points. Therefore, it has to be complemented by a difference scheme for mesh points on the boundary. Two types of boundary conditions will be treated here:

■ Mixed boundary conditions:

$$\alpha u + \beta u_\nu = \gamma \quad \text{on } \partial D \qquad\qquad (4.14)$$

■ Linearity boundary condition:

$$u_{\nu\nu} = 0 \quad \text{on } \partial D \tag{4.15}$$

More information on the linearity boundary condition can be found in [115]. Discretization of each of the boundary conditions will be described for the case $d = 2$ for clarification. For boundary condition (4.14) there are two possible schemes. The first one replaces the derivative in (4.14) by a one-sided difference quotient. As an example, the scheme for the points on the left side of D consistent with (4.12) would be

$$\left(\alpha - \frac{\beta}{\Delta x_1}\right) u_{0,j}^{k+\frac{1}{2}} + \frac{\beta}{\Delta x_1} u_{1,j}^{k+\frac{1}{2}} = \gamma$$

$$u_{0,j}^{k+1} = u_{0,j}^{k+\frac{1}{2}}$$

Thereby, the tridiagonal structure of the system of linear equations is retained. An alternative scheme assumes a virtual mesh point $u_{-1,j}$ and takes central differences:

$$\alpha u_{0,j}^{k+\frac{1}{2}} + \beta \frac{u_{1,j}^{k+\frac{1}{2}} - u_{-1,j}^{k+\frac{1}{2}}}{2\Delta x_1} = \gamma$$

The value $u_{-1,j}$ can be eliminated by employing the discretized differential equation on the boundary point $(0, j)$

$$(1 - \theta M_{x_1}) u_{0,j}^{k+\frac{1}{2}} = \left(1 + (1 - \theta) M_{x_1} + M_{x_2} + M_{x_1 x_2}\right) u_{0,j}^{k}$$

The two equations above yield an equivalent equation of the form

$$q_1 u_{0,j}^{k+\frac{1}{2}} + q_2 u_{1,j}^{k+\frac{1}{2}} = q_3$$

with coefficients q_1, q_2, and q_3 that can be calculated. This system fits into the tridiagonal system (4.12).

Boundary condition (4.15) at a left boundary mesh point $(0, j)$ is discretized by employing the discretized differential equation while setting $u_{x_1,x_1} = u_{x_1,x_2} = 0$ and using only one-sided difference approximations for the remaining differentials in x_1-direction. Let the one-sided version of the difference operator be defined by

$$M_{x_1}^+ u_{0,j} = \lambda_{x_1} b_1 (u_{1,j} - u_{0,j}) + (c\Delta t) u_{i,j}$$

Then scheme (4.12) is complemented by

$$(1 - \theta M_{x_1}^+)u_{0,j}^{k+\frac{1}{2}} = \left(1 + (1 - \theta)M_{x_1}^+ + M_{x_2}\right)u_{0,j}^k$$

$$(1 - \theta M_{x_2})u_{0,j}^{k+1} = u_{0,j}^{k+\frac{1}{2}} - \theta M_{x_2}u_{0,j}^k$$

(4.16)

The schemes for the other parts of the boundary are constructed in a similar way.

4.5   CONVERGENCE AND PERFORMANCE

In this section, the convergence and performance of the θ-scheme, with Biconjugate Gradient Stabilized (BCGS) solver, and the ADI scheme will be examined. As example, we take the Black-Scholes two-stock model (4.1) for an outperformance option. The payoff at maturity is

$$P(S_T^1, S_T^2) = \max\left(w_1\frac{S_T^1}{S_0^1} - w_2\frac{S_T^2}{S_0^2} - K, 0\right)$$

where w_1 and w_2 are weights and K is the strike. As an analytical solution is available, we can compute the numerical pricing error. In the examples we use $r = 0.05$, $\sigma_1 = 0.3$, $\sigma_2 = 0.15$, $K = -0.2$, $T = 1$, and $p_1 = p_2 = 0$.

Figures 4.1 and 4.2 show the convergence w. r. t. the space discretization for the ADI and the BCGS schemes, respectively, calculated with 100 time

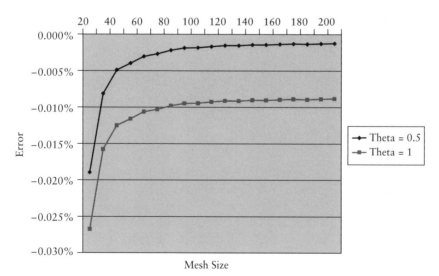

FIGURE 4.1   ADI scheme: convergence for $dx, dy \rightarrow 0$.

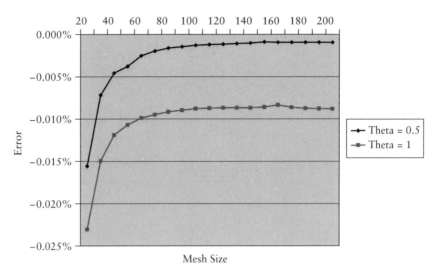

FIGURE 4.2 BCGS scheme: convergence for $dx, dy \to 0$.

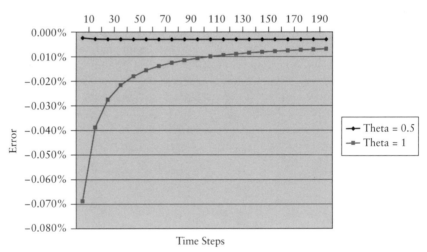

FIGURE 4.3 ADI scheme ($\rho = 0$): convergence for $dt \to 0$.

steps per year. In this example we set $\rho = 0$, but the result does not change much for different choices of ρ. Both schemes exhibit a similar convergence.

The convergence w. r. t. the time discretization is shown in Figure 4.3 for the case $\rho = 0$ (no mixed derivatives). The result for the BCGS scheme looks very much the same, so the corresponding graph is not shown here. For the choice $\theta = 0.5$, the convergence is of second order in dt, whereas for $\theta = 1$ it is of first order, resulting in a slower convergence. Setting $\rho = 0.7$,

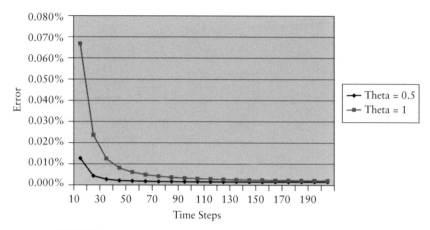

FIGURE 4.4   ADI scheme ($\rho = 0.7$): convergence for $dt \to 0$.

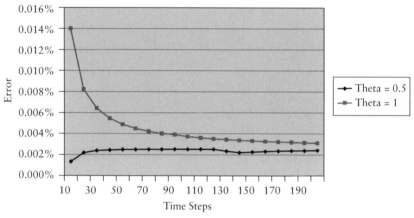

FIGURE 4.5   BCGS scheme ($\rho = 0.7$): convergence for $dt \to 0$.

the ADI scheme is only of first order in dt regardless of the choice of θ because of the mixed derivative term. The graphs for this case are shown in Figures 4.4 and 4.5. Here one can see that the ADI scheme converges considerably slower than the BCGS scheme.

As a last issue, the computing time is compared for the ADI and the BCGS scheme. Figure 4.6 shows the time needed to price the outperformance option described earlier as a function of the mesh size. The ADI method is much faster, especially for a larger number of mesh points. Using a better preconditioner, such as incomplete lower triangular-upper triangular (ILU) decomposition, the performance of the BCGS scheme might be improved.

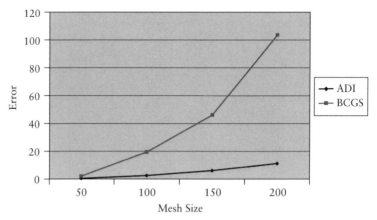

FIGURE 4.6   Computing time for ADI and BCGS schemes.

This surely will be the case if the coefficients are taken to be constant in time, such that the preconditioning has to be done only once. If a new coefficient matrix is taken for each time step, then the ILU preconditioner usually does not improve the efficiency.

4.6   DIVIDEND TREATMENT IN STOCHASTIC VOLATILITY MODELS

In modeling equity markets, there are two important features to be taken into account that go beyond the classical Black-Scholes theory:

- There is a pronounced volatility skew, usually in the form in which implied volatility is monotonically decreasing as a function of the strike of the option.
- The stock periodically pays dividends.

A class of models that exhibits a volatility skew are the level-dependent or stochastic volatility models, both of which can be written in the form

$$dS_t = (r_t - p_t)S_t \, dt + \sigma_t S_t \, dW_t \tag{4.17}$$

$t \in [0, T]$, where r_t denotes the continuously compounded interest rate, p_t the repo rate, and σ_t the instantaneous volatility—all of which may be stochastic processes. Examples are the level-dependent or local volatility model $\sigma_t = \sigma_{loc}(S_t, t)$ or the Heston model, where σ_t is given by another stochastic differential equation.

Modeling Dividends

To fix the notation, let $D_1, \ldots, D_n$ be the cash dividends at times $t_1, \ldots, t_n$, $0 < t_1 < \ldots < t_n \leq T$. Until further notice, the quantities D_i are allowed to be stochastic. We denote the present value of all future dividend payments up to maturity T by I_t and the accumulated dividends from 0 to time t by $\tilde{I}_t$, formally

$$I_t = \sum_{i=1}^{n} \mathbb{E}\left[D_i e^{-\int_t^{t_i} r_\tau \, d\tau} \mid \mathcal{F}_t \right] 1_{[0,t_i)}(t)$$

$$\tilde{I}_n = \sum_{i=1}^{n} D_i e^{\int_{t_i}^{t} r_\tau \, d\tau} 1_{[t_i,\infty)}(t)$$

To actually use dividend models for numerical pricing, one has to be more specific about the dividends. One possible assumption is that the dividend payments are linear functions of the spot price before it goes "ex dividend,"

$$D_i = a_i + b_i S_{t_i-}$$

Let $\delta_1, \ldots, \delta_n$ be dividend estimates. For short-term, dividend estimates are quite accurate, so one could set b_i to zero, such that the dividends are deterministic and equal $a_i = \delta_i$. For long-term options, a pragmatic approach is to introduce a blending function λ_i, taking the value 1 for the first two years and then decreasing linearly to 0. Then one sets $a_i = \lambda_i \delta_i$. The coefficients b_i can then be fitted to the forward curve $F_T = \mathbb{E} S_T$ by using the iterative scheme

$$F_T = \mathbb{E}\left[S_T \mid \mathcal{F}_0 \right]$$

$$= \mathbb{E}\left[\mathbb{E}\left[S_T \mid \mathcal{F}_{t_n-} \right] \mid \mathcal{F}_0 \right]$$

$$= \mathbb{E}\left[\left(S_{t_n-}(1 - b_n) - a_n \right) e^{\int_{t_n}^{T} r_t - p_t \, dt} \mid \mathcal{F}_0 \right]$$

$$= ((1 - b_n) e^{\int_{t_{n-1}}^{t_n} r_t - p_t \, dt} F_{t_{n-1}} - a_n) e^{\int_{t_n}^{T} r_t - p_t \, dt}$$

Stock Process with Dividends

Obviously, to prevent arbitrage, the stock price has to jump by an amount $-D_i$ at time t_i. However, there are numerous ways to incorporate that jump into the nondividend model (4.17).

Jump process   This is the most obvious extension to (4.17), where we just add the jump to the SDE by means of the Dirac delta function $\delta(x)$:

$$dS_t = \left((r_t - p_t)S_t - \sum_{i=1}^{n} D_i \delta(t - t_i)\right)dt + \sigma_t S_t \, dW_t \qquad (4.18)$$

Yield model   The dividend yield model consists of adding a function q ("dividend yield") to the repo rate p:

$$dS_t = (r_t - p_t - q_t)S_t \, dt + \sigma_t S_t \, dW_t \qquad (4.19)$$

In this model the forward curve is continuous and given by

$$F_T = S_o e^{\int_0^T r_t - p_t - q_t \, dt}$$

for all T. A discontinuous forward curve due to discrete dividend payments can be approximated by the yield model. If one assumes a piecewise constant dividend yield function q_t, taking constant values q_k on intervals (s_{k-1}, s_k) $(k = 1, \ldots, m)$, then one can match all forwards F_{s_k} by solving the equation

$$q_k(s_{k+1} - s_k) = -\log F_{s_{k+1}} + \log F_{s_k} + \int_{s_k}^{s_{k+1}} r_t - p_t \, dt$$

for q_k.

Exclude future dividends   From the original stock process, one can define the continuous "ex dividends" process

$$\tilde{S}_t = S_t - I_t \qquad (4.20)$$

The process $\tilde{S}_t$ starts at S_0 minus the present value of all expected future dividend payments up to maturity, and ends at $\tilde{S}_T = S_T$. The assumption for the stock process is that $\tilde{S}$ satisfies the SDE

$$d\tilde{S}_t = (r_t - \tilde{p}_t)\tilde{S}_t \, dt + \tilde{\sigma}_t \tilde{S}_t \, dW_t \qquad (4.21)$$

THEOREM 4.1

Let $D_1, \ldots, D_n$ be deterministic. Then the dividend models (4.18) and (4.21) describe the same process if

$$\sigma_t = \tilde{\sigma}_t \frac{\tilde{S}_t}{S_t} \qquad \text{and} \qquad (4.22)$$

$$p_t = \tilde{p}_t \frac{\tilde{S}_t}{S_t} \qquad (4.23)$$

PROOF

By assumptions, the process I_t is deterministic, with differential

$$dI_t = \left(\sum_{i=1}^{n} rD_i e^{-r(t_i - t)} 1_{[t_0, t_i)}(t) - D_i \delta(t - t_i) \right) dt$$

$$= \left(rI_t - \sum_{i=1}^{n} D_i \delta(t - t_i) \right) dt$$

Then, from (4.18) it follows that

$$d\tilde{S}_t = dS_t - dI_t$$

$$= (r_t - p_t)S_t \, dt + \sigma_t S_t \, dW_t - rI_t \, dt$$

$$= (r_t \tilde{S}_t - p_t S_t) \, dt + \sigma_t S_t \, dW_t$$

$$= \left(r_t - p_t \frac{S_t}{\tilde{S}_t} \right) \tilde{S}_t \, dt + \sigma_t \frac{S_t}{\tilde{S}_t} \tilde{S}_t \, dW_t$$

Comparing this equation to (4.21), one easily sees that the models are the same if and only if

$$\tilde{\sigma}_t = \sigma_t \frac{S_t}{\tilde{S}_t} \quad \text{and} \quad \tilde{p}_t = p_t \frac{S_t}{\tilde{S}_t}$$

proving the theorem.

A main application of dividend model (4.21) is to obtain closed-form solutions to European options.

THEOREM 4.2

Let $\tilde{C}_{K,T}(\tilde{S}_t, t)$ be the price of a European call option with maturity T and strike K written on the underlying $\tilde{S}$ satisfying (4.21). Then, the price of the same European call option written on the stock $S_t = \tilde{S}_t + I_t$ is given by

$$C_{K,T}(S_t, t) = \tilde{C}_{K,T}(S_t - I_t, t) \tag{4.24}$$

In particular, if all coefficients are constant, Black-Scholes formula yields

$$C_{K,T}(S_t, t) = (S_t - I_t)e^{-p(T-t)}N(d_1) - Ke^{-r(T-t)}N(d_2)$$

where

$$d_1 = \frac{\log((S_t - I_t)/K) + (r - D + \sigma^2/2)(T - t)}{\sigma\sqrt{T - t}}$$

$$d_2 = d_1 - \sigma\sqrt{T - t}$$

PROOF

The price $C_{K,T}(S_t, t)$ is given by

$$C_{K,T}(S_t, t) = \mathbb{E}\left[e^{-\int_t^T r_\tau d\tau}\max(S_T - K, 0) \mid \mathscr{F}_t\right]$$

$$= \mathbb{E}\left[e^{-\int_t^T r_\tau d\tau}\max(\tilde{S}_T - K, 0) \mid \mathscr{F}_t\right] \qquad \text{(using } S_T = \tilde{S}_T)$$

$$= \tilde{C}_{K,T}(\tilde{S}_t, t)$$

since $\tilde{S}_t$ can be considered as non–dividend-paying stock. Equation (4.24) now follows from the identity $\tilde{S}_t = S_t - I_t$. The rest follows directly from the Black-Scholes pricing formula for European call options applied to the underlying $\tilde{S}_t$.

Include past dividends   This model is similar to model (4.20), (4.21), except that instead of the "ex dividends" process, one considers the continuous capital gains process $\hat{S}_t$, modeling the value of one stock plus the value of all dividends immediately reinvested. It is defined by

$$\hat{S}_t = S_t + \tilde{I}_t \tag{4.25}$$

in particular $\hat{S}_0 = S_0$. The assumption now is that the process $\hat{S}_t$ satisfies the SDE

$$d\hat{S}_t = (r_t - \hat{p}_t)\hat{S}_t\,dt + \hat{\sigma}_t\hat{S}_t\,dW_t \tag{4.26}$$

Similar to Theorem 4.1, the following theorem holds:

THEOREM 4.3

The dividend models (4.18) and (4.26) describe the same process if

$$\sigma_t = \hat{\sigma}_t \frac{\hat{S}_t}{S_t} \quad \text{and} \tag{4.27}$$

$$p_t = \hat{p}_t \frac{\hat{S}_t}{S_t} \tag{4.28}$$

Again, this dividend model can be used to derive closed-form solutions for European options. The result, corresponding to Theorem 4.4, is:

THEOREM 4.4

Let $\hat{C}_{K,T}(U_t, t)$ be the price of a European call option with maturity T and strike K written on the underlying $\hat{S}$ satisfying (4.26). Then the price of the same European call option written on the stock $S_t = \hat{S}_t - \tilde{I}_t$ is given by

$$C_{K,T}(S_t, t) = \hat{C}_{K+\tilde{I}_t, T}(S_t, t) \tag{4.29}$$

PROOF

The price $C_{K,T}(S_t, t)$ is given by

$$
\begin{aligned}
C_{K,T}(S_t, t) &= \mathbb{E}\left[e^{-\int_t^T r_\tau \, d\tau} \max(S_T - K, 0) \mid \mathcal{F}_t \right] \\
&= \mathbb{E}\left[e^{-\int_t^T r_\tau \, d\tau} \max(\hat{S}_T - \tilde{I}_T - K, 0) \mid \mathcal{F}_t \right] \quad \text{(using (4.25))} \\
&= \hat{C}_{K+\tilde{I}_T, T}(\hat{S}_t, t) \\
&= \hat{C}_{K+\tilde{I}_T, T}(S_t, t) \quad \text{(since } \hat{S}_t = S_t\text{)}
\end{aligned}
$$

proving the theorem.

Local Volatility Model with Dividends

In the local volatility model without dividends the stock price satisfies

$$dS_t = (r_t - p_t)S_t \, dt + \sigma_{loc}(S, t)S_t \, dW_t \tag{4.30}$$

where r_t and p_t are assumed to be deterministic, and σ_{loc} is a known function of spot and time. In the presence of dividends, one can use the dividend models from Section 4.6 with $\sigma_t = \sigma_{loc}(S, t)$. Using model (4.25), the function $\sigma_{loc}(S, t)$ can be calibrated analytically using Dupire's formula (cf. [38]) and Theorem 4.3. The result is:

THEOREM 4.5

Let $\hat{S}_t = S_t + \tilde{I}_t$ satisfy equation (4.26), with the instantaneous volatility $\hat{\sigma}$ being a function

$$\hat{\sigma} = \hat{\sigma}_{loc}(\hat{S}_t, t)$$

Let a continuum of European call prices be given, denoted by

$$\{C_{K,T} \,|\, K \geq 0, T \geq t_0\}$$

Assume that the prices $\hat{C}_{E,T} := C_{E-\tilde{I}_T,T}$ define a smooth surface in E and T. Then, the local volatility $\hat{\sigma}_{loc}$ can be calculated as

$$\hat{\sigma}_{loc}^2(E, T) = \frac{\dfrac{\partial}{\partial T}\hat{C}_{E,T} + (r - d)E\dfrac{\partial}{\partial E}\hat{C}_{E,T} + p\,\hat{C}_{E,T}}{\dfrac{1}{2}E^2\dfrac{\partial^2}{\partial E^2}\hat{C}_{E,T}} \tag{4.31}$$

PROOF

For the European option, the following identity holds:

$$C_{E-\tilde{I}_T,T} = \mathbb{E}\left[e^{-\int_t^T r_\tau d\tau}(S_T - (E - \tilde{I}_T))_+\right] = \mathbb{E}\left[e^{-\int_t^T r_\tau d\tau}(\hat{S}_T - E)_+\right] = \hat{C}_{E,T}$$

Now one has exactly the same situation as in the case without discrete dividends, with the stock process being replaced by $\hat{S}_t$, and the given European call prices being replaced by the quantities $\hat{C}_{E,T}$.

The Feynman-Kac partial differential equation for either of the dividend models discussed above can be derived in a straightforward way. The (one-factor) PDE for the fair price $u(t, S_t)$ of an option on S corresponding to the jump model (4.18) is

$$u_t + (r - p)Su_S + \tfrac{1}{2}\sigma_{loc}^2(S, t)S^2 u_{SS} = ru \qquad (4.32)$$

between two dividend payments. On a dividend payment date, there is an additional jump condition

$$u(S, t_i^-) = u(S - D_i, t_i^+)$$

Note that the option price is continuous over a sample spot path, since the spot price drops by the amount D_i at time t_i.

The PDE for model (4.21) is most naturally written for the function $\tilde{u}(t, \tilde{S}) = u(t, S)$:

$$\tilde{u}_t + (r - \tilde{p})\tilde{S}\tilde{u}_{\tilde{S}} + \tfrac{1}{2}\tilde{\sigma}^2(\tilde{S}, t)\tilde{S}^2 \tilde{u}_{\tilde{S}\tilde{S}} = r\tilde{u} \qquad (4.33)$$

Since $\tilde{S}_t$ is a continuous process there are no jump conditions needed for $\tilde{u}(t, \tilde{S})$. However, sometimes it is more convenient to formulate the equation in the original coordinates (t, S) instead of $(t, \tilde{S})$. This might be the case for barrier-type options where one has a boundary condition on a fixed spot level, such as

$$u(S, t)\big|_{S=B} = R \qquad \text{for all } t \qquad (4.34)$$

In coordinates $\tilde{S}$ the boundary would be moving (or rather jumping at a dividend payment date). Transforming (4.33) into coordinate S yields

$$u_t + \big(rS - \tilde{p}(S - I_t)\big)u_S + \tfrac{1}{2}\tilde{\sigma}^2(S - I_t, t)(S - I_t)^2 u_{SS} = ru$$
$$\text{for} \qquad t \notin \{t_1, \ldots, t_n\} \qquad (4.35)$$

There are now additional jump conditions at the dividend dates

$$u(S, t_i^-) = u(S - D_i, t_i^+)$$

The treatment of model (4.26) is similar.

Heston Model with Dividends

In the Heston model, the instantaneous volatility σ_t is given by

$$\sigma_t = \sqrt{v_t}$$

where the instantaneous variance process v_t and S_t follow a system of SDEs

$$dS_t = (r_t - p_t)S_t\, dt + \sqrt{v_t}\, S_t\, dW_t^S \tag{4.36}$$

$$dv_t = \kappa(\theta^2 - v_t)\, dt + \gamma\sqrt{v_t}\, dW_t^v \tag{4.37}$$

The correlation between the two Brownian motions W_t^S and W_t^v is denoted by ρ. Again, one can use the dividend models from the previous section.

As an example, we assume model (4.26). This is equivalent to assuming that $\hat{S}_t$ follows a Heston process. The advantage now is that there are analytical solutions for European options that can be used for an efficient calibration of the Heston parameters to market data. Let $C_{K,T}^H$ denote the fair price of a European call option on S, and $\hat{C}_{K,T}^H$ denote the fair price of a European call option on $\hat{S}$. Since $\hat{S}$ is a Heston process (without dividends), the price of $\hat{C}_{K,T}^H$ is given by an analytical formula. By Theorem 4.4, the price $C_{K,T}^H$ is given by

$$C_{K,T}^H = \hat{C}_{K+\tilde{I}_t,T}^H$$

After the Heston parameters have been calibrated, exotic options can be priced using a two-dimensional PDE. Writing the equation in terms of $\hat{S}$, no jump conditions on dividend dates are needed, and the equation has exactly the form (4.6).

CHAPTER 5

Convertible Bonds and Asset Swaps

5.1 CONVERTIBLE BONDS

Introduction

The history of convertible bonds (CBs) dates back over 100 years, although the real boom in sales has only occurred over the last two decades. Figure 5.1 shows that the issued volume grew from just over 23 billion U.S. dollars in 1995, to more than 100 billion by 2000, when the market capitalization stood at over 450 billion U.S. dollars. European and U.S. markets are currently the main contributors to new issuance, as shown in Figure 5.2. Issuance in Japan was considerable during the 1980s, and the capitalization of the Japanese CB market remains the largest in the world, although economic circumstances have caused Japanese CB issuance to decline greatly in recent years. In Europe, France has the largest convertible bond market, with about 30% market share. The average deal size goes up steadily: In 2000 the average was over 600 million Euros, with ten deals going over one billion Euros. Most convertible bond issuers are of investment grades (BBB or better), with only about 10 percent of issuers in Europe in subinvestment (junk bond) grades.

Convertible bonds are bonds issued by a company that pay the holder regular coupons and that may be converted into the underlying shares, normally at the holder's discretion. They are widely traded on the secondary market. Having equity, interest rate, and credit exposure, the convertible bond is a challenging hybrid security to value. They are usually subject to default risk, that is generally represented by a credit spread, and that influences the discount rate which should be used to value the bond. The choice of approach used to model this influence is of paramount importance.

In addition to the conversion feature, most convertible bonds have call and put features. The call feature allows the issuer to buy back the bond

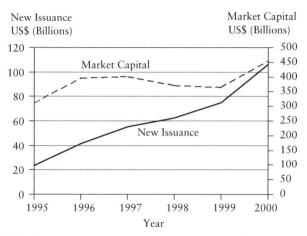

FIGURE 5.1 New issuance and market capital over the past six years.

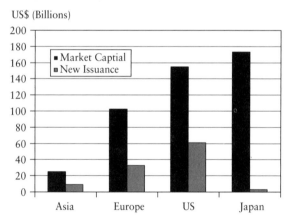

FIGURE 5.2 New issuance and market capital in different regions in year 2000.

for a predetermined price. Such call is normally protected by a threshold (trigger level) and is frequently available only after a certain date. The bond holder has the right to convert the bond once the call is announced, so the call feature is mainly used to force early conversion. The put provision, by contrast, allows the bond holder to sell back the bond in exchange for the put price. Again, it is available only during certain periods and it will be exercised when the yield curve steepens: The bond holder then redeems the bond and reinvests at a higher rate. Furthermore, many convertibles have extra features to make them more attractive to investors. These include conversion price resets, cash at conversion, and *make whole* provisions. In general, it is not optimal to convert a bond before maturity (compare to an American-style call option) except when called.

Merton [85] proposed to value a defaultable bond based on the face value of the bond and the value of the firm. Hull [62] outlined a convertible bond model to calculate the discount rate from the probability of conversion, which is assumed to satisfy the Black-Scholes equation [58]. Intuitively, since a high stock price means conversion is more likely, the discount rate should then be close to the risk-free rate. In 1997, Jarrow, Lando, and Turnbull [64] proposed pricing defaultable bonds by considering the credit-rating transition-probability. The default probability is linked to the transition-probability from one grade to another. The risk-neutral transition-probabilities used in the model are calibrated to a series of zero-coupon risky and risk-free bonds and to the historical credit-rating transition-probability matrix. Later, Tsiveriotis and Fernandes [116] priced convertible bonds by creating an artificial Cash Only Convertible Bond, the cash flows of which are discounted back at the full risky rate (risk-free rate + credit spread). We will outline an alternative method that considers an artificial portfolio which consists of a long position in a convertible bond and a short position in Δ number of shares.

There are also a number of papers which introduce multifactor models pricing convertibles [30]. Their advantage is that the additional factors allow a more realistic representation of the market. Their disadvantages are that they typically postulate variables unobservable in the market, whose calibration can be difficult, and that they are generally computationally expensive to run when compared with one-factor models.

In this chapter, we look at one-factor models implemented in a finite difference framework and examine various choices of credit-spread treatment. Additionally, we examine the effect of the volatility skew on the pricing of convertible bonds, approached in a deterministic local volatility model.

Deterministic Risk Premium in Convertible Bonds

Incorporating the credit-worthiness of the issuer into the valuation of convertible bonds presents a special problem. This arises because the holder can obtain value from the bond in two ways: either from receiving cash payments (coupons, repayment of principal at maturity, and early redemption at the holder's option), or from converting the bond into equity. It is generally held that these processes are differently affected by the credit-worthiness of the issuer, in that the ability of an issuer to make cash payments is certainly affected by his cash flow situation, but his ability to issue new shares, in any situation short of actual default, is not.

A quantity s_t, the credit spread, is defined to quantify the market's view on the likelihood of an issuer being able to meet an obligation to make a cash payment on its due date. We define it by reference to the market price of a defaultable zero-coupon bond $P^d(0, t)$ and of a risk-free bond maturing at the same date t, thus:

$$s_t = \frac{\partial}{\partial t} \left[\log \frac{P(0, t)}{P^d(0, t)} \right] \tag{5.1}$$

In one-factor convertible bond models, this quantity is explicitly assumed to be deterministic. Given this assumption, one may consider a number of approaches for incorporating it into the valuation algorithm.

In the following section we consider three such approaches. Bear in mind that the aim of all these is to use a single deterministic number, credit spread, in such a way as to discount the value to the bond-holder of the fixed payments but not the value he obtains from conversion to equity.

Conversion probability approach   The first approach involves making an adjustment to the discount rate used in the numerical scheme. In this approach the credit spread is weighted according to the (risk-neutral) probability of conversion of the bond, and the effective "defaultable" discount rate r_t^d is given by

$$r_t^d = r_t + (1 - p_t)s_t = r_t + \hat{s} \tag{5.2}$$

in which r_t is the risk-free rate, p_t the conversion probability, and we introduce the *conversion-adjusted credit spread* $\hat{s} = (1 - p_t)s$. The conversion probability is itself clearly a derivative of the underlying asset price S_t and as such satisfies the PDE

$$\frac{\partial p_t}{\partial t} + \frac{\sigma^2 S^2}{2} \frac{\partial^2 p_t}{\partial S^2} + (r - q)S \frac{\partial p_t}{\partial S} = 0 \tag{5.3}$$

At low values of S, it is clear that $p_t \to 0$ and thus the discount rate is the full risky rate $r_t + s_t$, which corresponds well with our understanding that a deeply out-of-money convertible bond is essentially a pure bond with little equity content (i.e., the option to convert is worth little). At high values of S, by contrast, the risk-free rate is used in discounting the conversion and coupon value, which conflicts with the aim of applying risky discounting to fixed payments. Refer also to Hull [62] in connection with this approach.

Tsiveriotis-Fernandes approach   Tsiveriotis and Fernandes have proposed [116] an approach which addresses the high-S limit by decomposing the convertible bond into a cash-only part (the *cash-only convertible bond*, denoted V_{co} or $COCB$) and a share-only part V_{so}. The COCB is a hypothetical (not a real) instrument which is defined such that its holder would receive those fixed payments (i.e., coupons, redemption, etc.) which would be received by an optimally behaving holder of the full convertible bond, but would not benefit from shares received on conversion. The share-only convertible bond is precisely the converse, yielding only the corresponding conversion cash flows. The full convertible bond value is given by $V = V_{co} + V_{so}$.

The core of the method is to separately discount the two parts at the risky and riskless rates respectively. As derivatives of S, they obey the following pair of Black-Scholes equations, which are coupled through the application of free boundary conditions.

$$\frac{\partial V_{co}}{\partial t} + \frac{\sigma^2 S^2}{2} \frac{\partial^2 V_{co}}{\partial S^2} + (r - q)S\frac{\partial V_{co}}{\partial S} = (r + s)V_{co}$$

$$\frac{\partial V_{so}}{\partial t} + \frac{\sigma^2 S^2}{2} \frac{\partial^2 V_{so}}{\partial S^2} + (r - q)S\frac{\partial V_{so}}{\partial S} = rV_{so} \qquad (5.4)$$

where s is the credit spread of the bond, r the risk free interest rate, and q the dividend yield.

Free boundary conditions are determined by the behavior of V: If the bond is optimal to convert, V_{co} is set to zero (in the backward induction scheme) and V_{so} to the conversion value.

From the above two equations, it is clear that

$$\frac{\partial V}{\partial t} + \frac{\sigma^2 S^2}{2} \frac{\partial^2 V}{\partial S^2} + (r - q)S\frac{\partial V}{\partial S} = (r + \hat{s})V \qquad (5.5)$$

in which the conversion-adjusted credit spread is given by

$$\hat{s} = s\frac{V_{co}}{V} \qquad (5.6)$$

It can thus be seen that the Tsiveriotis-Fernandes approach is equivalent to a form of scaling the credit spread according to the moneyness of the bond, similarly to the conversion probability approach.

The low-S limit is the same, in that the bond will not convert and therefore $V_{so} \rightarrow 0 \implies V = V_{co}$. In the high-$S$ limit, V_{co} contains only coupon payments and not the principle repayment, and as such is generally substantially smaller than V.

Delta-hedging approach   We have found in practice that the above two approaches have drawbacks at high-credit spreads, say 500 bp or more. For this reason, we introduce a third approach based on the delta hedging of a CB position.

As stated earlier, the aim of these deterministic credit-spread treatments is to apply an adjustment to s_t that has the effect of discounting fixed payments but not those cash flows resulting from conversion. In the Tsiveriotis-Fernandes approach, this is achieved by splitting the CB price into two components, separately discounted. The approach outlined here proposes an alternative split of the CB into components taken to be riskless and risky.

Consider a long-CB position which is delta-hedged by shorting Δ_t shares. As such, we require that the portfolio $V_t - \Delta_t S_t$ is instantaneously independent of stock price movements, i.e.,

$$\frac{\partial}{\partial S_t}(V_t - \Delta_t S_t) = 0 \iff \Delta_t = \frac{\partial V_t}{\partial S_t} \tag{5.7}$$

We may now split the bond price V_t into two parts: a stock part $\Delta_t S_t$, that is discounted at the risk-free rate r_t, and a bond part (stock-independent by the above equation) $V_t - \Delta_t S_t$ that is discounted at the risky rate.

Proceeding similarly to the Tsiveriotis-Fernandes case, we find the conversion-adjusted credit spread

$$\tilde{s} = \left(1 - \frac{\Delta_t S_t}{V}\right)s \tag{5.8}$$

Comparison between the approaches   For comparing the risk premium methodologies, we take as a test case an idealized bond that exhibits the most important features encountered in real bonds. Explicitly, we consider a bond having four years remaining until maturity, having notional equal to 100, paying a 4 percent annual coupon and having conversion ratio 1.0. We consider it to be noncallable for the next two years and thereafter callable at 110, with a trigger at 130. We let the credit spread on the bond take the relatively high value of 5 percent to clarify its effects in the different treatments.

In Figure 5.3 we show the effects of choice of credit-spread treatment as the spread widens: At low spreads, as much as 400 bps, the effect is small and the treatments are not very distinct. At higher spreads, the effect is quite marked, amounting to several percent. It is occasionally necessary in practical situations (perhaps a bond issue by a young company in a risky sector) to wish to price a bond at spreads well in excess of 500 bps, so the range of spreads shown in Figure 5.3 is not unreasonable.

To further illustrate the consequences of spread treatment choice, we show in Figure 5.4 a graph of price versus volatility for our example bond. It can be seen that two of the three treatments lead to negative vega

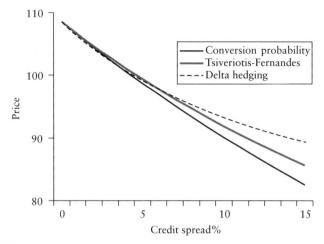

FIGURE 5.3 CB price versus credit spread for three credit-spread treatments.

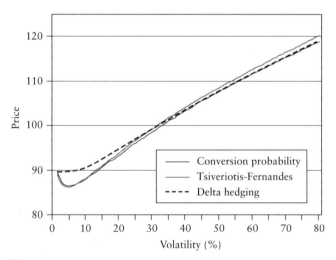

FIGURE 5.4 CB price versus volatility for three credit-spread treatments at 500 bps spread.

at low volatilities—a counterintuitive side effect of these methodologies. Fortunately, this generally occurs at volatilities too low to be of much real-market significance.

An intuitive understanding of this behavior can be gained (Figure 5.5) by noting that with zero credit spread, the present value of the payoff at maturity is a continuous function of the value S_T of spot at that time, because the discounting is unaffected by whether this payoff is from conversion or

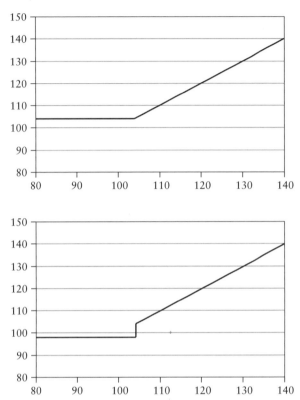

FIGURE 5.5 Discounted payoff at maturity versus S_T for a noncallable convertible bond at zero-credit spread (top graph) and at a high-credit spread (bottom graph) in the conversion-probability credit-spread treatment. The right-hand profile can easily show negative vega.

redemption (depending on whether S_T is greater or less than the notional plus final coupon). This payoff is strictly nonnegative vega. By contrast, if a severe discounting is applied to value obtained from redemption of the bond, then although the magnitude of the payoff at maturity is a continuous function of S_T, its present value is not. This discounted payoff profile may be vega-negative.

Non–Black-Scholes Models for Convertible Bonds

Convertible bonds are complex hybrid securities whose pricing in real markets is affected by a number of factors. Indeed they are probably the most complex widely traded instruments. A complex convertible-bond model would probably take into account stochasticity of the equity, interest rates, and default probability. In view of this, it is clear that convertible-bond models must go well beyond simple Black-Scholes.

In this section, we apply the Vasicek model outlined in Chapter 4 to the challenging case of the convertible bond, and in addition consider a deterministic local volatility model. The former is a two-factor model while the latter is a single-factor model in which a large number of parameters are introduced in order to reproduce the market-implied volatility surface.

The effect of interest rate stochasticity on convertible-bond valuation   Since CBs are coupon-bearing instruments typically of five years' maturity or longer, it has for a long time been seen as natural to model them under some stochastic interest-rate model.

Using the Vasicek model (4.2), we can obtain pricing differences between this model and Black-Scholes. The numerical solution can efficiently be calculated using the two-dimensional finite difference ADI method described in Section 4.4. Our test case is a four-year noncallable bond yielding a 4 percent coupon and having a conversion ratio of 1.0, priced at 100 bps credit spread.

In Figure 5.6, we set the correlation ρ in (4.2) to -0.7 and we vary the equity price between deeply out-of-money and deeply in-the-money values,

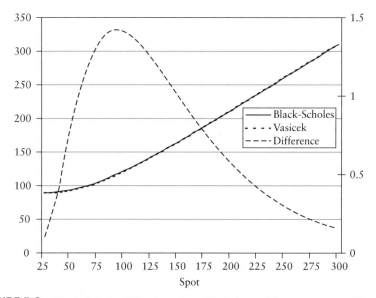

FIGURE 5.6   Black-Scholes CB price minus Vasicek model price over a wide range of spot prices. (Prices on left-hand axis; difference on right.)

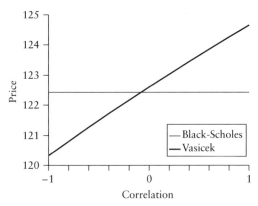

FIGURE 5.7   Black-Scholes CB price and Vasicek model price over the full ranges of correlation.

observing little effect from stochastic interest rates at either extreme, a result we intuitively expect in the limits when the bondholder's receipt of the bond's cash payments is independent of the behavior of the equity. The peak difference occurs around the point at which the bond is at the money (equity price equal to conversion price).

To see the effect of varying the correlation, in Figure 5.7 we vary the correlation ρ of Equation (4.2) between ± 1: The effect is almost exactly linear. In general, we see around a 1 percent price difference for our four-year test case: The effect becomes larger as maturity increases and its magnitude depends on the parameters of the Vasicek model.

The effect of volatility skew on convertible-bond valuation   It is well known that the presence of skew in implied volatilities requires us to go beyond the Black-Scholes model in equity markets. Furthermore, it is also well known that models which yield implied volatility skew in European options also yield prices for many other structures which can be very far from those given by the Black-Scholes model applied to the same structure.

The trivial example of such a structure is the call spread, which is just $C(K_1, T, \sigma_1) - C(K_2, T, \sigma_2)$, i.e., long a call struck at K_1 and short a call struck at $K_2 > K_1$, having a common maturity T. For clarity, we explicitly list the volatilities $\sigma_{1,2}$ used to price the options. Each of the options in this structure is by definition fairly priced at the implied volatility $\hat{\sigma}$ observed in the market for that strike and maturity: $\sigma_i = \hat{\sigma}(K_i, T)$. The price of this combination is therefore clearly not the Black-Scholes price if $\hat{\sigma}(K_1, T) \neq \hat{\sigma}(K_2, T)$, i.e., if there exists volatility skew for the underlying.

Figure 5.8 illustrates the effect of skew on a two year 100 percent–120 percent spread on German insurer Allianz, showing the price of this

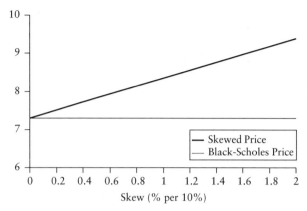

FIGURE 5.8   Skew effect on a call spread structure, showing price versus skew with the unskewed (Black-Scholes) market for comparison.

structure in percent of notional against skew, measured in percent volatility per 10 percent change in strike. The actual Allianz option market in August 2001 had a skew of around 1 percent volatility per 10 percent change in strike at two years maturity, exactly in the center of the graph.

Another example is afforded by barrier options: No derivatives business today would use a Black-Scholes model for barrier option in a skewed market.

In this section, we investigate the effect of volatility skew on convertible bonds. Since there are many models which attempt to account for skew, we here focus on one important case: the deterministic local volatility model of Dupire [38]. The stochastic volatility model of Heston [61] is another important case which could also be considered and would not be expected to give identical results.

Since implied volatilities are derived from liquid European option prices, in the cases of most convertible bonds, there will not be sufficient information in the market to derive implied volatilities, as the stock of most convertible-issuing companies worldwide will not have liquid traded options. The investigation of the effects of skew is therefore principally applicable to major blue-chip companies where there is an option market.

The numerical solution can again be obtained using a finite difference algorithm. For the local volatility model the standard one-factor implicit scheme or Crank-Nicolson scheme may be used. For the Heston model (4.6) one can use the two-factor schemes described in Chapter 4. There is an additional difficulty that arises for the Heston model. The boundary condition on the boundary $v = 0$ (short volatility of zero) is (see [61])

$$u_t + (r - p)S u_S + \kappa\theta^2 u_v = ru$$

This boundary condition does not fall into one of the standard classes of Dirichlet or Neumann boundary conditions for parabolic equations. Letting $v \to 0$ the diffusion terms $\frac{1}{2}vS^2 u_{SS}$ and $\frac{1}{2}\gamma^2 v u_{vv}$ vanish. The same, of course, happens for the Black-Scholes equation letting $S \to 0$, but by using new variables $x = \log(S)$, those problems can quickly be amended. Trying the same for the Heston equation one faces the problem that the u_v drift term becomes large compared to the diffusion term, which also may lead to numerical problems. A general strategy is to use a scheme based on the implicit (or Crank-Nicolson) scheme and restrict the computation to an appropriate region in the (S, v) plane.

Intuitively, we expect that the effect of skew is greatest on callable bonds. These contain an embedded out-of-the-money call option, and it is the implicit presence of an out-of-the-money strike which suggests the comparison with the call spread.

To illustrate this with a numerical example, we choose a bond very similar to the one used previously, i.e., four years to maturity, paying a 4 percent coupon and noncallable for the next two years, and thereafter callable at 110, with a trigger at 130. Since we are concerned only with major corporate issuers for volatility skew effects, we set the credit spread to zero. (This is not reasonable even for major corporate issuers but, for our present purposes, it is convenient to separate the effects of credit-spread treatment from those due to volatility skew).

In Figure 5.9 we illustrate convertible-bond pricing under the deterministic local volatility model. The parameters used for the calculations are approximately those of Siemens during August 2001. The graph compares

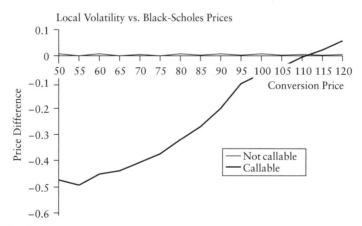

FIGURE 5.9   Skew effects on callable and noncallable convertible bonds, shown as deviations from the Black-Scholes price using at-the-money term structure.

local volatility pricing against Black-Scholes pricing for the bond detailed above and for a sequence of otherwise identical bonds differing only in their conversion prices. On the same graph we show the comparison for a second sequence of bonds identical with the first except for removal of the issuer call provision.

It is clear that the noncallable bond shows no deviation from the Black-Scholes price except numerical imprecision. This is because the bondholder will not exercise early under any circumstances, so the option is effectively European. Since we calibrate the local volatility surface to match market European option prices, we expect these to be repriced exactly.

The callable bond behaves quite differently. The holder of a convertible bond can elect to convert it to stock when he receives a call from the issuer, and it will generally be optimal for him to do so. The effect of the call feature therefore is not to cap the value of the bond at the call price—so it is quite different from a call spread in this respect—but to force early conversion and consequent loss of coupons and remaining optionality.

5.2 CONVERTIBLE BOND ASSET SWAPS

Introduction

A convertible bond asset swap (CBAS) is a construction used to separate the convertible bond (CB) into an equity option component and a bond component, both of which can separately be sold to different clients. Thereby the CBAS separates the equity market risk and credit risk inherent in the convertible bond, and thus has become a popular tool for risk management with a large impact on the convertible-bond market. The investor holding the credit risk will be referred to as the credit investor or credit buyer, and the investor holding the equity risk will be referred to as the stub investor or credit seller. Credit buyers are typically fixed income funds, commercial banks, and insurance companies, whereas the credit sellers are equity funds, hedge funds, or trading desks.

To illustrate the CBAS construction suppose a bank in possession of a convertible bond wants to use a CBAS construction to sell the credit component to a credit investor and the equity component to a stub investor. We make the assumption that the convertible bond has a nominal amount and a redemption value of 100. Then the bank enters into the following two contracts (see Figure 5.10):

Callable asset swap The bank enters with the credit investor into a callable asset swap, where the asset is the convertible bond. The credit investor buys the convertible bond from the bank for the nominal amount of 100. He is,

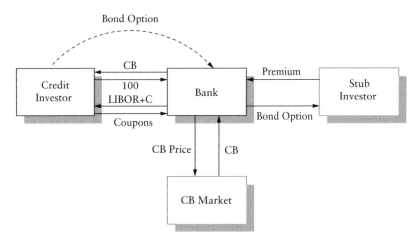

FIGURE 5.10   Convertible-asset swap transactions.

however, not entitled to exercise the option component of the convertible bond. At the same time he swaps the coupon payments for LIBOR (London Interbank Offered Rate), plus a spread reflecting the credit risk. The asset swap can be called before expiry in exchange for the bond floor of the convertible bond, calculated with the agreed credit spread of the asset swap.

Bond option   The bank sells to the stub investor a bond option on the convertible bond for a price reflecting the equity option component. In simple cases the strike of the option is the bond floor calculated with the agreed credit spread of the asset swap.

Depending on the prevailing market conditions over the lifetime of the CBAS, and the behavior of the parties involved, one of the following events may occur:

- **Option expires**   If the stub investor does not exercise the bond option and the convertible bond is not called by the issuer, then the bond option and the asset swap both expire and the credit investor redeems the bond.
- **Option exercised**   If the stub investor exercises the option, then the bank calls the asset swap and gives the convertible bond to the stub investor in exchange for the bond floor. The stub investor then can convert the bond into shares.
- **Issuer call**   If the issuer calls the convertible bond, then this event forces the option to be exercised with all consequences described earlier.

- **Issuer default** Should the convertible bond issuer default, the credit investor is left with the recovery value of the convertible bond plus the interest swap, which he then may choose to unwind as per market conventions.

In practice, convertible asset swap terms can be individually negotiated and may have different or additional features to the ones described here. The following remarks intend to clarify some of the terms mentioned earlier and give examples of possible variants:

- The bond floor is calculated from the fixed income flows of the convertible bond using an initially agreed-upon credit spread.
- Since the strike of the bond option is (in simple cases) equal to the bond floor, the option contains both an equity call option and a bond put option.
- Instead of fixed/floating, the asset swap could also be fixed/fixed.
- If the bond is called between floating rate payment dates, the credit investor is compensated by an adjusted accrual amount.
- To protect the credit investor in case the asset swap is being called, a lockout clause may be added to the contract. This may require that the credit investor be paid an additional cash amount should the bond be called before a specified lock-out date, or it may simply prohibit the call before that date. Another feature to protect the credit investor is a make-whole clause specifying a minimum number of coupons the credit investor receives even if the bond is called before the corresponding coupon payment dates.

Convertible-asset swap constructions give a number of benefits to both the credit buyer and the credit seller. For the credit buyer, the CBAS opens a new range of investment opportunities, often at better prices than he could achieve in the straight-bond market. Some companies have only issued convertible bonds, such that investments in straight bonds are not possible. For the stub investor the main advantage is the removal of the credit risk from the convertible bond. Using the CBAS as a risk management component, it can help to exploit arbitrage opportunities arising from undervalued convertible bonds. Since by entering into the CBAS position, the stub investor sells the bond part of the convertible bond to the credit investor, the CBAS immediately monetizes this part of his convertible-bond position. Another advantage to equity investors might arise from the fact that convertible bonds often have long times to maturity, such that the CBAS gives access to long-term equity options that otherwise for many underlying stocks would not be available.

It should be mentioned that another possibility to hedge the credit risk of a convertible bond is to buy a credit protection by means of a credit default swap (CDS) (see Figure 5.11) that also have a well-established market.

FIGURE 5.11   Credit-default swap.

In contrast to the CBAS, the CDS usually is not callable such that the CDS has to be unwound if the protection is no longer needed. Moreover, the CDS often does not contain an initial payment, which means that the convertible-bond investor has additional financing costs.

Pricing and Analysis

Breaking down the convertible-asset swap construction into its constituents and taking the fixed income parts for granted, we concentrate in this section on the convertible-bond option part held by the stub investor. In the following, by the notation CBAS we mean the value of this bond option part. Generally, the CBAS can be seen as a compound option on the convertible bond, where the payoff is given by

$$CBAS_t = \max(CB_t - K_t, 0) \tag{5.9}$$

Here, CB_t denotes the convertible-bond value and K_t the strike, that is calculated as the sum of the following terms:

- Strike notional N_K (usually the nominal of the convertible bond).
- Adjusted accrual amount A.
- Unwinding value U of a given swap.
- Lockout amount L (optional).

The adjusted accrual amount is given by $A = N \times (L_0 + C) \times R$ for the fixed-floating case. N stands for the bond notional, L_0 for the LIBOR rate, C for the accrual spread, and R for the time elapsed since the last coupon payment date of the swap long leg. The unwinding value U is the termination payment that would have to be paid to unwind a swap, that pays fixed amounts equal to the coupon payments of the bond and receives floating rate payments of LIBOR plus a spread defined in the asset swap terms. In the fixed-fixed case, the floating-rate payments are replaced by fixed-rate payments. The lockout amount L compensates the investor for the return he would have received during the lockout period had the call not occurred: In the usual case of the fixed-floating swap, it is equal to the present value of the spread payments during the remainder of the period.

A numerical solution for the CBAS price can easily be calculated from the appropriate pricing PDE using a finite difference scheme on a two-layer mesh. One layer holds the convertible-bond price as described in the previous section, the other layer holds the CBAS price. Starting with the payoff (5.9) at maturity, the Black-Scholes equation is solved backwards in time, as usual.

At each time step within the exercise period, the current CBAS value is forced to be greater or equal to the exercise value (5.9). The strike K_t in (5.9) can be evaluated just by discounting cash flows. The CB value CB_t is taken from the first layer of the mesh. That still leaves us with the choice of the appropriate stochastic model. If we restrict ourselves for practical purposes to one-factor and two-factor models, the obvious possibilities are

- One-factor stock process (Black-Scholes, local volatility).
- Two-factor stock process (stochastic volatility).
- One-factor stock process, one-factor short rate process.
- One-factor stock process, one-factor credit spread process.

To analyze the effects of spot price, interest rate, and credit-spread changes, we start with the Black-Scholes model and look at how the price changes with respect to those market parameters. The impact of the skew on the price of the convertible bond has been treated earlier and will be left out here.

To set up a test case we take as underlying convertible bond the example from an earlier section. It was a 4 percent coupon 4-year bond with conversion price 100, that is callable after two years for a price of 110 with call trigger 130. The static market data is

- Spot: 80.
- Interest rate: 6 percent.
- Credit spread: 300 bps.
- Volatility: 30 percent.

The convertible-asset swap is exercisable over the whole lifetime of the convertible bond and has the following underlying swap structure:

- Notional: 100.
- Type: fixed-floating.
- Fixed rate: 4 percent.
- LIBOR spread: 300 bps.

Figure 5.12 shows how the CBAS option price moves with the equity price. As you would expect, the form of the graph is similar to that for a

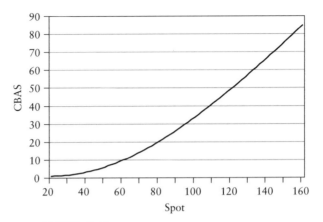

FIGURE 5.12   CBAS option value versus spot.

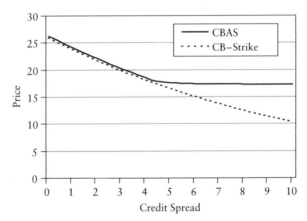

FIGURE 5.13   CBAS option value versus credit spread.

call option. In fact, the CBAS price is very close to the CB price minus
the CBAS strike. This effect will be explained later in more detail. Figure
5.13 is a graph showing the CBAS option and CB prices against the credit
spread. As shown in the graph, when the credit spread is low, the CBAS
price moves by approximately the same amount as the CB price when the
spread changes. This means no extra optionality exists for the CBAS option.
When the credit spread is higher than a certain level, however, the CBAS
option value is almost independent of the credit spread, while the CB value
keeps decreasing as the credit spread gets higher. This is due to the fact that
the CBAS will not get exercised when the credit spread increases. Since we

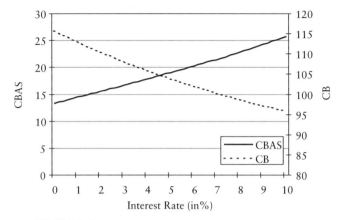

FIGURE 5.14 CBAS option value versus interest rate.

kept the spot price constant while moving the credit spread, in this case the CBAS resembles a European option (see end of this chapter). This shows one of the limits of the simple Black-Scholes model, because in reality it is unlikely that the spot price stays constant when the credit spread increases. The impact of interest rate changes on the CBAS value is shown in Figure 5.14. In contrast to the CB value the CBAS value goes up with increasing interest rates. The reason is that the strike of the CBAS is roughly equal to the bond floor of the CB and decreases as interest rates rise. It was already remarked earlier that the CBAS in this sense implicitly contains a bond put option.

In some cases, the CBAS option price is simply taken as its intrinsic value, which is the convertible bond price minus the bond floor calculated with credit spread equal to the fixed swap spread q_0. This intrinsic value is also called the *stripped convertible bond*. We now discuss the cases in which this simplification holds, and make the following assumptions:

- The CB has a nominal N, coupons c, and no call or put features.
- The CB is optimally exercised at maturity.
- The current credit spread is q.

To ensure the assumption that the CB is optimally exercised at maturity, it can be shown that this will be the case, if the coupons are higher than the stock dividends. The argument is similar to that for an American call option.

At maturity T, the CB and CBAS options have payoffs:

$$CB_T = \max(S_T, K) \tag{5.10}$$

$$CBAS_T = \max(CB_T - K_T, 0) = \max(S_T - K, 0) \tag{5.11}$$

$$\text{where } K = K_T = N + c \text{ at maturity } T$$

Now consider a time t before maturity with stock value S_t. It can be shown that the convertible bond value is:

$$CB_t = S_t e^{-y\Delta t} N(d_1) - K e^{-(r+q)\Delta t} N(d_2) + BF_t(q) \tag{5.12}$$

where $BF_t(q)$ is the bond floor price with credit spread q, y is the stock dividend yield, and $\Delta t = T - t$. The functions $N(d_1)$ and $N(d_2)$ are cumulative normal distribution functions and $d_{1,2}$ are defined as $(\log \frac{S_t}{K} + (r - y \pm \frac{1}{2}\sigma^2)\Delta t)/(\sigma \sqrt{\Delta t})$. The CBAS option intrinsic value at time t is

$$\widetilde{CBAS}_t = CB_t - K_t$$
$$= S_t e^{-y\Delta t} N(d_1) - K e^{-r\Delta t} N(d_2) + A \tag{5.13}$$

where

$$A = K e^{-r\Delta t} N(d_2) - K e^{-(r+q)\Delta t} N(d_2) + BF_t(q) - BF_t(q_0) \tag{5.14}$$

Assume Δt is the smallest discrete time period, so no exercise opportunity exists between time t and T. The CBAS option value at time t is simply a European option with payoff defined in (5.11):

$$CBAS_t = S_t e^{-y\Delta t} N(d_1) - K e^{-r\Delta t} N(d_2) \tag{5.15}$$

Clearly this value is independent of the credit spread. By comparing (5.13) and (5.15), we can judge whether it is optimal to exercise early or not.

- Case 1: $q \leq q_0$ In this case, $BF_t(q) \geq BF_t(q_0)$ and $\widetilde{CBAS} \geq CBAS_t$, so $A > 0$, which means the intrinsic value is always larger than the unexercised option value. Therefore, the stripped convertible bond value (SCNV) is equal to the CBAS option value.
- Case 2: $q \gg q_0$ In this case $BF_t(q) \ll BF_t(q_0)$. The extra term A in the intrinsic value is negative, so the CBAS option will not be exercised early. The CBAS option is simply a European option, which is naturally independent of the credit spread.

■ Case 3: $q \sim q_0$ The exact boundary q_b below which it is optimal to exercise the CBAS option can be found by solving the equation $A = 0$ for q. For $q\Delta t$ sufficiently small and no (or neglectable) coupons during the period Δt we have the approximation

$$A = Ke^{-r\Delta t}N(d_2)q\Delta t + Ke^{-r\Delta t}(q_0 - q)\Delta t \qquad (5.16)$$

yielding the spread boundary

$$q_b = \frac{q_0}{1 - N(d_2)} \qquad (5.17)$$

CHAPTER 6

Data Representation

T he representation of financial market data in the context of equity derivatives is a difficult task due to the multitude of instruments and the various parameters which define them. The added burden of sharing this data across trading, risk management, and settlement systems required in a derivatives house complicates the process of defining such data.

Derivative products, with many parameters defining each specific contract, can result in extremely complex data structures. Also, their dependence on market data such as the underlying stock and interest rate curves means that the total amount of data to price such a derivative is large, as depicted in Figure 6.1.

With software running on different operating systems, written in different programming languages, and utilizing different data storage, the transfer of data between multiple systems potentially involves transformation of the data at every stage in the entire business flow (refer to Figure 6.2).

Certainly in most institutions, it is unlikely that a consistent software platform will exist across business areas. The needs of the front-office and back-office are quite different, and to expect one software package to fulfill these different requirements is unrealistic. It is also necessary to communicate with external systems; for a front-office system this may be to a live price or trade feed, for a back-office system this may involve overnight uploads to an external clearing house.

These interdependencies result in a large development effort in transforming data from one system to another, and a potential maintenance nightmare when system data structures change. Although this development effort cannot be eliminated, through the use of new constructs such as the Extensible Markup Language (XML) which is rapidly emerging as a de facto data representation tool, it can be reduced through the use of common and easily transformable data structures (Figure 6.3).

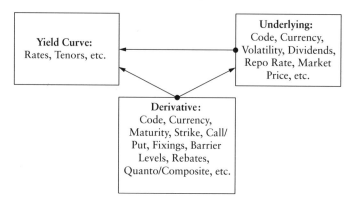

FIGURE 6.1   Dependency on yield curve and underlying data.

FIGURE 6.2   Software systems in the various business units.

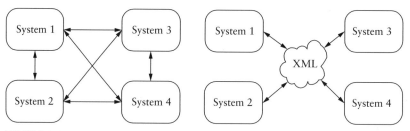

FIGURE 6.3   Transferring to an XML-based data structure reduces integration costs.

The following sections will provide an introduction to XML, first by presenting an overview of the language itself, and then moving into other associated standards useful for describing and manipulating XML data. Finally, some discussion on methods for describing equity derivatives will be presented as a prelude to the following chapters on application connectivity and web-based pricing applications.

6.1 XML

The Extensible Markup Language is a specification published by the World Wide Web Consortium (W3C)[1] that specifies a markup language for documents containing structured information [59]. Like the Hypertext Markup Language (HTML), a well known specification for displaying content in a web browser, XML has it origins from the Standard Generalized Markup Language (SGML). As a way of defining different special-purpose markup languages, SGML was first considered, however it was decided that due to its complexity, something simpler was needed: enter XML.

The introduction of XML was hailed by many as a revolution in computing, and it has now become a critical component in developing web-based and distributed systems. Architectures such as Java and .NET are incorporating XML as a fundamental component of their class libraries, and XML libraries are available for virtually all other programming languages. The success of XML has not only been due to the support of industry, but also due to its strength in structured information representation, and its independence from any programming language or operating system.

Unlike HTML, where specific markup and grammar are defined, the XML specification does not provide these definitions. Tags found in HTML, such as `<body>` and `<table>` have a clear definition and indicate a display layout which should be consistent across all HTML parsers. For example, the following piece of HTML processed by a web browser will display a three row, two column table, displaying stock price data.

```
<html>
  <body>
    <h1>Prices for stock DBKG.F</h1>
    <table>
      <tr><td>Bid</td><td>89.2</td></tr>
      <tr><td>Ask</td><td>89.4</td></tr>
      <tr><td>Last</td><td>89.4</td></tr>
    </table>
  </body>
</html>
```

These tags, their corresponding closing tags, and the hierarchy provide layout information to the web browser. However, the markup is really only describing the layout of a table on an HTML page; there is no capability of adding further markup to provide additional descriptive information about the content. The fact that the content is representing the bid, ask, and last prices for a particular stock code is irrelevant to the HTML parser; it is

---

[1]Refer to http://www.w3.org.

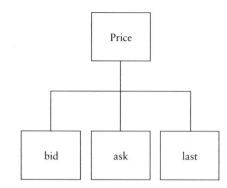

FIGURE 6.4   Tree structure for an XML document.

simply text. Now, by concentrating on the data representation, and not the presentation, an XML document for defining the bid, ask, and last prices for a stock might look like:

```
<?xml version="1.0"?>
<price code="DBKG.F">
  <bid>89.2</bid>
  <ask>89.4</ask>
  <last>89.4</last>
</price>
```

Rather than the tags describing visual layout in the form of tables, rows, and columns, the tag specifications and structure describe the actual data. For instance, from looking at the XML data it is clear that 89.2 is a bid price for the stock DBKG.F.

For XML to be parsed correctly, it must be *well formed*, that is, tags must be closed, and no tags must be out of order. Also, an XML document must contain a single root node, and this node can contain one or more child elements. The structure of an XML document forms a tree, as shown in Figure 6.4.

In this diagram, the root node is <price> and the other tags <bid>, <ask>, and <last> are children of this node.

Tags and Elements

- *Start-tag.* A start-tag has the general form <name...>, where *name* is the name that identifies the type of the element, and where ... corresponds to optional *attributes* (discussed later). An example start-tag without any attributes is <american>.

- *End-tag.* An end-tag is required for every start-tag and has the form `</name>`. The *name* value must correspond exactly with the *name* defined in the start-tag. End-tags may not contain attributes. The corresponding end-tag for the above start-tag is `</american>`.
- *Empty-element tag.* If no data is contained between the start- and end-tags, then an empty-element tag can be defined that has no corresponding end-tag, and that allows attributes in the form of `<name.../>`. An example of this tag type is `<american/>`.

Attributes

Start-tags and empty-element tags can also contain *attributes,* which specify extra property information for the particular tag. For example, to add the code attribute to the `<price>` tag is as follows:

```
<price code="DBKG.F"/>
```

Note the use of the empty-element tag in the above example.

Namespaces

Namespaces are an important part of XML, as they provide a mechanism for identifying the context of the markup. For instance, it is quite probable that the tag `<price>` could mean something completely different in a domain outside finance. By specifying a namespace, it is possible to more clearly describe the tags and attributes. Namespaces are declared using the `xmlns:`*someidentifier* and are added to a tag as in the following example.

```
<ns:price xmlns:ns="some-uri">data</ns:price>
```

The identifier *ns* is bound to the Uniform Resource Identifier (URI) *some-uri*. The namespace declaration is considered to apply to the element where it is specified, and to all elements within the content of that element, unless overridden by another namespace declaration.

A default namespace can also be specified which applies to all child elements as in the following.

```
<price xmlns="some-uri">data</price>
```

For further details regarding XML namespaces, refer to the W3C specification at http://www.w3.org/TR/REC-xml-names.

Processing Instructions

Processing instructions are strings inserted into an XML document to provide a way to send a message to an external application providing content relevant to the processing of the document. The content, however, might not be relevant to the document itself. Processing instructions take the form:

```
<? target-name string-of-chars ?>
```

Although the `<?xml version="1.0"?>` declaration has the same format as a processing instruction, it is actually not one, but is optionally used at the start of an XML document to indicate the version of the XML [16].

Comments

Comments can be placed anywhere in an XML document in the form:

```
<!-- some comment here -->
```

and are ignored by the XML parser. They are simply used for descriptive purposes.

```
<price>
  <!-- Define a list of stock prices. -->
  <bid>89.2</bid>
</price>
```

Nesting

Nesting gives XML a powerful way to represent complex data structures. For example, in the case of a more complex data structure, such as an American option, an XML document may take the following form:

```
<?xml version="1.0"?>
<american>
  <code>FTSE_OTC</code>
  <underlying>
    <code>FTSE</code>
    <currency>GBP</currency>
  </underlying>
  <expiry>2005-06-30</expiry>
  <strike>6000.0</strike>
  <cp>Call</cp>
</american>
```

As stated earlier, element tags must not overlap, but

```
<underlying><code>FTSE</code></underlying>
```

is legal, however

```
<underlying><code>FTSE</underlying></code>
```

is invalid.

Parsing XML

The above sections have given a brief overview of XML and the various constructs which define a document. It is clear that as the data to be represented increases in size and complexity, so too does the XML document. To be able to utilize the benefits of XML, tools must exist to simplify the process of reading and writing XML. Fortunately for the developer, class libraries and tools are available to do exactly this. Two techniques for parsing XML have become popular—DOM (Document Object Model) and SAX (Simple API for XML)—and each has a different approach to parsing. The size and content of the XML often helps determine which is more suitable.

Document Object Model (DOM) The Document Object Model provides a tree structure in memory for the developer to access the XML document. The DOM interface provides a straightforward mechanism to access and manipulate the object in memory. Usually the DOM is instantiated, whereby the XML document is read into memory and parsed. If the XML document is valid, a set of nodes is created, with each node containing certain properties depending on type. It is now possible to access nodes from the DOM; the various XML parsers available provide methods for this purpose.

Simple API for XML (SAX) The DOM provides a simple way of accessing content, but requires the entire XML document to be initially read into the object. For extremely large documents this may be inefficient. The Simple API for XML (SAX) was thus developed as an alternative event-driven model for processing XML. This allows SAX to process an incomplete document without the need to validate the entire XML document. This event-driven model, comes at a cost however, as in the implementation it is necessary to keep state across events.

Choosing a parser type is in many ways dependent on the type of data being processed, as both of the above models offer advantages for different situations. Other XML parsers have been written, offering other speed and usability optimizations. For further details on parsing, refer to [16] and [84].

Multiple Representation

The flexibility to create any entity definition in XML is obviously very powerful, as it provides a representation of complex data structures. However, this flexibility can also be its biggest weakness, as the likelihood of having multiple representations to describe the same data is high. For instance, there is no reason for someone else not to define a completely different set of tags and layout for the previous stock price example. In the following XML definition, the use of attributes determines whether the price is a bid, ask, or last, and the root tag of <pricelist> is different:

```
<?xml version="1.0"?>
<pricelist>
    <code>DBGK.F</code>
    <price type="bid">89.2</price>
    <price type="ask">89.4</price>
    <price type="last">89.4</price>
</pricelist>
```

There are endless permutations of how to describe the same data, and on initial thought it would appear that the transformation nightmare is simply transferred, rather than reduced as was promised with the use of XML. Also, the above XML provides no programmatic information, such as the data types of each element. When mapping to languages such as C++ and Java, it would be nice to have the ability to map between the data and program variables such as integers, strings, dates, and more complex types such as arrays and classes.

Fortunately, other specifications which are part of the XML family, and defined by the World Wide Web Consortium, provide consistent mechanisms to describe and transform XML document content. The two main specifications which will be discussed below are XML Schema and Extensible Stylesheet Language Transformation (XSLT).

6.2 XML SCHEMA

It is unusual for XML to exist in the raw form as discussed in the previous section, without some mechanism to describe and constrain the XML representation. For instance, when describing a particular piece of data it is necessary to define what constitutes that data and the structure of the data. By using XML Schema it is possible to formally define the types and the context of an XML document. The XML specification currently includes Document Type Definitions (DTDs) that fulfill the same role, however XML Schema has begun to take over this role, as it provides a number of benefits not available with DTDs. In particular, unlike DTDs, XML Schema descriptions are XML documents themselves, and therefore can be parsed and created using the same tools used for the underlying XML document that they describe. Although DTDs are in use today and are part of the XML specification, it is anticipated that XML Schemas will replace DTDs for the purpose of XML description, and therefore DTDs will not be further discussed.

An XML Schema document is opened with a `<schema>` element, along with a namespace identifier[2] as follows:

```
<xsd:schema xmlns:xsd="http://www.w3.org/2000/10/XMLSchema">
```

The best approach to providing an overview of XML Schema is to work through an example. In this case, XML Schema will be used to describe and constrain the following XML document representing a trade execution:

```
<?xml version="1.0"?>
<trade date="2001-06-21">
  <code>DBKG.F</code>
  <quantity>1000</quantity>
  <price>90.10</price>
  <buySell>buy</buySell>
  <account>
    <reference>C1232</reference>
    <brokerage>0.01</brokerage>
  </account>
</trade>
```

The initial step after the `<schema>` element is to examine the `<trade>` element and determine its type. As it consists of a `date` attribute and several child elements it is defined as a complexType as follows:

```
<xsd:element name="trade">
  <xsd:complexType>
    <xsd:sequence>
```

Groupings in XML Schema are defined using compositors, of which there are three kinds (sequence, choice, and all). In the above example the `<sequence>` compositor is used to indicate an ordered list of child elements. For the child nodes, such as `<code>`, a *simpleType* is defined:

---

[2]The namespace refers to the version of XML Schema at the time of writing. Refer to http://www.w3.org/XML/Schema for the latest release.

```
<xsd:element name="code" type="xsd:string"/>
<xsd:element name="quantity type="xsd:integer"/>
<xsd:element name="price" type="xsd:decimal"/>
<xsd:element name="buySell" type="xsd:string"/>
```

In the above, the `type` attribute is used to specify the data type of the element—in this case one of the predefined XML Schema data types.

The `<account>` element is another complexType and so the format is the same as for the `<trade>` root element. For this tag, it would be useful to define a mechanism whereby the definition allows for one or two lots of account details. This might be applicable in the case of a cross trade, whereby the broker is both the buyer and the seller. By adding extra attributes to define the minimum and maximum occurrences (known as cardinality), this can be achieved.

```
<xsd:element name="account" minOccurs="1" maxOccurs="2">
  <xsd:complexType>
    <xsd:sequence>
```

By default, both the `minOccurs` and `maxOccurs` attributes have a value of one.

Finally, for the `date` attribute of the `<trade>` element, an `<xsd:attribute>` section is used in a similar fashion to the simple type element definition.

Therefore, after working through the document, the complete XML Schema document is:

```
<?xml version="1.0"?>
<xsd:schema xmlns:xsd="http://www.w3.org/2000/10/XMLSchema">
  <xsd:element name="trade">
    <xsd:complexType>
      <xsd:sequence>
        <xsd:element name="code" type="xsd:string"/>
        <xsd:element name="quantity" type="xsd:integer"/>
        <xsd:element name="price" type="xsd:decimal"/>
        <xsd:element name="buySell" type="xsd:string"/>
        <xsd:element name="account"
                  minOccurs="1" maxOccurs="2">
          <xsd:complexType>
            <xsd:sequence>
              <xsd:element name="reference"
                  type="xsd:string"/>
              <xsd:element name="brokerage"
                  type="xsd:decimal"/>
            </xsd:sequence>
          </xsd:complexType>
        </xsd:element>
```

```
    </xsd:sequence>
    <xsd:attribute name="date" type="xsd:date"/>
   </xsd:complexType>
  </xsd:element>
</xsd:schema>
```

By utilizing such a schema, it becomes possible to bind XML documents to programming constructs such as classes in C++ and Java. This allows for the autocreation of class libraries from XML documents, also applicable to the the next chapter, the process of marshaling (converting objects into XML) and unmarshaling (the reverse process), both of which make use of the XML Schema paradigm.

6.3 XML TRANSFORMATION

Clearly, XML provides a flexible mechanism for the representation of data, however it has been shown that it is often necessary to translate XML data from one format into another. When sharing data between disparate systems, a transformation from one XML format into another format might be required, or even the conversion from an XML document into an HTML page for display purposes on a web site. Due to the frequency of this transformation task, the W3C created the Extensible Stylesheet Language Transformation Working Group.

Initially there was the Extensible Stylesheet Language Working Group, responsible for the development of:

■ A language for transforming XML documents.
■ An XML vocabulary for specifying formatting semantics.

However, due to its usefulness, the W3C decided that the process of transforming XML documents into other documents should be defined in a separate specification. As a result, the XSLT Working Group was established, with the development of a recommendation currently at version 1.0.[3] This recommendation defines the syntax and semantics for providing a language for the transformation of XML documents into other documents (which may or may not be XML).

An XSLT stylesheet, itself a well-formed XML document, contains one or more XSLT templates. XSLT instructions are always qualified with the XSLT namespace URI (http://www.w3.org/1999/XSL/Transform), which is typically mapped to the namespace prefix xsl. Defining a minimum stylesheet would be as follows:

---

[3]http://www.w3.org/TR/xslt.html

```
<?xml version="1.0"?>
<xsl:stylesheet
    xmlns:xsl="http://www.w3.org/1999/XSL/Transform"
    version="1.0">
</xsl:stylesheet>
```

In order to make use of XSLT, a translation engine is required which accepts input in the form of an XSL document and an XML document. By processing the XSLT instructions, an output file is generated based on the content of the XML input (see Figure 6.5).

XML Document Transformation

The example below will demonstrate the use of a stylesheet for the transformation of one XML representation into another representation. The input XML document in the process is the original price description and the result is the variation defined with a root element of pricelist. These are repeated below for ease of reference:

- Input document.

```
<?xml version="1.0"?>
<price code="DBKG.F">
  <bid>89.2</bid>
  <ask>89.4</ask>
  <last>89.4</last>
</price>
```

- Required output document.

```
<?xml version="1.0"?>
<pricelist>
    <code>DBKG.F</code>
    <price type="bid">89.2</price>
    <price type="ask">89.4</price>
    <price type="last">89.4</price>
</pricelist>
```

The stylesheet presented below uses a series of XSLT instructions for matching and extracting elements from within the original document such as:

- xsl:template used to define a pattern-based rule.
- xsl:value-of used to output the string corresponding to an associated select expression.

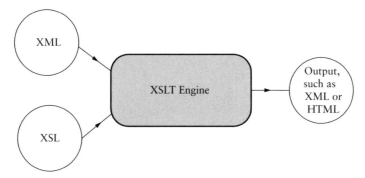

FIGURE 6.5 XSLT engine architecture.

It also includes instructions for generating elements and attributes into the output document:

- ■ `xsl:element` used for emitting elements.
- ■ `xsl:attributes` used for generating attributes.

Also included is the `xsl:output` instruction that is used to specify how the result tree should be created, in this example as XML.

```
<?xml version="1.0"?>
<xsl:stylesheet
   xmlns:xsl="http://www.w3.org/1999/XSL/Transform"
   version="1.0">
  <xsl:output method="xml"/>
  <xsl:template match="/price">
      <xsl:element name="pricelist">
          <xsl:element name="code">
              <xsl:value-of select="@code"/>
          </xsl:element>
          <xsl:element name="price">
              <xsl:attribute name="type">bid
                  </xsl:attribute>
              <xsl:value-of select="bid"></xsl:value-of>
          </xsl:element>
          <xsl:element name="price">
              <xsl:attribute name="type">ask
                  </xsl:attribute>
              <xsl:value-of select="ask"></xsl:value-of>
          </xsl:element>
          <xsl:element name="price">
              <xsl:attribute name="type">last
                  </xsl:attribute>
              <xsl:value-of select="last"></xsl:value-of>
```

```
          </xsl:element>
        </xsl:element>
      </xsl:template>
</xsl:stylesheet>
```

Transformation into HTML

For conversion into a displayable format such as HTML, an XSLT document and the associated transformation engine allow web developers an easy mechanism for publishing XML content. As client-side web browsers understand HTML, and currently offer less support for XML (although this is changing), the transformation usually takes place on the web server. Using technologies such as Active Server Pages (ASP) or Java Server Pages (JSP), HTML pages can either be statically or dynamically rendered. In the latter approach, more interactive pages can result, due to the ability to sort and filter data based on user input (see Figure 6.6).

In the following, a stylesheet is presented that transforms the output of the previous example into an HTML document. The transformation mechanism introduces new instructions for providing looping and function calling ability.

- `xsl:for-each` evaluates to create a node set based on the `select` attribute.
- `xsl:call-template` invokes a template, acting like a function call.

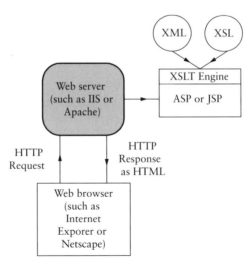

FIGURE 6.6 Generation of HTML output to a web client from a web server application.

As the output is HTML, it is possible to include tags such as `<table>` and `<body>`, provided that the entire stylesheet remains well formed. The transformation engine will simply pass content directly through to the output if it is not an XSLT instruction.

```
<?xml version="1.0"?>
<xsl:stylesheet
  xmlns:xsl="http://www.w3.org/1999/XSL/Transform"
  version="1.0">
  <xsl:output method="html"/>
    <xsl:template match="/pricelist">
      <html>
        <body>
          <h3>
            <xsl:text>Prices for stock </xsl:text>
            <xsl:value-of select="code"/>
          </h3>
          <table border="1">
            <xsl:for-each select="price">
              <xsl:call-template name="output_row"/>
            </xsl:for-each>
          </table>
        </body>
      </html>
    </xsl:template>
    <xsl:template name="output_row">
      <tr>
        <td>
          <xsl:value-of select="@type"/>
        </td>
        <td>
          <xsl:value-of select="."/>
        </td>
      </tr>
    </xsl:template>
</xsl:stylesheet>
```

The resulting output would now be in an HTML format directly displayable by a web browser:

```
<html>
  <body>
    <h3>Prices for stock DBGK.F</h3>
    <table border="1">
      <tr>
        <td>bid</td>
        <td>89.2</td>
```

```
      </tr>
      <tr>
        <td>ask</td>
        <td>89.4</td>
      </tr>
      <tr>
        <td>last</td>
        <td>89.4</td>
      </tr>
    </table>
  </body>
</html>
```

XSLT is the equivalent of a programming language, and therefore a thorough analysis of the technology is beyond the scope of this book. For further details, refer to some of the excellent references now available on this topic [16], [70].

6.4 REPRESENTING EQUITY DERIVATIVE MARKET DATA

With XML as the data representation, and specifications such as XSLT and XMLSchema, it becomes possible to design systems modeled on the actual business representations, independent of particular system or process representations. It is important to appreciate that systems and processes are modeled around the data, and not vice versa. From an equity derivatives perspective, the first consideration is how one would represent the data, that is, how does one describe an American option or an Asian option? This is opposed to first building an application, and then exporting data in a system-specific format. An XML definition for an American option should be completely independent of system. It is the responsibility of the individual applications to ensure that internal data structures can process the XML data representation.

In a derivative pricing system, it is necessary to have access to market data for yield curves, underlyings, and derivative instruments. As such, example XML representations will be presented here, and will be referenced in the following chapters where system connectivity and pricing services are described in more detail.

■ Yield curve.

```
<?xml version="1.0"?>
<yieldcurve>
    <currency>GBP</currency>
```

```
    <today>2001-06-27</today>
    <rates>
      <rate><term>2001-06-28</term><value>5.00</value>
         </term></rate>
      <rate><term>2001-07-27</term><value>5.20</value>
         </term></rate>
      <rate><term>2001-10-27</term><value>5.32</value>
         </term></rate>
      <rate><term>2002-06-27</term><value>6.00</value>
         </term></rate>
    </rates>
</yieldcurve>
```

■ Underlying.

```
    <?xml version="1.0"?>
    <underlying type="Index">
        <code>.FTSE</code>
        <currency>GBP</currency>
        <dividendyield>3.8</dividendyield>
        <volatility>30.0</volatility>
    </underlying>
```

■ American option.

```
    <?xml version="1.0"?>
    <option type="American">
        <code>FTSE_OTC</code>
        <underlying>.FTSE</underlying>
        <maturity>2005-06-30</maturity>
        <strike>6000.0</strike>
        <callput>Call</callput>
    </option>
```

■ Barrier option.

```
    <?xml version="1.0"?>
    <option type="Barrier">
        <code>FTSE_OTC</code>
        <underlying>.FTSE</underlying>
        <maturity>2005-06-30</maturity>
        <strike>6000.0</strike>
        <callput>Call</callput>
        <barrier updown="down" inout="out">5000.0</barrier>
        <rebate type="maturity">100.0</rebate>
    </option>
```

- Asian option.

```xml
<?xml version="1.0"?>
<option type="Asian">
    <code>FTSE_OTC</code>
    <underlying>.FTSE</underlying>
    <maturity>2005-06-30</maturity>
    <strike>6000.0</strike>
    <callput>Put</callput>
    <fixings>
        <fixing date="2001-05-20" weight="5">5932.4
            </fixing>
        <fixing date="2001-06-20" weight="4">5950.0
            </fixing>
        <fixing date="2001-09-20" weight="3"/>
        <fixing date="2001-12-20" weight="2"/>
    </fixings>
</option>
```

The definitions defined above have been used in this context for the purpose of introducing the use of XML for equity derivative representation. In real world use, it is likely that further information would be required, such as counterparty and settlement details. At the time of writing, industry initiatives such as FpML (www.fpml.org) for defining derivative products are helping to cement the use of XML as a cross-system and cross-company platform.

CHAPTER 7

Application Connectivity

In the financial industry, where software development time scales are generally short, it is important to balance quick delivery of systems to the desktop with the incorporation of general software engineering practices. This balance is often difficult to achieve because to quickly deliver systems often results in less time spent on analysis and design. To overcome this, and to avoid mismanagement of development resources, it is important to create a framework whereby common components are developed and reused. For example, in the derivatives area, it makes sense to centralize the development of pricing models, due to their high mathematical content and speed requirements. Other systems dependent on the derivative pricing library can integrate the library with little or no knowledge of the implementation. Also, from another perspective, the use of the same pricing models across business areas avoids inconsistencies in risk and profit and loss calculations.

The reuse paradigm has always been a primary objective of the software industry, and when successful, provides for more rapid development and deployment of applications and better use of programming skill sets. Through the evolution of programming languages and frameworks, the fulfillment of this objective is coming closer.

Object-oriented languages such as C++, Java, and Smalltalk have been used by developers for many years as a way of encapsulating functionality within objects. For example, in the C++ language, the construct `class` represents the mechanism for declaring objects. This approach hides the implementation, and a public interface provides the mechanism for using the object. When developing derivative pricing models, usually implemented in C++ for better control over code optimizations, a large number of classes is required to implement and represent the derivatives, market data, and mathematical routines. These classes are then compiled into either an executable or a reusable set of components.

7.1   COMPONENTS

When developing in C++ on the UNIX platform, the primary method of sharing components is via static or shared libraries, which, along with the C++ header files describing the class interface, can be given to other developers for incorporation into their systems. Static libraries are linked into an executable at compile time, whereas shared libraries are loaded into the executable at run time. The advantage of using shared libraries is that if a change occurs in the implementation, it is possible to replace the shared library without a recompile of the host program. However, any change that results in a change in interface or a different memory layout will require a recompile. On the Windows platform, Dynamic Link Libraries (DLLs) are the equivalent of shared libraries. Products such as Microsoft Excel, arguably one of the most used applications within the finance industry, provide a mechanism for incorporating add-ins that provide extra functions to the spreadsheet. By following certain interface criteria defined by Microsoft, Excel can load and access a DLL. This method is often used for adding C++ pricing functions into the spreadsheet.

Although reuse through libraries and DLLs is continuing today, versioning difficulties soon become apparent in multiple systems that use the same component. Often these components are installed in a common system directory, and so any upgrade to the component, perhaps from an installation of a new system, could overwrite the existing component. If the component is a different version from the one required by existing systems, this may cause these systems to crash. *DLL Hell* is a term used to describe this problem under Microsoft Windows.

To overcome issues such as versioning, and to provide increased language independence, Microsoft developed the Component Object Model (COM), a binary mechanism capable of use across multiple programming languages. By enforcing an immutable interface on the COM component, the client application can be assured that any upgrade to the component will not break the connectivity between the component and the application. For the component development, this provides easier distribution. As long as the public interface remains the same across all versions of the component (it must, otherwise it wouldn't be a COM component), then the developer is safe in the knowledge that existing users of the component will not be affected.

To extend the functionality of the component new interfaces can be added. Figure 7.1 illustrates the addition of a new interface (IPrice2) to the component, with no modification to the existing interface. Existing client applications dependent on the first version of the component will happily continue using the existing interface (IPrice), while new applications can use the new interface.

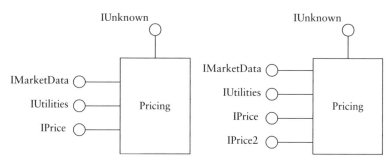

FIGURE 7.1   Initial object is extended to include a new price (IPrice2) interface without breaking existing users of the object.

Other component models, such as JavaBeans, provide similar encapsulation to that just described. For the Java platform, JavaBeans provides a platform-independent component methodology, and it can be utilized in builder tools by exposing their features in a specific manner. This allows developers to examine and modify a JavaBean directly through a user interface without writing a line of code.

7.2   DISTRIBUTED COMPONENTS

Shared libraries, DLLs, and COM provide a mechanism of adding external functionality into an application via an in-process mechanism. This means that the code runs in the address space of the application. Out-of-process components provide a further segregation by providing distributed connectivity across different address spaces or computers. To achieve component reuse across process boundaries, DCOM (Distributed Component Object Model) and CORBA (Common Object Request Broker Architecture) are commonly used. Distributed computing provides a number of advantages over traditional in-process mechanisms, including:

- **Reliability.** Server-based systems allow for better administration, and potentially incorporate better hardware infrastructure such as fault-tolerant disk arrays and fail-over. Also, a problem in the component will not cause the host application to crash, as is the case with in-process components.
- **Performance.** Moving the business logic from the client desktop onto more powerful server machines can increase speed and scalability, depending on the particular application.
- **Deployment.** Cost in rolling out software to desktop machines is reduced. Usually a small client-stub is required on the client machine instead of the full component.

These advantages, however, can be negated in many respects, as the overall system can be bound by the network. It is essential when designing distributed systems to ensure that the network is reliable and efficient.

DCOM and CORBA

The Distributed Component Object Model is an extension to COM, allowing objects to reside out-of-process either on another machine or in a different address space on the same machine. Objects are usually hosted within an executable or as a DLL hosted within a surrogate (Microsoft Transaction Server (MTS) is one example). DCOM is primarily Microsoft-specific, and although implementations do exist for other platforms, it would be rare to utilize this protocol on mixed operating system environments.

CORBA is an open, vendor-independent distributed architecture that has gained popularity across multiple platforms and is now included in frameworks such as Java. The architecture has been in existence for several years and is found in large distributed systems, usually written in third-generation languages such as C++ and Java.

Other remoting architectures such as Java's RMI (Remote Method Invocation) provide a simple interface for client/server connectivity and offer many of the features found in DCOM and CORBA. However, the use of RMI, although cross-platform, is really only applicable where the client and server are both written in Java.

These protocols, although providing functionality for state management, garbage collection, and security, are in many instances quite heavy in terms of resources and deployment. The rapid rise of the Internet has created a new platform for distributed components and, as a very large area network and stateless mechanism (through the standardization of HTTP), has resulted in a rationalization and simplification of transport protocols.

The following sections will describe the Simple Object Access Protocol (SOAP) as a lightweight alternative to the above, for the development of reusable web-based services in a loosely-coupled environment. Although the remaining sections will focus on SOAP, the authors are not advocating its use for all application domains. The extra built-in services offered by protocols such as DCOM and CORBA may provide a more appropriate fit, in some cases. For further details regarding such protocols, refer to [41] and [113].

7.3   SOAP

The Simple Object Access Protocol, based on XML, defines a lightweight mechanism for the communication of information between multiple systems

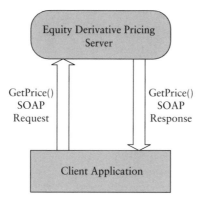

FIGURE 7.2   SOAP request and response for GetPrice(string code) function.

in a distributed environment. Initially developed by DevelopMentor, IBM, Lotus Development Corporation, Microsoft, and Userland Software, the product has been submitted to the World Wide Web Consortium [15]. At the time of writing, the SOAP 1.1 specification has been submitted as a W3C Note.[1] An XML Protocol working group has also been established to consolidate XML-based messaging systems, of which SOAP is a part.[2]

Using SOAP, an application can connect to services of other distributed applications regardless of operating system or programming language. The use of XML to describe the SOAP message format avoids relying on heavy infrastructure as is often the case with other distributed protocols such as DCOM and CORBA, described in Section 7.2. Although these other architectures offer more complex services as part of the standard, the objective of SOAP was to maintain a simple, yet extensible definition for distributed services. By maintaining simplicity, the protocol is instantly available to languages such as C++, Java, Visual Basic, and Perl, as a base implementation, while available toolkits provide further functionality and hide implementation details.

A SOAP message, which must be valid XML, represents a function call available on a remote service. As of version 1.1 of the specification, the underlying communication protocol is not enforced, however, most implementations currently available are on top of HTTP (Hypertext Transfer Protocol), which is the most used protocol on the Internet. However, SOAP implementations provide transport over message queues and SMTP (used for e-mail).

To understand SOAP, it is perhaps best to start with a simple example for getting the price of a stock or index, as depicted in Figure 7.2.

---

[1]The current SOAP specification can be found at http://www.w3.org/TR/SOAP.
[2]The W3C XML Protocol Working Group address is http://www.w3.org/2000/xp.

The exposed function residing on the server, perhaps written in C++, might have the following prototype:

```
double GetPrice(string code);
```

To call this function remotely over HTTP, the client would generate a SOAP request similar to the following:

```
POST /PriceServer HTTP/1.1
Host: www.unique-price-server.com
Content-Type: text/xml; charset="utf-8"
Content-Length: nnn
SOAPAction: "some-uri"

<SOAP-ENV:Envelope
  xmlns:SOAP-ENV="http://schemas.xmlsoap.org/soap/envelope/"
  SOAP-ENV:encodingStyle="http://schemas.xmlsoap.org/soap/
  encoding/">
  <SOAP-ENV:Body>
    <m:GetPrice xmlns:m="some-uri">
      <code>.FTSE</code>
    </m:GetPrice>
  </SOAP-ENV:Body>
</SOAP-ENV:Envelope>
```

Ignoring the namespace declarations for now, it can be seen that XML tags exist for defining the function GetPrice and the parameter code. The SOAP server process on receipt of this XML can extract the required function name and parameters and invoke the corresponding internal function. The layout of the response is similar and is:

```
HTTP /1.1 200 OK
Content-Type: text/xml; charset="utf-8"
Content-Length: nnn

<SOAP-ENV:Envelope
  xmlns:SOAP-ENV="http://schemas.xmlsoap.org/soap/envelope/"
  SOAP-ENV:encodingStyle="http://schemas.xmlsoap.org/soap/
  encoding/">
  <SOAP-ENV:Body>
    <m:GetPriceResponse xmlns:m="some-uri">
      <result>6005.0</result>
    </m:GetPriceResponse>
  </SOAP-ENV:Body>
</SOAP-ENV:Envelope>
```

In this case, the important XML sections to note are GetPriceResponse and result. The client application can process this XML and extract the return value.

The majority of SOAP implementations currently available hide the details of the SOAP packet, so, for example, the client request for the above might be as simple as:

```
string result = GetPrice(".FTSE");
```

The fact that a SOAP packet is being sent over HTTP to a remote server, is hidden from the client developer. Based on an interface description as discussed later in Section 7.4, a particular toolkit can generate client-side wrapper functions for generating a particular SOAP message.

SOAP Structure

A SOAP message definition is constructed from a number of XML sections:

- **Envelope.** This mandatory section is the top element of the XML document representing the message.
- **Header.** Optional, the header provides an extensible section for including extra message information such as transaction and authentication details. If included, the header section must be the first child element of the Envelope.
- **Body.** The body details the actual function call and parameter representation, and is a compulsory child section of the Envelope.

```
<SOAP-ENV:Envelope>
  <SOAP-ENV:Header>
    <!-- Optional header element -->
  </SOAP-ENV:Header>
  <SOAP:Body>
    <!-- Function, parameter details -->
  </SOAP:Body>
</SOAP-ENV:Envelope>
```

When sending a SOAP request message, the function name appears in the body section, and the equivalent SOAP response message by convention includes the function name with an appended `"Response"` string. This can be seen in the `GetPrice()` example in the previous section.

To indicate error or status information, the SOAP fault element in a message is used. The element is contained within the SOAP body and should convey appropriate information to the recipient of the message. In the example below, a server has returned a fault back to the client to indicate that a call has been attempted on an invalid function.

```
<SOAP-ENV:Envelope
  xmlns:SOAP-ENV="http://schemas.xmlsoap.org/soap/envelope/"
  SOAP-ENV:encodingStyle="http://schemas.xmlsoap.org/soap/
  encoding/">
  <SOAP-ENV:Body>
    <SOAP-ENV:Fault>
      <faultcode>SOAP-ENV:Server</faultcode>
      <faultstring>Function not found.</faultstring>
    </SOAP-ENV:Fault>
  </SOAP-ENV:Body>
</SOAP-ENV:Envelope>
```

Section 5 of the SOAP 1.1 specification deals with type encoding, and much of this follows the XML Schema data types specification as discussed in Section 6.2 of Chapter 6. For further explanation of SOAP and data type support, refer to the specification or [111]. As SOAP implementations mature, and XML class serialization is integrated more fully into frameworks such as .NET and Java, the conversion will be transparent from the developer's perspective.

In Section 6.4, market data and product details were described in XML. In order to send raw XML as a parameter within XML, it is convenient to use a CDATA section. By defining this, the XML parser will ignore the contents of the particular section. In the case of the market data functions, this avoids expansion of the XML data. For the creation of an underlying, the prototype would be:

```
string SetUnderlying(string xmldata);
```

and the SOAP message:

```
<SOAP-ENV:Envelope
  xmlns:SOAP-ENV="http://schemas.xmlsoap.org/soap/envelope/"
  SOAP-ENV:encodingStyle="http://schemas.xmlsoap.org/soap/
  encoding/">
  <SOAP-ENV:Body>
    <m:SetUnderlying xmlns:m="some-uri">
<![CDATA[<underlying type="Index"><code>.FTSE</code>
      <currency>GBP</currency><dividendyield>3.8
      </dividendyield>
      <volatility>30.0</volatility></underlying>]]>
    </m:SetUnderlying>
  </SOAP-ENV:Body>
</SOAP-ENV:Envelope>
```

SOAP Security

At the time of writing, version 1.1 of the SOAP specification does not address the issue of security. Eliminating the complexities of encryption, authentication, and authorization from the specification helps ensure that the protocol remains simple. However, due to its importance, it would be inappropriate not to discuss the current thoughts and methods on securing SOAP.

Encryption   A SOAP message defined as text-based XML has several advantages in terms of implementation and debugging, however, from a security standpoint, it is therefore obvious that these messages can be easily intercepted and understood by an impostor. Although SOAP itself does not define a mechanism for encryption, it is possible to use the security mechanisms of the actual underlying transport mechanism. Common transports such as SSL (secure sockets layer) provide a mechanism whereby the client and server create an encrypted channel. From a web-based perspective, this is achieved using the `https://` prefix that should be recognized when entering passwords on secure Internet sites. Provided both the client and server applications can transact over this transport, this is an effective security mechanism. However, the downside of sending SOAP using this method is that performance is reduced, due to the overhead of the SSL layer.

Authentication   Although transport layers such as SSL help secure the actual SOAP messages sent across the network, they do not determine the validity of the user. A secure system needs to authenticate users to ensure that they are who they say they are. Within SOAP, it is possible to use the optional header section to include authentication information. For example, before executing any functions on the server it might be a prerequisite to perform an initial login as follows:

```
<SOAP-ENV:Envelope
  xmlns:SOAP-ENV="http://schemas.xmlsoap.org/soap/envelope/"
  SOAP-ENV:encodingStyle="http://schemas.xmlsoap.org/soap/
  encoding/">
  <SOAP-ENV:Body>
    <login>
      <user>someuser</user>
      <password>somepassword</password>
    </login>
  </SOAP-ENV:Body>
</SOAP-ENV:Envelope>
```

The client would send the above message to the server, and because it contains password details, it is likely that this request would be over a secure transport. Once the validation of the user name and password has been successful, the response from the server would be:

```
<SOAP-ENV:Envelope
    xmlns:SOAP-ENV="http://schemas.xmlsoap.org/soap/envelope/"
    SOAP-ENV:encodingStyle="http://schemas.xmlsoap.org/soap/
    encoding/"
    xmlns:SOAP-ENC="http://schemas.xmlsoap.org/soap/encoding/">
    <SOAP-ENV:Header>
      <authentication SOAP-ENV:mustUnderstand="true"
                xsi:type="SOAP-ENC:base64">
    PGhlbGxvPjxnb29kYnnllPg==
      </authentication>
    </SOAP-ENV:Header>
    <SOAP-ENV:Body>
      <loginResponse>ok</loginResponse>
    </SOAP-ENV:Body>
</SOAP-ENV:Envelope>
```

The important section in the above message is the use of an authentication tag in the SOAP header. The mustUnderstand attribute is defined as part of the SOAP specification and is used to indicate whether the header is mandatory or optional to process. In this example, it is a requirement for the client to process the header section. The data contained with the authentication section is base 64, a common method for encoding binary data for transport over a text-based protocol such as SOAP or HTTP. The purpose of returning this data is so that subsequent calls to the server can include the data for use as a unique reference. A subsequent client call would therefore include a SOAP header, and could then be executed over a standard nonsecure transport.

```
<SOAP-ENV:Envelope
    xmlns:SOAP-ENV="http://schemas.xmlsoap.org/soap/envelope/"
    SOAP-ENV:encodingStyle="http://schemas.xmlsoap.org/soap/
    encoding/"
    xmlns:SOAP-ENC="http://schemas.xmlsoap.org/soap/encoding/">
    <SOAP-ENV:Header>
      <authentication SOAP-ENV:mustUnderstand="true"
                xsi:type="SOAP-ENC:base64">
    PGhlbGxvPjxnb29kYnnllPg==
      </authentication>
    </SOAP-ENV:Header>
    <SOAP-ENV:Body>
      <GetPrice>
        <code>.FTSE</code>
      </GetPrice>
    </SOAP-ENV:Body>
</SOAP-ENV:Envelope>
```

To allow for session timeouts so that the same authentication key cannot be used indefinitely, the server could have some mechanism for adding an encrypted time stamp into the key, or for performing some other rudimentary check.

Authorization Even though a user can successfully log in to the server, it might still be necessary to restrict certain users' access to all functions. For example, in a trading system it might be inappropriate to grant access to trade entry or modification. To achieve this, the server may either hide the function details from the specific client, or perform validation checking at each function call.

State and Scalability

The request-response mechanism of HTTP, the most popular transport for SOAP messages, provides a scalable mechanism for client to server interaction. By keeping the server stateless, that is, by maintaining no information about the client, scalability is simplified as multiple servers can independently handle client requests. This improves performance and simplifies the development of the server-based application.

Unfortunately, it is not always optimal to maintain this stateless environment. Where large amounts of data are required to achieve the appropriate functionality, as is the case with option pricing, it becomes extremely inefficient to transport the entire data set for each SOAP request. Also, the burden on the client application increases, contravening the philosophy of segregating the user-interface logic and business logic. To avoid this, the server application needs to provide some form of state management.

The simplest method for keeping server data synchronized with the client is to pass a unique key back to the client after the first function call. This might be done, for example, when the user initiates a login request to a particular server. This unique key is often known as a *cookie*. As with authentication, the SOAP header could include an entry as follows:

```
<SOAP-ENV:Header>
  <cookie>some-unique-cookie</cookie>
</SOAP-ENV:Header>
```

Upon receipt of a SOAP message, the server would extract the cookie value and map this to the appropriate data structure applicable to that user. In Figure 7.3, three consecutive calls are executed. The first two create state in the server by defining yield curve and underlying definitions. The third call relies on this data for a successful fair-price calculation. Through the use of a cookie value sent with each message, the server can maintain a unique reference to the data structures to be used in the final calculation.

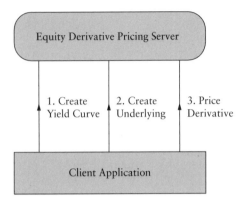

FIGURE 7.3 Remote calls to initialize market data and price a derivative.

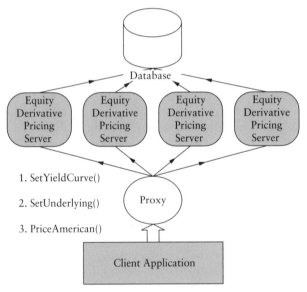

FIGURE 7.4 A proxy is used to distribute function calls into a server farm. A database is used to manage and share state information such as yield curve and underlying information.

Without this, multiple users of the pricing server could potentially update the same market data.

The difficulty with this approach is that it ties the client to one instance of the server, and therefore scalability and load-balancing become more problematic. To overcome this, further logic would need to be added into the server to utilize some form of shareable store such as shared memory or a database such as in Figure 7.4. This would allow multiple servers to access the same data, however, would introduce performance and synchronization issues.

Many distributed system designs try to maintain stateless objects where possible to avoid the difficulty in state management, and to improve scalability. In reality, there will be a combination of both, and it is important for the system architect to realize the appropriate design to ensure maximum scalability and performance.

7.4   WEB SERVICES

Through the use of SOAP and XML, a mechanism for achieving a loosely coupled distributed architecture for derivative pricing has been shown. Once this architecture has been put in place, it becomes possible to expose this functionality to a wide range of clients in a simple fashion. This concept, when used over the Internet, has been coined web services, and it is this that is currently driving the next generation of web-based applications. In conjunction with other XML based standards, SOAP provides the foundations for function invocation over the Internet. For this to be successful however, two new concepts need to be introduced:

- **Interface description:** describing the programmatic interfaces of web services.
- **Discovery:** a registry for indexing web services, so that their descriptions can be located.

Two primary standards are emerging to satisfy these concepts: the first is WSDL, and the second, UDDI.

WSDL

The Web Services Description Language (WSDL)[3] defines an XML grammar for describing network services as collections of communication endpoints capable of exchanging messages. The role of WSDL is functionally equivalent to that of IDL (Interface Definition Language) found in CORBA. An XML document contains a number of sections, including:

- `<types>`: usually using XML Schema datatypes for representing data definitions.
- `<message>`: abstract definitions of data being communicated.

---

[3]Currently a W3C Note at http://www.w3.org/TR/wsdl.

- `<portType>`: an abstract set of operations supported by the web service endpoints.
- `<binding>`: a concrete representation for a specific port type.
- `<service>`: a grouping of related endpoints.

Leaving the messages and portType sections completely independent of the binding allows concrete protocols (such as SOAP) to reuse the data and operation definitions. The web services infrastructure built into Microsoft.NET, for example, provides concrete protocols in the same WSDL document for SOAP, HTTP Post, and HTTP Get.

Using the existing SOAP example for `GetPrice()`, the corresponding WSDL document would be as follows:

```
<?xml version="1.0"?>
<definitions xmlns:s="http://www.w3.org/2000/10/XMLSchema"
  xmlns:http="http://schemas.xmlsoap.org/wsdl/http/"
  xmlns:soap="http://schemas.xmlsoap.org/wsdl/soap/"
  xmlns:soapenc="http://schemas.xmlsoap.org/wsdl/soap/encoding"
  xmlns:s0="some-uri" targetNamespace="some-uri"
  xmlns="http://schemas.xmlsoap.org/wsdl/">
  <types>
    <s:schema attributeFormDefault="qualified"
       elementFormDefault="qualified"
               targetNamespace="some-uri">
      <s:element name="GetPrice">
        <s:complexType>
          <s:sequence>
            <s:element name="code" type="s:string"/>
          </s:sequence>
        </s:complexType>
      </s:element>
      <s:element name="GetPriceResponse">
        <s:complexType>
          <s:sequence>
            <s:element name="GetPriceResult" type="s:double"/>
          </s:sequence>
        </s:complexType>
      </s:element>
      <s:element name="string" type="s:string"/>
    </s:schema>
  </types>
  <message name="GetPriceIn">
    <part name="parameters" element="s0:GetPriceXML"/>
  </message>
  <message name="GetPriceOut">
    <part name="parameters" element="s0:GetPriceResponse"/>
```

```
  </message>
  <portType name="MarketDataServiceSoap">
    <operation name="GetPrice">
      <input message="s0:GetPriceIn"/>
      <output message="s0:GetPriceOut"/>
    </operation>
  </portType>
  <binding name="PricingService" type="s0:PricingService">
   <soap:binding
   transport="http://schemas.xmlsoap.org/soap/http"
   style="document"/>
    <operation name="GetPrice">
      <soap:operation soapAction="some-uri/GetPrice"
                  style="document"/>
      <input><soap:body use="literal"/></input>
      <output><soap:body use="literal"/></output>
    </operation>
  </binding>
  <service name="PricingService">
    <port name="PricingService" binding="s0:PricingService">
      <soap:address location="http://localhost"/>
    </port>
  </service>
</definitions>
```

The above document is quite verbose for defining one public method on
a web service, however, in the majority of cases this definition is hidden with
the use of tools on both the client and server. A consumer of the service, that
is, a client or a development environment can read the WSDL document
and generate code stubs either dynamically or statically. Therefore, from
the programmer's perspective, the entire act of marshaling data, creating a
SOAP request, and handling the SOAP response is handled transparently, so
that the entire action simply looks like a local method call. More advanced
client-side tools allow for automatic generation of asynchronous calling so
that an event is triggered on receipt of the SOAP response from the server.
This allows the client to continue local processing without blocking.

UDDI

The Universal Description, Discovery, and Integration (UDDI)[4] addresses
the problem of how to locate web services [107], and has the backing
of major corporations including Ariba, IBM, and Microsoft [2]. UDDI

---

[4]Refer to http://www.uddi.org.

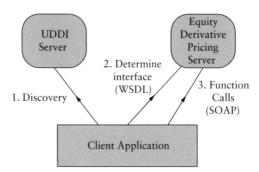

FIGURE 7.5 Process of finding an interface and dynamically binding to a service to execute a remote procedure call.

Registries on the Internet act like search engines for locating descriptive and programmatic information about web services. A registry can be used to determine whether a given business partner or company has a particular web service and to then further determine the technical details about an exposed web service. It would be possible for a derivatives house to offer web services via the registry and allow discovery and connectivity. In Figure 7.5, an application developed by an external client utilizes a UDDI server to discover and to determine an interface to a pricing service offered by an equity derivatives pricing application. A user of the service could be charged based on a subscription or transaction basis, or the service could be offered as part of a wider overall sales strategy.

This chapter has provided a grounding in SOAP as a protocol for communication between loosely-coupled systems. SOAP provides a straightforward mechanism to enhance reusability, and, for the finance domain allows for quicker rollout of systems to the desktop. Also, by exposing systems such as web services through the use of WSDL and UDDI, potential new marketing and business opportunities are created. Chapter 8 will present some of these opportunities, and the way they utilize XML as a data representation and SOAP as a communications protocol, in combination with other technologies.

CHAPTER 8

Web-Based Quantitative Services

In this chapter we will look at applications of a derivatives pricing web service, and contrast the ways in which pricing calculations are integrated into a monolithic application with the thin-client approaches possible through use of a web service. In this section, where we refer to calculations of price, this should be understood to refer to price, risk sensitivities, implied volatility, and so forth: the entire range of calculations typically performed in respect of derivative securities.

For the present purpose, we will define a client application as any which makes use of derivative pricing calculations, irrespective of whether it is more or less complex an application than the calculation engine itself. The classification of client applications into "thin" and "thick" clients is made on the basis of the amount of processing performed by the application beyond the simple displaying of results: We will look at examples of both.

Monolithic, or single-tier, applications are those in which the user interface, business logic, and data access are all implemented within a single layer: Thus there is no separate process responding to requests from one or more clients. Even if the data are stored elsewhere, an application is monolithic if the rules for managing it are implemented within the same process as the business logic and user interface. In a two-tier application, the data access is managed by a separate process, often on a physically distinct computer, but the interface and business logic remain tied together. Stored procedures, however, do provide a mechanism for shifting some business logic onto the database server.

Web services fit within a three- or n-tier architecture, shown in Figure 8.1, in which the interface is separated both from the business logic and from the data access. This very commonly applied paradigm separates the heart of an application, its business logic, from the database which maintains the persistent state of the system, and from the user interfaces. Obviously, this separation enables the data to be accessed from any suitable application, and potentially enables a number of different user interfaces to be created. In development terms, the technologies used to implement the core business logic and the interfaces might be quite different, as is particularly clear in

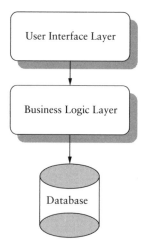

FIGURE 8.1   The common three-tiered model of system architecture: Business logic is separated from the data and from the user interface.

the case of those web-based applications in which the front-end is just an HTML page (see Section 8.3). It should be noted in passing that, although we logically decompose an application into three tiers, it is not necessary that these are physically located on three distinct computers. Often the deployment will be physically two-tier, with either a thick client running both the presentation layer and the business logic, or else a thick server in which the business logic is implemented entirely in stored procedures.

A web pricing service in this context clearly corresponds to the middle layer since it provides neither the user interface nor the persistent data. However, the model as shown in Figure 8.1 is too simple, and needs modification if the pricing server acquires its data from another web service rather than a database.

A slightly fuller description of the architecture of a pricing web service is shown in Figure 8.2, the essence of which is that the business logic, in this case the implementations of pricing algorithms, are hidden behind a translator that maps SOAP messages onto function or method calls.

At the extreme of the thick clients are the complex trading and risk management systems discussed in Section 8.2. Such applications are typically implemented in C++ (or possibly Java) and offer a full range of functionality and complex user interfaces. On a slightly smaller scale, a Value at Risk engine (for example) needs prices of complete portfolios under a variety of different scenarios, and extracts from the distribution of returns a Value at Risk number. Thus, while pricing is a critical part of such an application, it performs a substantial amount of additional logic as well. At the opposite

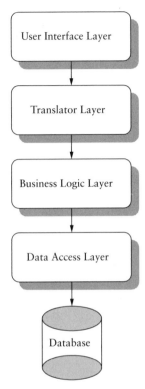

FIGURE 8.2   The business logic—that is, implementations of pricing algorithms— lies behind a layer that maps SOAP messages onto function calls. The data access may be provided by another web service.

end of the scale is the single ASP or JSP page, which makes a call to a pricing server by composing a SOAP message and integrating the response into an HTML response (Section 8.3).

8.1   WEB PRICING SERVERS

A derivatives analytics library will generally be developed as a general-purpose tool, by design not tightly coupled to any particular application or environment. Such a general-purpose package is intended for use in a web server, or in other environments: It can be statically linked into a trading and risk management application (Section 8.2) or registered as a dynamic linked library in a spreadsheet package, and can function as a web service only if sheltered behind a layer that accepts SOAP messages, parses them, and maps them onto corresponding method calls (Figure 8.2). Of course, client applications will need a corresponding layer to convert requests into SOAP messages.

This client-server separation is not a new idea, and indeed, technologies other than SOAP and web services can achieve it (e.g., DCOM and CORBA as discussed in Section 7.2), but for the present purpose we focus on SOAP and XML as the mechanism for communicating requests and their responses between client and server processes. The requirement for a wrapper that marshals and unmarshals requests from the network is common to all these technologies.

The content of these network messages may be of three types in the domain of derivative pricing, corresponding to the three easily distinguished categories of information that must be passed into a derivatives calculation engine:

1. Market data—the information on market observables required as inputs to the pricing algorithms.
2. Static data—the definitions of tradeable instruments (derivatives and their underlyings).
3. Control information—instructions that the server carry out a specified calculation, for example, determining the implied volatility of a specified option, given sufficient market and static data.

While it is possible for a client to supply market and static data with (i.e., at the same time as) the request, this is probably not optimal as, in all likelihood, the next request will again require the same market data (a request to price another, perhaps very similar, derivative on the same underlying asset), or the same static data and almost identical market data (a request to price the same derivative after the underlying price has ticked up, for example). It is clearly better if market data are supplied in a separate message from static data, and better yet if the independent items of market data are supplied in separate XML messages of the types given in Section 6.4. This trivially allows an application to transmit a yield curve (for example) that is thereafter in memory in the server and is referenced as needed by future requests. It may, of course, later be updated by the applications, perhaps in response to a real-time event. Static data may be treated similarly: The client transmits the definition of a derivative and associates with it a unique identifier. Thereafter, requests to price that security contain little more than its name and a list of the quantities that the client requires from the library, that is, price and typically a selection of "greeks" (sensitivities of price to changes in market-observed data).

We may now envisage two approaches: Either the application can extract market data from its database and fire it across to the pricing server in messages, prior to the requests that need it, or the server itself

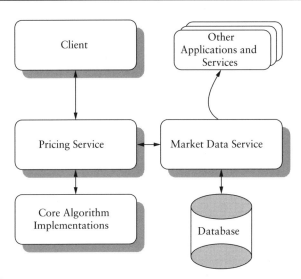

FIGURE 8.3 A market data service provides data to the pricing service and to other applications and services.

can request from a data source those market data items that it needs. This latter approach is most naturally implemented as a market data service, which lends itself to reuse in other applications and servers (Figure 8.3). In the case that the client is a complex application such as a trading and risk-management system supplied by a third party, the market data are probably already in memory, in which case it may be more appropriate to send market data messages from the system instead of from a separate market data server.

Splitting the required data set into separate messages raises the issue of the maintenance of state in web services. For a discussion of this, and in particular the example of a derivatives pricing service, see Section 7.3.

As ever with distributed processing, there is the objection that it is subject to an overhead imposed by the network, and the object of minimizing the number and size of messages is precisely to minimize this effect. If market data are updated much less frequently than they are used, and the static data describing a security are updated rarely if at all (perhaps only in response to a misbooking), then the commonest messages will be the requests for a calculation and the response. As mentioned above, the calculation request need contain little other than the identifier of the security to be priced, and the response will be similarly lightweight. The objection, however, has most force if the security to be priced has a trivial or very fast pricing algorithm, such as an index future, a stock, or a European option. For such cases, there is an argument for the client not making use of the pricing server, but instead performing the calculations locally. The trade-off is between performance and development and maintenance costs.

Thread Safety Issues in Web Servers

In some applications, more than one flow of control can exist simultaneously in the code. Such applications are said to be *multithreaded* and may have threads of control executing many different code paths at the same time (running genuinely in parallel on different CPUs or time-sharing on a single CPU) while sharing at least some data. *Thread-safe* code is structured in such a way as to function correctly in a multithreaded environment.

In a situation where a server accepts a stream of messages that may be updates to market data or may be requests for a calculation, it is obviously possible that a subsequent message may arrive before the previous calculation has completed. This will be the case if the client application is multithreaded, or if there are many clients making requests. Two avenues are open in this case. If the pricing library is thread-safe, then each message simply triggers the spawning of a new thread to carry out the calculation. When the calculation is complete, the thread generates the response message and terminates. If the library is not thread-safe, then the server has to buffer the messages. The advantage of a thread-safe library is that when a particularly intensive computation (a Monte Carlo simulation, perhaps) is requested by one client, then the response to the remaining clients is not frozen until it completes. Instead, the response to the other clients degrades slightly, instead of going through periods when they get no service at all. The latter may very well be completely unacceptable to some clients, notably real-time listed option market-making systems.

When creating a thread-safe server, the problems are with the shared data that may change, that is, market data objects. The most obvious danger comes from messages that update market data: This would be disastrous while one or more threads were accessing that data item. For this reason, a thread that needs to use a market data object in a pricing calculation must read-lock it. A message that updates a market data item requires a write lock, and is therefore blocked until no other thread is using it.

Another problem concerns the fact that, for many models, expressions for greeks are not available in closed form and must instead be calculated by perturbation of market data objects. If each thread has its own copy of any market data objects it needs, then no problem arises. More likely, however, is that all threads will share a single instance, thus avoiding excessive duplication of objects. In this case, a thread needing to perturb the instance would require a write lock, would be blocked until all other threads had completed, and would then block all other threads until it had itself completed. This is far from ideal since calculation of greeks by perturbation is very common in the more complex models. The solution is to either aggressively clone (i.e., to create temporary copies of) all market data objects in a thread-safe version of the library (but not in the non–thread-safe versions, to preserve the performance gains versus cloning), or to adopt a copy-on-write approach, whereby a market data object is read-locked until such time as a perturbation is requested, at which time it is cloned and the lock released—an approach that might be called *lazy cloning* (Figure 8.4). If no perturbation is ever requested by the thread, then of course no clone operation is performed and no overhead is incurred. Finally, note that the tests for thread safety given in the figure are not necessarily performed at run time: Thread-safe and non–thread-safe builds of the library may be more appropriate, so that single-threaded applications incur no overhead at all.

8.2   MODEL INTEGRATION INTO RISK MANAGEMENT AND BOOKING SYSTEMS

Of central importance to the operation of any derivatives business is a trading and risk management system whose principal functions include:

- The booking of deals, and their maintenance throughout their life.
- The aggregation of deals into portfolios and other groupings.
- The calculation and display of profit and loss on positions.
- The calculation and display of risk parameters for positions—these latter calculations, at least, invariably required in real time.

Invariably also, a major component of this system will be a large, complex database containing the details of securities (derivative and otherwise), positions, trades, market data, and a whole host of other information. Broadly, therefore, such applications can be crudely represented by Figure 8.5, in which we explicitly show the pricing component as separable from the main business logic segment, and assume that market and static data services exist and are available to other applications. The pricing component is potentially implemented as a web service, as discussed in Section 8.1. This also anticipates the following discussion, and reflects the fact that the pricing component is invariably produced by a model development group distinct from the core system implementation group.

In view of the cost and complexity of developing the whole system, frequently it is supplied off-the-shelf by an external vendor, although it may be developed "in-house" by a specialist group of developers who generally have prior experience of the business area. Both approaches have

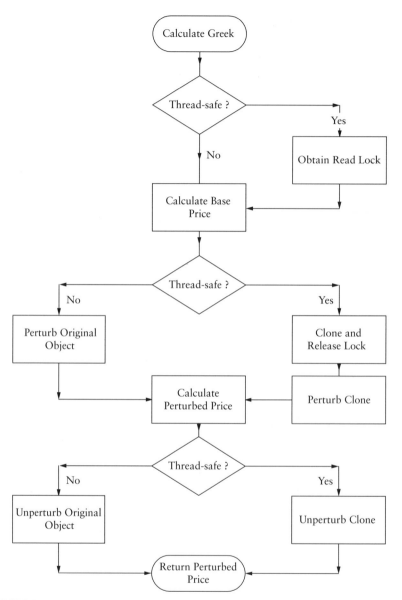

FIGURE 8.4   Cloning of a market data object when necessary for thread safety.

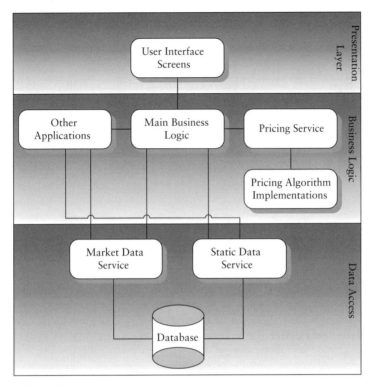

FIGURE 8.5   Elements of a trading and risk management system.

their adherents, and both have their advantages and disadvantages: It is far outside our scope to examine these issues.

In-house solutions will certainly require a model library to be provided, which may itself be provided in-house or by an external vendor. In either case, there will exist some process of integrating that library into the application. Commercially available trading and risk systems, by contrast, come with model libraries incorporated, but it is common for purchasers of those solutions to wish to incorporate their own models: For this reason, these systems typically provide a mechanism to enable this.

Section 7.1 discusses the consequences of delivering an analytics library as a static library, shared library, or component for in-process use: Section 7.2 extends this to distributed components. These considerations apply fully to analytics integration into a trading and risk management system. In practice, one finds that in-process approaches impose significant coupling between the build environments and other dependencies (such as third-party libraries) of the analytics library and its various client applications, making it hard for either library or client to change its build procedures

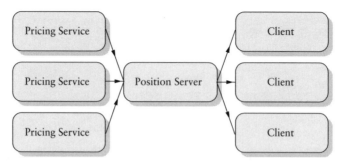

FIGURE 8.6   A position server collating the results of several pricing services and distributing these to clients.

independently. This is a classic case of a convoy moving at the speed of the slowest ship. In-process approaches also require that a version of the library be maintained for each platform on which clients run, which can be an appreciable maintenance overhead.

All these issues are addressed by implementing a pricing service via a network, although this is not a universal solution: Few practitioners would advocate that a trading and risk management system should run even fast models remotely under all circumstances.

A Position Server

In a multiuser environment such as the derivatives trading business of a financial institution, the pricing service does not fully answer one of the problems that arises. Consider the situation when a number of users of a particular application that is a client of the pricing server (or of an in-process pricing library) view a particular portfolio or other, larger aggregation of positions. When their display is initially built, and thereafter whenever a relevant real-time event triggers an update, these users will all carry out identical calculations: The computer resources (memory and CPU cycles) thus used redundantly can and should be put to better use.

This inefficiency is unfortunate, but in itself is hardly fatal. A worse consequence, however, is that users suffer decreased performance because of this effect, and the effect is worst when the calculation load is heaviest, that is, in quickly moving markets.

The obvious solution is to cache the results of the calculations, and to make the cache available as a web service. This can be compared to using pointer indirection in programming languages that support it: Instead of referring directly to the pricing service, you refer to a service that itself refers to it. This caching service can be called a *position server*. It can itself refer to a number of calculation engines, as shown in Figure 8.6, with the result that a unified view of the capabilities of multiple pricing sources is available to all clients.

Additionally, the position server can add extra functionality that does not properly belong in a pricing server. To avoid excessive and redundant calculations in response to every tick of the market, it can store for each instrument a number of recently calculated prices and the corresponding spot values: This makes interpolation possible on this array if the current spot value lies within the bounds of the array. If deltas are available as well as prices, which is often the case, these can be used to refine the interpolation by using a third-order polynomial. While clearly the cache must be emptied if there is an update to another item of market data, such as a yield curve, for many applications this is rare, compared to ticks in the underlying price. Furthermore, pricing algorithms implemented on a finite difference grid (see Chapter 4) can export to the position server the complete $t = 0$ boundary, which supports interpolation in a wide range without any further recalculations.

8.3   WEB APPLICATIONS AND DYNAMIC WEB PAGES

Hitherto we have considered the use of web services by "thick" clients: those that perform a substantial amount of processing around the service itself. In the remainder of this chapter we outline a technology available for the creation of the thinnest of thin clients: a case where the client application is just a web browser. We outline the application of this technology for financial institutions to deliver lightweight pricing applications to users within and without the institution.

It is obvious that the provision of static web pages is no longer the state of the art in web sites. E-commerce sites in particular, such as the online booksellers and other online stores, have much more the feel of a traditional application, responsive to commands and requests entered by the user, than just a static repository of information that the user can view. The distinction arises because the HTML page that is delivered to a user's web browser contains information specific to that user, and even to his or her recent actions within the web site. An excellent example of this is the ubiquitous "shopping basket" on e-commerce sites.

Furthermore, this transformation from a web dominated by static pages to one dominated by dynamic web applications has occurred in an astonishingly short time.

The technology that allows this is the use of a scripting language to generate HTML pages immediately before they are transmitted back to the client by the web server. If a web server is asked for a simple HTML page, it locates the page and transmits it back to the requester in an HTTP

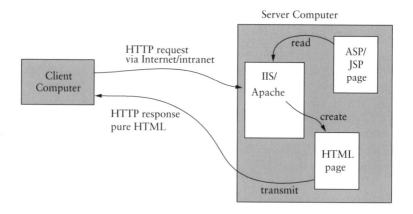

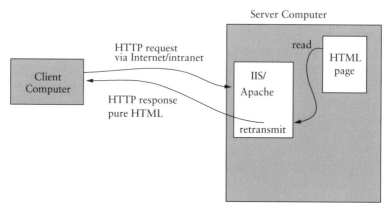

FIGURE 8.7 Scripting technologies such as ASP and JSP introduce an extra step into the generation of a pure HTML HTTP response to a user.

message. With a scripting language such as ASP or JSP, the web server executes commands contained in the requested file, generates HTML, and then proceeds as before in transmitting the response back to the requester. Thus an extra step shown in Figure 8.7 has been introduced, and the script may take advantage of whatever information (which might have been supplied by a user via form fields) is available to it to construct a different page each time. We can call web pages generated in this way *dynamic* web pages since the users can see different content each time they request the page. For a good introduction to this technology, see [22].

However, this is not sufficient for a true web application. An application maintains state and, as indicated in Section 7.3, HTTP is stateless. A scripting language, or rather the support for it provided by a web server, allows state

to be maintained, to be read and written by the script, and to persist between page requests. This allows for the writing of true applications with user interfaces extending entirely across the Internet or corporate intranet. The great advantage of this is that the computer of the user need have no software installed on it other than a web browser. This is an appreciable consideration even within a corporation, lowering as it does the barriers between a potential user of a service and his or her access to it, but is a very great advantage indeed if services are to be provided outside the corporate boundaries.

Among the benefits of this approach are the universal access it offers, and the guarantee that all users instantly have access to the latest version of the application. With no client machines on which to install anything, the cost and complexity of managing the application is dramatically reduced, compared with a thick-client approach.

Furthermore, because only pure HTML is sent in the response to the client, the server-side script used to generate the page is not available to the client—this is generally very desirable in a proprietary web application. As applied to finance, such server-side script could expose details of the calculation that the business might not want to make available to clients or competitors.

Applying this to derivatives pricing over the web requires that the script embedded in the page itself make a call to a web server by constructing a SOAP message and incorporating the response into the HTML page sent back to the requester. Were the calculations required for derivatives pricing very much simpler, then it would be possible to implement them directly in the scripting language and avoid the extra step of referring to a separate web service. In practice, however, scripting languages are unsuitable for implementing derivatives pricing algorithms, and a general programming language such as C++ is used. The natural approach is therefore to make use of an available web service for the calculation.

A more full picture of the functioning of a thin-client derivatives pricing application would therefore look like Figure 8.8, indicating the extra step involved in referring to a pricing service from the server-side script. The pricing service may or may not run on the same computer as the web server.

One can see this as a way of using different technologies for the things they are best at: Scripting is ideal for creating dynamic web pages, whereas C++ is good at complex calculations.

Option Calculator Pages

Despite the prominence often given to complete trading and risk management systems offering a full range of functionality, for the needs of many

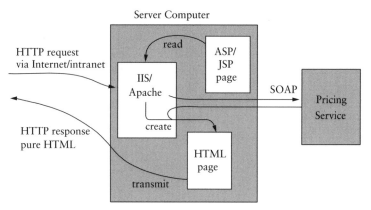

FIGURE 8.8 Server-side script generates a SOAP message, delegating the calculation to a pricing service, and incorporating the response into the generated HTML (compare to Figure 8.7).

business users much of this functionality is redundant and may even add complexity to no good purpose. Furthermore, if the system is supplied by a third party, there will generally be quite a high cost in providing it to each additional user. In view of this, there are motivations, of cost and suitability, to develop lightweight applications of restricted functionality.

An example is provided by the requirements of an over-the-counter (OTC) derivatives sales desk. It will often be the case that salespeople repeatedly price a restricted range of fairly standardized products (for example, vanilla, quanto and composite options, Asian options, reverse convertibles, and equity swaps) and need to do this quickly and flexibly, with the ability to vary the structure's defining parameters and see the effect on the price. In addition, it helps greatly if they can base their calculations on market data in use at the trading desk, that is, on the same database used by the main trading and risk management system. (Without this connection, any prices they might calculate are not even indicative.) This sort of lightweight pricing application is called an *option calculator*.

Although there are, of course, many possible solutions to this common problem, for the reasons of low maintenance, zero installation costs, and instant, universal access given above, the type of web-based browser-client application we have been discussing is an attractive one. A typical home page for such a calculator is pure HTML and contains links to (for example) ASP pages that are specialized for a particular option type. A reasonable layout for these pages is to split them into two regions: The first contains form fields with which the user defines the structure, and the second displays the results returned by the server, typically the calculated price and selected greeks.

Market data can be provided by a market data service (Figure 8.3), although it is possible to build in the facility in the client to provide override market data. Indeed, if the market data service connects to the live database of the main trading and risk management system, any prices calculated are zero-P&L prices: It will be necessary manually to override (at least) the volatility in order to generate tradeable prices.

Providing Pricing Applications to Clients

In the case of providing services to clients that are corporate entities separate from that of the service provider, the advantages of a technology that is purely browser based are considerable. Although it is of course possible to develop client applications in Visual Basic, C++, or the programming language of your choice, all of these would need to be installed on the client computers. This is not difficult within the corporate boundaries, but assumes a different set of problems if the client is in a different organization.

Computers belonging to a company other than the service provider are supported by a different staff and are configured to that company's in-house standards. At best it is inconvenient to install an application onto clients' computers, at worst impossible. On-site support would be inconvenient and expensive, the service provider would have to provide support on multiple platforms, and it might simply not be acceptable to the client to have support staff install or maintain applications on computers in restricted areas in offices. Nor might it be acceptable to download and install certain applications onto business-critical computers.

It is clear from the above that a web-based approach to providing services to clients of a derivatives business addresses most of these issues. The issues it raises, however, are those of security, authentication, and authorization: These are discussed in Section 7.3. The provision of such services to clients, particularly major clients, can be an important *added value* from the viewpoint of the client, and as such forms a part of the relationship between client and service provider.

Calculator pages Just as certain categories of users within a derivatives sales and trading business need a lightweight pricing application, clients of that business have similar needs. Much of the above discussion of option calculators therefore extends to providing this service outside the corporate boundaries.

A major issue for an application intended for clients and potential clients is the provision of market data. This arises because, given a pricing service for vanilla options, it is not difficult to infer the yield curve, dividend estimates, and volatility surface in use by the pricing engine. While some of these data are accessible from widely available data sources (yield curves and spot exchange rates, for example), other data are not and must be estimated or interpolated (volatilities for stocks where there are no liquid options, for example, and the correlations needed for quanto option pricing). The main database for the trading and risk management system would seem an obvious choice as a source for such data, were it not for the fact that it contains the levels used to mark the firm's books, which are highly sensitive commercially. This choice of data source is thus not appropriate and, at least, the data must be adjusted in some way before exposure in this public interface.

The only other solution to this appears to be to require the service consumer to enter much of the required market data, which considerably diminishes the value of the service. Much of its value to the consumer lies in the assumption that the prices obtained are at least indicative of tradeable prices, which relies on the data in use being close to the data that the derivative supplier would use to price the structure.

The process of determining the terms of an OTC derivative contract is generally not a simple one, often involving a number of drafts of a term sheet and the involvement of a marketer with considerable experience of derivatives and preferably a well-established relationship with the client. Marketers often visit client offices and require there access to analytics so as to discuss possible structures, investigating the implications of varying certain parameters, both in market and static data.

One solution is, of course, the use of a laptop computer on which a suitable application is installed (perhaps an analytics DLL loaded into Excel, which offers a good combination of power and flexibility), but web technology opens up a new possibility. If calculator pages are made available on the web, perhaps with appropriate authentication, these can be accessed from a client office, and the requested calculations delivered to the browser. Furthermore, the market data source accessed can be chosen so as to generate reasonable indicative prices, which would not be readily achievable without the connection to the corporate internal network. If appropriate, the page viewed could be saved locally on the client's computer and could form the basis of a deal confirmation.

Position revaluation   A second service that can be offered addresses clients' extremely common requirement for periodic statements reporting the value of their outstanding positions with a derivatives business: One option for delivering this is to upload it to a web site. This is probably the simplest service that we can consider, in which the Internet simply substitutes for someone faxing or e-mailing the report: It does not constitute a web service in the sense we have been discussing.

All that is required is that an application (linked to the main trading and risk management system, and an example of the *Other Applications* of Figure 8.5) at the service provider's site generate a report, perhaps in the form of an HTML page or PDF file, at regular intervals (e.g., weekly) and publish it to a web site. At any time thereafter, upon authentication, the client can download it.

CHAPTER 9

Portfolio and Hedging Simulation

9.1 INTRODUCTION

The purpose of quantitative pricing libraries for derivatives is usually not only to provide "fair" option prices but also to provide support for the risk management of the derivative positions. This risk-management takes place on a portfolio level, where the portfolio risk is dynamically managed (hedged) using information from the pricing models (such as delta, gamma). For the traders as well as for controlling, it is important to validate the pricing model and hedging strategy in realistic scenarios and to get estimates of the residual risk. This can be done using an algorithm that simulates the portfolio management, given a market scenario and rules for the trading strategy. The market scenario can be generated randomly according to some stochastic model, or taken from historical market data for backtesting the models. If stochastic market data are chosen, then it is also possible to do a Monte Carlo analysis of the portfolio risk.

The specifications of the simulation engine include the following features:

- Initial portfolios consist of cash positions, shares, and options.
- Interest and dividend payments are booked into the portfolio.
- Options get settled on expiry (e.g., cash settlement).
- Multiple currencies are supported.
- Choice of hedging strategy to be applied (e.g., delta hedging) and flexibility to define new strategies.
- Various output formats.
- Connectivity to databases with historical market data.

9.2 ALGORITHM AND SOFTWARE DESIGN

To meet the specifications listed above, the simulation engine is modularized into the following main components (see also Figure 9.1):

199

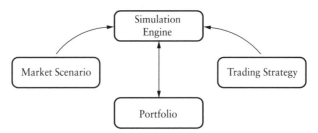

FIGURE 9.1   Simulation driver: main components.

- **Market scenario.** Provides access to the complete market data for each simulation date. This includes all yield curves, underlying information (spot price, dividends, repo rates, volatilities, etc.), and correlation matrices.
- **Portfolio.** List of all positions and their current quantities in the portfolio. Given the market data, the portfolio can be priced and the resulting prices and sensitivities can be extracted for each constituent.
- **Position.** Abstract base class for assets in the portfolio. A concrete derived class implements the method *event* that produces a list of trades that affect the portfolio. Those trades can be interest or dividend payments or the expiry of the option.
- **Trading strategy.** Given the portfolio and the market scenario, a list of trades is constructed to implement the particular trading (hedging) strategy. This component is implemented as an abstract base class from which specific strategies can be derived.

The basic algorithm of the simulation engine loops through the list of simulation dates, checks for events of each of the positions, and applies the trading strategy. The basic flowchart is shown in Figure 9.2. The step `calc. portfolio` also calculates all sensitivities necessary for the trading strategy. If the trading strategy is delta hedging, then all deltas have to be calculated. Let $S_1, \ldots, S_n$ be the underlyings and $\Delta_1, \ldots, \Delta_n$ the aggregated portfolio deltas with respect to those underlyings. Then the delta-hedging strategy would produce n trades to buy a number $-\Delta_i$ of underlying S_i for each $i = 1, \ldots, n$, such that the portfolio is delta flat in each underlying.

More advanced hedging strategies could be the following:

- Delta hedging is done only if delta exceeds given thresholds to decrease the number of trades being made.
- For cross-currency products, also hedge FX delta.
- For hedging exotic options, use liquid plain vanilla options to reduce the gamma or vega exposure.

■ Consider interest rate risk.
■ Take transaction costs into account.

9.3   EXAMPLE: DISCRETE HEDGING AND VOLATILITY MISSPECIFICATION

The Black-Scholes theory of option pricing and hedging is based on the ideal assumptions that the market is monitored continuously and that the portfolio is continuously rebalanced to adjust the delta hedge. In practice, the portfolio can be rebalanced only periodically. Besides the obvious reason that the trader has a certain time of reaction to market moves, other reasons are

■ Transaction costs.
■ Illiquid market.

The situation of an illiquid market occurs either for large trading volumes compared to the daily turnover, or for assets that have no continuous market at all, such as some investment funds whose prices are only periodically published.

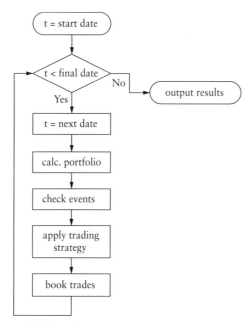

FIGURE 9.2   Simulation driver: flowchart.

The naive discrete delta-hedging strategy from Black-Scholes theory is to trade a number of stocks to make the total portfolio delta zero on each of the finite number of trading dates. Clearly there is a residual market risk due to the lack of hedging continuity. The question now is whether this simple delta-hedging strategy is optimal. If optimality means the minimization of the portfolio variance, then the hedging strategy can be improved by choosing (see chapter 20 in [108])

$$\Delta = \frac{\partial \Pi}{\partial S} + \left(\mu - r + \frac{1}{2}\sigma^2 \right) \frac{\partial^2 \Pi}{\partial S^2}$$

It should be emphasized that the hedging now depends explicitly on the drift of the stock, that is, it is not possible to use risk-neutral pricing. In most practical cases, the adjustment to be made for the delta can be neglected. Only for assets with large risk premium and comparably small volatility, the effect might be relevant.

Pricing the option under the discrete hedging assumptions can take into account the modified delta hedging. If the value is just defined as an expected value, then the value can be derived from the Black-Scholes price using a modified volatility

$$\sigma^* = \sigma \left(1 + \frac{\Delta t}{2\sigma^2} (\mu - r)(r - \mu - \sigma^2) \right)$$

More sophisticated models could, of course, take into account the risk preferences of the option holder or issuer.

As an example of the simulation driver, the effect of volatility mis-specification and discrete hedging will be considered. The test scenario is a three-month period of underlying stock prices S_t, where the stock prices are log-normal with a volatility of 0.3 and $S_0 = 100$. Interest rate is constant at 5 percent per year. The product to be simulated is a European call option struck at 100 with one year time to maturity. The hedging strategy is delta hedging applied once each day during the simulation period.

Let Π_t be the portfolio value at time t, $0 \le t \le T = 1$. Then the relative discounted P&L of the hedging strategy is defined as

$$P\&L_{rel} = \frac{e^{-rT}\Pi_T - \Pi_0}{\Pi_0}$$

To find the probability distribution of the P&L for that hedging strategy, a Monte Carlo approach is followed, that is, the portfolio simulation is

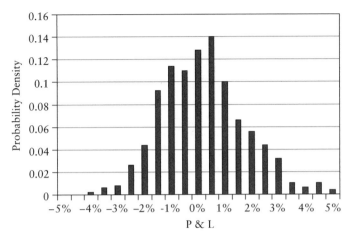

FIGURE 9.3   P&L distribution: discrete hedging with correct volatility.

iterated for many sample stock paths. The resulting probability distribution after 500 iterations is shown in Figure 9.3. The P&L is centered around 0 and looks very much like a normal distribution with mean zero.

The next step is to examine the effect of a wrong volatility specification. As market scenario we take the same as before, but the pricing and hedging is based on a volatility assumption of 0.25 instead of 0.3. The absolute P&L resulting from this misspecification is given by the following theorem (see [20] for more details):

THEOREM 9.1

Let the stock price S_t be given by the SDE

$$dS_t = \mu S_t \, dt + \sigma_t S_t \, dW_t$$

and let $\hat{V}(t, S)$ be the Black-Scholes price at time t of an option with European payoff $h(S_T)$ based on the assumption that the stock price volatility is $\hat{\sigma}(t)$ instead of σ_t. Let Π_t be the Black-Scholes value (based on $\hat{\sigma}(t)$) of the hedge portfolio, that is, Π consists of the following assets:

$$\Pi : \begin{matrix} 1 & \text{option} \\ -\hat{V}_S & \text{shares} \end{matrix}$$

plus a cash position making the strategy self-financing. Then the discounted P&L of the portfolio is given by

$$B^{-1}(T)\Pi_T - \Pi_0 = \frac{1}{2}\int_0^T B^{-1}(T)(\sigma_t^2 - \hat{\sigma}^2(t))S_t^2 \hat{V}_{SS}\, dt \qquad (9.1)$$

where $B^{-1}(t) = \exp\left(-\int_0^t r_\tau\, d\tau\right)$ is the discount factor.

REMARK

The cash position is used to finance stock trades being made during the lifetime of the option. The amount of cash, denoted by ψ_t, therefore equals the portfolio value minus the value of the option minus the value of the stocks:

$$\psi_t = \Pi_t - \hat{V}(t, S_t) + S\hat{V}_S(t, S_t)$$

By definition, the strategy is then self-financing; no external capital flows into or out of the portfolio.

PROOF

For a proof of (9.1) we use the identities

$$d\Pi = -\hat{V}_S\, dS + r(\Pi - \hat{V} + S\hat{V}_S)\, dt + d\hat{V}$$
$$d\hat{V} = \left(\hat{V}_t + \tfrac{1}{2}\sigma_t^2 S_t^2 \hat{V}_{SS}\right) dt + \hat{V}_S\, dS$$

Substituting the second equation into the first yields

$$d\Pi = r\Pi\, dt + \left(\hat{V}_t + rS_t\hat{V}_S + \tfrac{1}{2}\sigma_t^2 S_t^2 \hat{V}_{SS} - r\hat{V}\right) dt$$

Now using the Black-Scholes PDE for $\hat{V}$ that holds with $\hat{\sigma}$ instead of σ_t we get

$$d\Pi = r\Pi\, dt + \tfrac{1}{2}\left(\sigma_t^2 - \hat{\sigma}(t)^2\right)S_t^2 \hat{V}_{SS}\, dt$$

The rest now follows from discounting on both sides, and integrating from 0 to T.

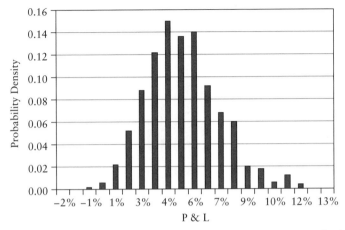

FIGURE 9.4   P&L distribution: discrete hedging with incorrect volatility.

By the above formula, the realized P&L depends on the particular stock path and the value of $\Gamma = V_{SS}$ along the path. In the example considered here, we have $\sigma = 0.3$ and $\hat{\sigma} = 0.25$ and a positive gamma, so we expect a positive P&L. Those theoretical considerations agree with the simulation results shown in Figure 9.4.

9.4   EXAMPLE: HEDGING A HESTON MARKET

In this example, we assume that the stock price follows a Heston process, but the hedging is still based on Black-Scholes prices with an estimated constant volatility. The Heston process is given by the SDEs

$$dS_t = (r_t - p_t)S_t \, dt + \sqrt{v_t}S_t \, dW_t^S$$
$$dv_t = \kappa(\theta^2 - v_t) \, dt + \gamma \sqrt{v_t} \, dW_t^v$$

with parameters

$$\kappa = 1.5 \quad \text{reversion speed}$$
$$\theta = 0.3 \quad \text{long volatility}$$
$$\gamma = 100 \quad \text{volatility of volatility}$$
$$\rho = 1.5 \quad \text{correlation between } W_t^S \text{ and } W_t^v$$
$$\sqrt{v_0} = 0.3 \quad \text{short volatility}$$

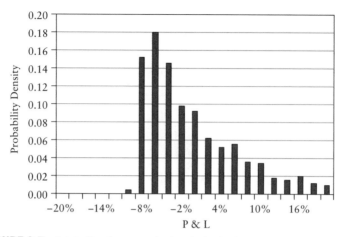

FIGURE 9.5 P&L distribution: Black-Scholes hedging in a Heston market.

As the volatility estimation used in the hedging strategy, the long volatility of 0.3 is taken. The fair value of the option calculated within the Black-Scholes framework is 14.20, the fair value in the Heston framework is 12.40. The P&L results from hedging the option using the Black-Scholes prices and deltas are shown in Figure 9.5.

9.5 EXAMPLE: CONSTANT PROPORTION PORTFOLIO INSURANCE

Portfolio insurance strategies are investment strategies for downside protection of a risky portfolio. One way of doing this is to decrease the investment in the risky asset when the portfolio value approaches the floor level guaranteed to the investor. To fix some notation, let S_t be the price of the risky asset and $B(t) = e^{rt}$ the price of the risk-free asset. Then the portfolio value is given by

$$\Pi_t = \alpha_t S_t + \beta_t B_t$$

In the Constant Proportion Portfolio Insurance (CPPI) strategy (see [11] and [12]), the weight α is chosen in such a way that the proportion of the investment in the risky asset with respect to the excess wealth over the floor level $F_t = F(t)$ is held constant:

$$\alpha_t S_t = M(\Pi_t - F_t) \tag{9.2}$$

The factor M determines the risk exposure of the investor. Given α, the weight β_t is determined by the assumption that the strategy is self-financing.

Then the portfolio value satisfies the SDE

$$d\Pi_t = r\left(\Pi_t - \alpha_t S_t\right) dt + \alpha_t \, dS_t \tag{9.3}$$

Substituting Equation (9.2) into (9.3) gives

$$d\Pi_t = r\left((1 - M)\Pi_t + MF_t\right) dt + M\left(\Pi_t - F(t)\right) \frac{dS_t}{S_t}$$

In the special case $F(t) = e^{rt}F_0$, the last equation can be further simplified. Using $dF(t) = rF(t) \, dt$ we get

$$d\left(\Pi_t - F_t\right) = r(1 - M)\left(\Pi_t - F_t\right) dt + M\left(\Pi_t - F_t\right) \frac{dS_t}{S_t}$$

or

$$\frac{d\left(e^{-r(1-M)t}(\Pi_t - F_t)\right)}{e^{-r(1-M)t}(\Pi_t - F_t)} = M \frac{dS_t}{S_t}$$

Now we assume that S_t is a log-normal process given by

$$\frac{dS_t}{S_t} = \mu \, dt + \sigma \, dW_t$$

Then the solution for Π_t can be explicitly written as

$$\Pi_t = F_t + (\Pi_0 - F_0) \, e^{\left(r + M(\mu - r) - \frac{1}{2}M^2\sigma^2\right)t + M\sigma W_t} \tag{9.4}$$

From Equation (9.4) it can be seen that M serves as a leverage factor for the risk premium and the volatility.

In practice, the portfolio is not rebalanced continuously, but always at the beginning of a certain period, which could be weekly. Therefore, there is a residual risk that the portfolio value falls below the floor. A realistic model for such a strategy also has to take into account transaction costs and bid/offer spreads.

Typical values for the multiplication factor M are between 3 and 5, and rebalancing is often done weekly, provided the prices have moved sufficiently to trigger a rebalancing. This extra proviso is attached to the strategy to avoid very small rebalancings. It is worth pointing out that the CPPI strategy will guarantee the initial capital if the asset never drops by more than $1/M$ in any period between rebalancing. In practice, a financial institution can sell CPPI structures with or without a capital guarantee

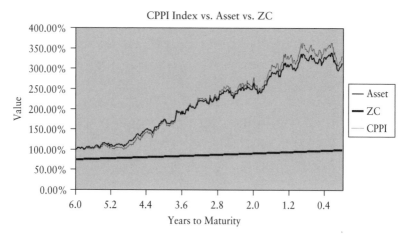

FIGURE 9.6 Asset, Zero-Coupon Bond, and CPPI in increasing market.

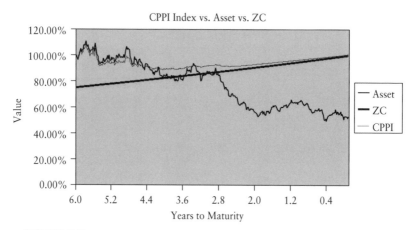

FIGURE 9.7 Asset, Zero-Coupon Bond, and CPPI in decreasing market.

against drops by more than $1/M$. The capital guarantee amounts to adding a series of put options to the CPPI.

Ignoring the risk of market drops in excess of $1/M$ between rebalancings, the performance of the CPPI compared to the underlying asset is illustrated in Figures 9.6, 9.7, and 9.8. Three different scenarios are possible: The asset performs well over the period, in which case the CPPI is also going to perform well (see Figure 9.6). The asset performs badly, but because of the CPPI trading strategy, the initial capital is retained for the CPPI (Figure 9.7). Finally, if the asset initially performs badly, but rallies later on, the CPPI *may* not be able to pick up the growth in the asset because the CPPI

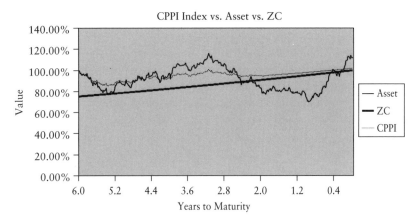

FIGURE 9.8   Asset, Zero-Coupon Bond, and CPPI in decreasing market that subsequently rallies.

will then be almost exclusively invested in the zero-coupon bond. This is the key drawback of the CPPI, illustrated in Figure 9.8.

9.6   SERVER INTEGRATION

Connected to a market data server, the simulation engine from Section 9.2 can be used to build backtesting systems and risk engines. A possible setup for the main components is shown in Figure 9.9. The scenario builder can either take historical data from the market data server or do projections into the future. The scenario builder should have some logic to produce extreme scenarios for stress testing. The functionality of the user interface may contain graphical output of the simulation results and statistical reports.

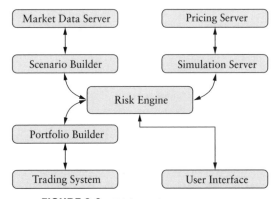

FIGURE 9.9   Risk-engine components.

The user should be able to define portfolios or select portfolios from the trading system and specify market scenarios.

The data exchange between the components is done via XML (see Chapter 6). The examples given there certainly apply for this application. From the simple XML definitions for market data and financial instruments, one can easily build up the scenario and portfolio data. An example for a portfolio definition in XML is

```xml
<?xml version="1.0"?>
<portfolio>
  <name>DAX-Option-Portfolio</name>
  <currency>EUR</currency>
  <positions>
    <position>
      <quantity>100</quantity>
      <code>DAX_OTC_01</code>
    </position>
    <position>
      <quantity>20</quantity>
      <code>DAX_OTC_02</code>
    </position>
  </positions>
</portfolio>
```

The market scenario comprises the XML definitions of the market data on each of the simulation dates:

```xml
<?xml version="1.0"?>
<marketscenario>
  <marketdata>
    <date>03-01-2001</date>
    <yieldcurve>...</yieldcurve>
    <underlying>...</underlying>
    ...
  </marketdata>
  <marketdata>
    <date>04-01-2001</date>
    ...
  </marketdata>
</marketscenario>
```

The communication between the components of the simulation and risk engine can be implemented with SOAP interfaces (see Chapter 7).

references

1. Ané, Thierry, and Hélyette Geman. "Stochastic Volatility and Transaction Time: An Activity-Based Volatility Estimator," *The Journal of Risk*, 2(1999).

2. Ariba, Inc., International Buisness Machines Corporation, and Microsoft Corporation. UDDI Technical White Paper. uddi.org (http://www.uddi.org), 2000.

3. Asmussen, Soren, and Jan Rosinski, *Approximations of Small Jumps of Lévy Processes with a View Towards Simulation*. Lund University, technical report, 2000.

4. Barndorff-Nielsen, Ole. "Processes of the Normal Inverse Gaussian Type," *Finance and Stochastics*, 2(1998): 41–68.

5. Bates, David. "Jumps and Stochastic Volatility: Exchange Rate Process Implicit in PHLX Deutschmark Options," *Review of Financial Studies*, 9(1996): 69–108.

6. Bellamy, Nadine, and Monique Jeanblanc. "Incompleteness of Markets Driven by a Mixed Diffusion, *Finance and Stochastics*, 4(2000): 209–222.

7. Bertoin, Jean. *Lévy Processes*. Cambridge, UK: Cambridge University Press, 1996.

8. Bertoin, Jean. "Subordinators: Examples and Applications," in P. Bernard, *Lecture Notes in Probability Theory and Statistics*. Volume 1717 of *Lecture Notes in Mathematics*. New York: Springer, 1999, pp. 1–91.

9. Billingsley, Patrick. *Probability and Measure*, 3rd ed. New York: Wiley, 1995.

10. Bingham, Nick, and Rüdiger Kiesel. "Risk-Neutral Valuation." Berlin, Heidelberg, New York, Springer, 1998.

11. Black, F., and R. Jones. "Simplifying Portfolio Insurance for Corporate Pension Plans," *Journal of Portfolio Management*, 14(1988): 33–37.

12. Black, F., and A. Perold. "Theory of Constant Proportion Portfolio Insurance," *Journal of Economic Dynamics and Control*, 16(1992): 403–426.

13. Black, F. and Myron Scholes. "The Pricing of Options and Corporate Liabilities," *Journal of Political Economy.* 81(1973): 637–654.

14. Bochner, S. *Harmonic Analysis and the Theory of Probability,* Berkeley: University of California Press, 1955.

15. Box, Don, David Ehnebuske, Gopal Kakivaya, Andrew Layman, Noah Mendelsohn, Henrik Frystyk Nielsen, Satish Thatte, and Dave Winer. *Simple Object Access Protocol (SOAP) 1.1.* W3C (http://www.w3.org/TR/SOAP), technical report, 2001.

16. Box, Don, Aaron Skonnard, and John Lam. *Essential XML Beyond Markup,* Reading, MA: Addison-Wesley, 2000.

17. Boyarchenko, Svetlana, and Sergei Levendorskii. *Perpetual American Options under Lévy Processes.* Technical report, 2000.

18. Brémaud, Pierre. *Point Processes and Queues, Martingale Dynamics.* Berlin, Heidelberg, New York: Springer, 1981.

19. Brockhaus, Oliver, Michael Farkas, Andy Ferraris, Douglas Long, and Marcus Overhaus. *Equity Derivatives and Market Risk Models.* Risk Books, 2000.

20. Brockhaus, Oliver, Andrew Ferraris, Christoph Gallus, Douglas Long, Reiner Martin, and Marcus Overhaus. *Modelling and Hedging Equity Derivatives.* Risk Books, 1999.

21. Bühlmann, Hans, Freddy Delbaen, Paul Embrechts, and Albert Shiryaev. *No-Arbitrage, Change of Measure and Conditional Esscher Transforms.* ETH Zürich, 1997.

22. Buser, David, John Kauffman, Juan T. Llibre, Brian Francis, David Sussman, Chris Ullman, and Jon Duckett. *Beginning Active Server Pages 3.0.* Wrox Press, 1999.

23. Carmona, Philippe, Frédérique Petit, and Marc Yor. "Sur Les Fonctionnelles Exponentielles de Certains Processus de Lévy," *Stochastics and Stochastic Reports,* (1994): 71–101.

24. Carmona, Philippe, Frédérique Petit, and Marc Yor. "On the Distribution and Asymptotic Results for Exponential Functionals of Lévy Processes," in Mark Yor, *Exponential Functionals and Principal Values of Brownian Motion.* Biblioteca de la Revista Matematica Iberoamericana, 1997.

25. Carr, Peter, Hélyette Geman, Dilip Madan, and Marc Yor. *The Fine Structure of Asset Returns: An Empirical Investigation.* Technical report, 2000.

26. Carr, Peter, and Dilip Madan. "Option Valuation Using the Fast Fourier Transform," *Journal of Computational Finance,* 2(1998): 61–73.

27. Chung, K. L., and R. J. Williams. *Introduction to Stochastic Integration,* 2nd ed. Boston: Birkhauser, 1990.

28. Cinlar, E., J. Jacod, P. Protter, and M. Sharpe. "Semimartingales and Markov Processes," *Zeitschrift für Wahrscheinlichkeitstheorie und verwandte Gebiete.* 54(1980): 161–220.

29. Craig, I. J. D., and A. D. Sneyd. "An Alternating-Direction Implicit Scheme for Parabolic Equations with Mixed Derivatives," *Computers and Mathematics with Applications,* 16(1998): 341–350.

30. Davis, Mark, and F. Lischka. *Convertible Bonds with Market Risk and Credit Risk.* Technical report, 2000.

31. Delbaen, F., P. Grandits, T. Rheinlander, D. Samperi, M. Schweizer, and C. Stricker. *Exponential Hedging and Entropic Penalties.* Preprint, 2000.

32. Delbaen, F., and W. Schachermayer. "A General Version of the Fundamental Theorem of Asset Pricing," *Mathematische Annalen,* 300(1994): 463–520.

33. Deutsche Bank Global Equities. *Convertible Bonds: Risk Treatments.* Deutsche Bank, technical report, 2000.

34. Dritschel, M., and P. Protter. "Complete Markets with Discontinuous Security Price," *Finance and Stochastics,* 3(1999).

35. Duffie, Darrell, Jun Pan, and Kenneth Singleton. *Transform Analysis and Asset Pricing for Affine Jump-Diffusions.* Palo Alto, CA: Stanford University, technical report, 1999.

36. Duffie, Darrell, and Kenneth Singleton. "Modeling Term Structures of Defaultable Bonds," *Review of Financial Studies,* 12(1999): 687–720.

37. Dufresne, Daniel. "The Distribution of a Perpetuity, with Applications to Risk Theory and Pension Funding," *Scandinavian Actuarial Journal* (1990): 37–79.

38. Dupire, Bruno. "Pricing with a Smile," *Risk,* 7(1994).

39. Eberlein, Ernst. *Applications of Generalized Hyperbolic Lévy Motions to Finance.* University of Freiburg, technical report, 1999.

40. Eberlein, Ernst, and Ulrich Keller. "Hyperbolic Distributions in Finance." *Bernoulli,* 1(1995): 281–299.

41. Eddon, Guy, and Henry Eddon. *Inside Distributed COM*. Redmond, WA: Microsoft Press, 1998.

42. El Karoui, Nicole, Hélyette Geman, and Jean-Charles Rochet. "Changes of Numeraire, Changes of Probability and Option Pricing," *Journal of Applied Probability*, 32(1995): 443–458.

43. El Karoui, Nicole, and Quenez, M.C. "Dynamic Programming and Pricing of Contingent Claims in an Incomplete Market," *SIAM Journal of Control Optimization*, 33(1995): 26–66.

44. Elliott, R. J. *Stochastic Calculus and Applications*. Berlin: Springer-Verlag, 1982.

45. Feller, William. *An Introduction to Probability Theory and Its Applications*, 2nd ed. New-York: Wiley, 1971.

46. Föllmer, H., and M. Yu. Kabanov. "Optional Decomposition and Lagrange Multipliers," *Finance and Stochastics*, 33(1998): 29–66.

47. Föllmer, H., and P. Leukert. "Quantile Hedging," *Finance and Stochastics*, 3(1999): 251–273.

48. Föllmer, H., and P. Leukert. "Efficient Hedging: Cost versus Shortfall Risk," *Finance and Stochastics*, 4(2000): 117–146.

49. Fristedt, Bert, and Lawrence Gray. *A Modern Approach to Probability Theory*. Boston: Birkhauser, 1996.

50. Geman, Hélyette, Dilip Madan, and Marc Yor. "Stochastic Volatility, Jumps and Hidden Time Changes," Finance and Stochastics. Forthcoming, 2001.

51. Geman, Hélyette, Dilip Madan, and Marc Yor. "Time Changes for Lévy Processes," *Mathematical Finance*, 11(2001): 79–96.

52. Geman, Hélyette, Dilip Madan, and Marc Yor. *Time Changes Hidden in Brownian Subordination*. Technical report, 2000.

53. Geman, Hélyette, and Marc Yor. "Bessel Processes, Asian Options, and Perpetuities," *Mathematical Finance* 3(1993): 349–375.

54. Geman, Hélyette, and Marc Yor. "Pricing and Hedging Double Barrier Options: A Probabilistic Approach," *Mathematical Finance*, 6(1996): 365–378.

55. Gerber, H., and E. Shiu. "Martingale Approach to Pricing Perpetual American Options," *ASTIN Bulletin*, 24(1994): 195–220.

56. Gerber, Hans, and Elias Shiu. "Pricing Perpetual Options for Jump Processes," *North American Actuarial Journal*, 2(1998): 101–112.

57. Gjessing, Hakon, and Jostein Paulsen. "Present Value Distributions with Applications to Ruin Theory and Stochastic Equations," *Stochastic Processes and Their Applications*, 71(1997): 123–144.

58. Goldman Sachs. *Valuing Convertible Bonds as Derivatives*. Goldman Sachs, technical report, 1994.

59. Graham, Ian S., and Liam Quin. *XML Specification Guide*. New York: Wiley, 1999.

60. Harrison, J. Michael, and Stanley Pliska. "Martingales and Stochastic Integrals in the Theory of Continuous Trading," *Stochastic Processes and Their Applications*, 11(1981): 215–260.

61. Heston, Steven. "A Closed-Form Solution for Options with Stochastic Volatility with Application to Bond and Currency Options," *Review of Financial Studies*, 6(1993): 327–343.

62. Hull, John. *Futures, Options, and Other Derivatives*, 3rd ed. Upper Saddle River, NJ: Prentice Hall, 1997.

63. Jacod, Jean, and Albert N. Shiryaev. *Limit Theorems for Stochastic Processes*. Berlin: Springer-Verlag, 1987.

64. Jarrow, Robert, David Lando, and Stuart Turnbull. "A Markov Model for the Term Structure of Credit Spreads," *Review of Financial Studies*, 10(1997): 481–523.

65. Jeanblanc, Monique, and Nicolas Privault. *A Complete Market with Poisson and Brownian Components*. Technical report, 2000.

66. Kallsen, Jan, and Albert N. Shiryaev. *The Cumulant Process and Esscher's Change of Measure*. University of Freibug, technical report, 2000.

67. Karatzas, Ioannis. *Lectures in Mathematical Finance*, American Mathematical Society, 1997.

68. Karatzas, Ioannis, and S. E. Shreve. *Brownian Motion and Stochastic Calculus*, 2nd ed. Berlin, Heidelberg, New York: Springer-Verlag, 1991.

69. Karatzas, Ioannis, and Steven Shreve. *Methods of Mathematical Finance*. New York: Springer-Verlag, 1998.

70. Kay, Michael. *XSLT Programmer's Reference*. Wrox Press, 2000.

71. Kloeden, Peter, and Eckhard Platen. *Numerical Solution of Stochastic Differential Equations*, New York: Springer, 1995.

72. Knudsen, Thomas, and Laurent Nguyen-Ngoc. *Pricing European Options in a Stochastic Volatility–Jump Diffusion Model*, Deutsche Bank,

technical report, 2000; submitted to *Journal of Financial and Quantitative Analysis*.

73. Kou, Steve, and Huio Wang. "First Passage Times of a Jump-Diffusion Process." Columbia University, 2001.

74. Kramkov, D. O. "Optional Decomposition of Supermartingales and Hedging Contingent Claims in Incomplete Security Markets," *Probability Theory and Related Fields*, 105(1996): 459–479.

75. Kunitomo, N., and M. Ikeda. "Pricing Options with Curved Boundaries," *Mathematical Finance*, 2(1992).

76. Lamberton, Damien, and Bernard Lapeyre. *Introduction au Calcul Stochastique Appliqué à la Finance*, Ellipses, 1992.

77. Lando, David. "On Cox Processes and Credit Risky Securities," *Review of Derivatives Research*, 2(1998): 99–120.

78. Lebedev, N. N. *Special Functions and Their Applications*. Dover, 1972.

79. Leblanc, Boris, and Marc Yor. "Lévy Processes in Finance: A Remedy to the Non-Stationarity of Continuous Martingales," *Finance and Stochastics*, 2(1998): 399–408.

80. Lukacs, Eugene. *Characteristic Functions*. Griffin Statistical Monographs and Courses, 1960.

81. Madan, Dilip, and Frank Milne. "Option Pricing with VG Martingale Components," *Mathematical Finance*, 1(1991): 36–56.

82. Madan, Dilip, and E. Seneta. "The Variance-Gamma (VG) Model for Share Market Returns," *Journal of Business*, 63(1990): 511–524.

83. Mandelbrot, Benoit. "Fractals and Scaling in Finance: Discontinuity, Concentration, Risk." Springer-Verlag, 1997.

84. McLaughlin, Brett. *Java and XML*, Sebastopol, CA: O'Reilly, 2000.

85. Merton, Robert. "On the Pricing of Corporate Debt: The Risky Structure of Interest Rates," *Journal of Finance*, 29(1974): 449–470.

86. Merton, Robert. "Option Pricing When Underlying Stock Returns are Discontinuous," *Journal of Financial Economics*, 3(1976): 125–144.

87. Miyahara, Yoshio. *Minimal Relative Entropy Martingale Measures of Geometric Lévy Processes and Option Pricing Models in Incomplete Markets*. Nagoya City University, Faculty of Economics, technical report, 1999.

88. Mordecki, Ernesto. "Optimal Stopping for a Diffusion with Jumps," *Finance and Stochastics*, 3(1999): 227–236.

89. Musiela, Marek, and Marek Rutkowski. *Martingale Methods in Financial Modelling.* Berlin, Heidelberg, New York: Springer, 1997.

90. Nguyen-Ngoc, Laurent. *"Produits Dérivés en Marché Incomplet: Quelques Exemples."* Master's thesis, Université Paris 6, 1999.

91. Nguyen-Ngoc, Laurent, and Marc Yor. *Wiener-Hopf Factorization and the Pricing of Barrier and Lookback Options under General Lévy Processes.* Université Pierre et Marie Curie, technical report 640, 2001.

92. Nilsen, T., and J. Paulsen. "On the Distribution of the Present Value of a Randomly Discounted Compound Poisson Process," *Stochastic Processes and Their Applications,* 61(1996): 305–310.

93. Norberg, Ragnar. "Ruin Problems with Assets and Liabilities of Diffusion Type," *Stochastic Processes and Their Applications,* 81(1999): 255–269.

94. Paulsen, Jostein. "Risk Theory in a Stochastic Economic Environment," *Stochastic Processes and Their Applications,* 46(1993): 327–361.

95. Paulsen, Jostein. "Sharp Conditions for Certain Ruin in a Risk Process with Stochastic Return on Invesments," *Stochastic Processes and Their Applications,* 75(1998): 135–148.

96. Pecherskii, E. A., and B. A. Rogozin. "On Joint Distributions of Random Variables Associated with Fluctuations of a Process with Independent Increments," *Theory of Probability and Its Applications,* 14(1969): 410–423.

97. Pelsser, Antoon. "Pricing Double Barrier Options Using Laplace Transforms," *Finance and Stochastics,* 4(2000): 95–104.

98. Prause, Karsten. *The Generalized Hyperbolic Model: Estimation, Financial Derivatives, and Risk Measures.* PhD thesis, Albert-Ludwigs-Universität Freiburg, 1999.

99. Press, William H., Saul A. Teukolsky, William T. Vetterling, and Brian P. Flannery. *Numerical Recipes in C,* 2nd ed. Cambridge, UK: Cambridge University Press, 1993.

100. Protter, Philip. *Stochastic Integration and Differential Equations: A New Approach.* Berlin: Springer, 1995.

101. Raible, Sebastian. *Lévy Processes in Finance: Theory, Numerics, and Empirical Facts.* PhD thesis, Albert-Ludwigs-Universität Freiburg, 2000.

102. Ray, Daniel. "Stable Processes with Absorbing Barriers," *Transactions of the AMS*. 89(1958): 16–24.

103. Revuz, Daniel, and Marc Yor. *Continuous Martingales and Brownian Motion*. New York: Springer-Verlag, 1999.

104. Rogers, L. C. G., and D. Williams. *Diffusions, Markov Processes and Martingales: Foundations*. Cambridge, UK: Cambridge University Press, 2000.

105. Rogers, L. C. G., and D. Williams. *Diffusions, Markov Processes and Martingales: Ito Calculus*. Cambridge, UK: Cambridge University Press, 2000.

106. Rosinski, Jan. *Series Representations of Lévy Processes from the Perspective of Point Processes*. Technical report, 1999.

107. Ryman, Arthur. *Understanding Web Services*. IBM, 2000.

108. Sato, Ken-Iti. *Lévy Processes and Infinitely Divisible Distributions*. Cambridge, UK: Cambridge University Press, 1999.

109. Schweizer, M. "Approximation Pricing and the Variance-Optimal Martingale Measure," *Annals of Probability*, 24(1996): 206–236.

110. Scott, Louis. "Pricing Stock Options in a Jump-Diffusion Model with Stochastic Volatility and Interest Rates: Applications of Fourier Inversion Models," *Mathematical Finance*, 7(1997): 413–426.

111. Scribner, Kennard, and Mark C. Stiver. *Understanding SOAP*. Sams, 2000.

112. Shiryaev, Albert N. *Essentials of Stochastic Finance*. World Scientific, 1999.

113. Siegel, Jon. *CORBA 3 Fundamentals and Programming*, 2nd ed. New York: Wiley, 2000.

114. Stuart, A., and K. Ord. *Kendall's Advanced Theory of Statistics*, Volume 1, 6th ed. London: Edward Arnold, 1994.

115. Tavella, D., and C. Randall. *Pricing Financial Instruments: The Finite Difference Method*. New York: Wiley, 2000.

116. Tsiveriotis, K., and C. Fernandes. "Valuing Convertible Bonds with Credit Risk," *Journal of Fixed Income*, 9(1998): 95–102.

117. Vasicek, Oldrich. "An Equilibrium Characterization of the Term Structure," *Journal of Financial Economics*, 7(1977): 117–161.

index

American option, 163
Applications
  Common Object Model (COM), 166
  Common Object Request Broker Architecture (CORBA), 168
  Distributed Component Object Model (DCOM), 168
  distributed components for, 167–168
  DLL Hell, 166
  Dynamic Link Libraries (DLLs), 166
  dynamic web pages, 191–197
  server-side scripts, 193, 194
  shared libraries, 166
  Simple Object Access Protocol (SOAP), 168–177
  single-tier, 181
  static libraries, 166
  "thick" clients, 181, 182, 191
  "thin" clients, 181, 191
  three-tier, 181–182
  two-tier, 181
Arbitrage, 19
Asian option, 164

Barrier option, 75–77, 163
Black-Scholes dynamics, 40
Black-Scholes (BS) model, 77–78
Brownian motion, 12, 14, 55
  hitting times, 63

Cadlag, 2
Canonical decomposition, 5

Canonical space, 1–2
Carr-Geman-Madan-Yor (CGMY) model, 86–87
Change of numéraire, 72
Compensator process, 6
Compound Poisson process, 65–66
Constant Proportion Portfolio Insurance (CPPI), 206–209
Convertible bond asset swaps, 137–145
  bond options, 138
  callable assets, 137–138
  issuer default, 139–140
  pricing and analysis, 140–145
Convertible bonds
  approach comparisons, 130–132
  conversion probability approach, 128
  defined, 125
  Delta-Hedging approach, 129–130
  deterministic risk premium, 127–132
  Interest Rate Stochasticity Effect, 133–134
  non–Black-Scholes models, 132–137
  Tsiveriotis-Fernandes approach, 128–129
  volatility skew effect, 134–137

Dividends
  Heston model, 123–124
  jump process, 118

Dividends (*Continued*)
  local volatility model, 122–123
  modeling, 117
  yield model, 118

Entropy, 59
  minimal entropy martingale
    measure (MEMM), 60
Esscher transforms, 58
Exotic derivatives
  barrier options, 75–77
  perpetual options, 74–75
  perpetuities, 73–74
Expectation, 2
Exponential formula, 57

Fast Fourier Transform (FFT), 95
Feynman-Kac theorem, 8, 103–104
Filtration, 2, 11

Girsanov's theorem, 10

Hedging, 43–45
  efficient, 39
  quantile, 39, 46–50
  super, 46–50
Heston model, 31, 37
Hull-White interest rate model, 31

Incomplete market pricing, 37–42
Intensity (λ), 13
Itō's formula, 9–10

Jump Diffusion (JD) model, 77–78,
    87

Lebesque integral, 2
Lévy-Khintchine representation, 53
Lévy, Paul, 12
Lévy measure, 53
Lévy processes, 51–102
  defined, 52

diffusion coefficient, 53
drift, 53
gamma process, 62
model combining volatility and
    jumps, 98–102
modeling, 68–72
with negative jumps, 66–68
numerical methods, 95–98
proof for, 54–55
subordinated, 64
subordinator, 61
Localizing sequence, 4

Market completeness, 19, 30–36
  defined, 19
Markov processes, 7–8
Martingale measures, 15–17
  with market completeness,
    28–30
  with no arbitrage, 28–30
Martingale restrictions, 79
Martingales, 4–7, 11
Merton's model, 81–83, 87
Monte Carlo simulation, 95–97

Normal Inverse Gaussian (NIG)
  model, 77–78, 83–85, 87

Object-oriented languages, 165

Parabolic Differential Equation
    (PDE), 103
  discretization, 106–109
Perpetual options, 74–75
Perpetuities, 73–74
Plim, 6
Poisson process, 13, 14, 55
  compound, 56, 65–66
Portfolio and hedging simulation
  algorithms, 199–201
  components, 200

Portfolio and hedging simulation
   (*Continued*)
   discrete hedging, 201–205
   Heston markets, 205–206
   portfolio insurance, 206–209
   server integration, 209–210
   volatility misspecification,
       201–205
Pricing
   European options, 70–72, 81
   variance-optimal method, 39,
       43–45
Pricing models, 103–106
   Alternating Direction Implicit
       (ADI) scheme, 110–113
   convergence and performance,
       113–116
   Crank-Nicolson scheme, 110
   explicit, 109
   Heston model, 106
   multiasset model, 104
   stock-spread model, 105
   Vasicek model, 106
Probability basis, 1–2
Probability space Ω, 1
Processes, 2–8
   adapted, 3
   Brownian motion, 12, 14
   canonical decomposition, 5
   compensator, 6
   compound Poisson, 56
   intensity (λ), 13
   Lévy, 51–102
   Markov, 7–8
   martingales, 4–7, 11
   Poisson, 13, 14
   predictable, 4
   progressive measurability, 17
   semimartingales, 4–7

Quadratic variation, 5–6, 7
Quantile hedging, 46–50

Risk management and booking
   systems, 187–191
   "in house" solutions, 187–189

Self-financing strategies, 17
   with market completeness,
       17–21
   with no arbitrage, 17–21
Semimartingales, 4–7
Simple Object Access Protocol
   (SOAP), 168–177
   described, 168–171
   security, 173–175
   state and scalability, 175–177
   structure, 171–172
Smile effect, 91
Stochastic calculus, 8–10
Stock processes
   with dividends, 117–118
   future dividends excluded,
       118–120
   past dividends included,
       120–121
Stopping time, 3
Super hedging, 46–50

Universal Description, Discovery,
   and Integration (UDDI),
       179–180
Uniform Resource Identifier (URI),
       151

Variance Gamma (VG) model,
       77–78, 85–86, 87
Variance-optimal pricing, 43–45
Volatilities, 79–80
   Carr-Geman-Madan-Yor
       (CGMY) model, 90–91
   ETR2 index, 92, 93
   Merton's model, 89, 93–94

Web pricing servers, 183–187
  position servers, 190–191
  thread safety issues, 186–187
Web services, 177–180
Web Services Description Language (WSDL), 177–179

XML (Extensible Markup Language)
  attributes, 151
  comments, 152
  compared with HTML, 149–150
  Document Object Model (DOM), 153
  Document Type Definition (DTD), 154–155
  empty-element tag, 151
  end tags, 151
  namespaces, 151
  parsing, 153
  processing instructions, 152
  representing equity market data, 162–164
  schema, 154–157
  Simple API for XML (SAX), 153
  start tags, 150
  transformation, 157–162
  transformed into HTML, 160–162
  well-formed, 150
  XSLT stylesheets, 157–158

Zero-coupon bonds, 208, 209